THE VILLAGE
NEWS

THE VILLAGE NEWS

THE TRUTH BEHIND ENGLAND'S RURAL IDYLL

TOM FORT

**SIMON &
SCHUSTER**

London · New York · Sydney · Toronto · New Delhi

A CBS COMPANY

First published in Great Britain by Simon & Schuster UK Ltd, 2017
A CBS COMPANY

1 3 5 7 9 10 8 6 4 2

Simon & Schuster UK Ltd
1st Floor
222 Gray's Inn Road
London WC1X 8HB

www.simonandschuster.co.uk
www.simonandschuster.com.au
www.simonandschuster.co.in

Simon & Schuster Australia,
Sydney

Simon & Schuster India,
New Delhi

A CIP catalogue record for this book
is available from the British Library

Hardback ISBN: 978-1-4711-5109-5
eBook ISBN: 978-1-4711-5111-8

Typeset in Bembo by M Rules
Printed in the UK by CPI Group (UK) Ltd, Croydon, CR0 4YY

To my sister, Elizabeth, and to Joe

CONTENTS

INTRODUCTION

The English village has been declared dead or dying so often that it seems almost heretical to declare that it is nothing of the sort. But I have to respect the evidence. And the evidence is that it remains very much alive – not necessarily kicking, but with a heartbeat that more often than not is regular and firm. Furthermore, barring some cataclysm that destroys society and all its structures, the village shows every sign of surviving into our foreseeable future.

I am not trying to be contrary. The village as a model for communal living is simply too strong to fail. It meets too many of our deep needs. It came into existence long before towns and cities so that people could live together but not necessarily under the same roof. It enabled them to work together and achieve results that would have been impossible had it been each man for himself. It provided a sense of security in the face of ever-present danger, and the reassurance of proximity without everyone having to eat and sleep side by side.

That fundamental, instinctive need – to be part of something larger and stronger – is as insistent as ever. So why have we been so ready to write the village off, to declare it redundant and therefore destined for a lingering passing from life? How did we lose sight of its indispensable nature?

I believe we allowed ourselves to be deceived about what the village was, and is, for. Because it developed in its familiar form so that those who worked the land would have somewhere close by to eat and rest and have occasional respite from their otherwise ceaseless round of toil, it became an article of faith that the bond with the land created the village. It seemed to follow that if and when that bond was broken, the village was doomed because its reason for being had been taken from it.

After two thousand years and more, the bond was ruptured beyond repair. For the sake of convenience let us date that breaking to 1945. In fact, of course, it had been weakening for a long time before that. But it is beyond dispute that since the end of the 1939–45 World War agriculture in this country has been transformed literally beyond recognition. Before 1914 it would have been unusual to find an able-bodied man in a country village who was not directly or indirectly employed on the land or in trades associated with it. Between the wars it would have been worthy of comment. Post 1945 the farm labourer has become a threatened species, and the associated traders – wheelwright, carter, blacksmith and the rest – have become virtually extinct.

The social consequences of the rupture were seismic. The agricultural labouring class, the bedrock of village life, disappeared, dispersed to towns and cities where there were factories and shops and jobs. The vacuum they left was filled by migrants from elsewhere: incomers, newcomers, newbies, call them what you will. The village dynamic was turned upside down. But the village did not die.

There had been times, long ago, when villages readily gave up the ghost. England is littered with the sites of deserted villages: prehistoric, Celtic, Roman, Saxon, Norman, medieval. In those far-off days people organised themselves for communal living in particular places because the circumstances – availability, good soil, favourable climate, absence of war and plague – supported the arrangement. But by its nature that arrangement was precarious, and there was nothing permanent about it. The notion of the settlement putting down roots to anchor it in its location would have struck those early peasants as highly fanciful. If the circumstances changed – a Saxon incursion, for instance, or the Norman invasion, or the Black Death, or simply the exhaustion of the soil by primitive farming methods – the village could easily become unviable. Its population diminished until those left decided to move and join another settlement, or try somewhere else altogether. Their village decayed and vanished, sometimes within a generation, sometimes over a more extended period.

It took centuries for a village to acquire history. In time, though, the churchyard took possession of succeeding generations, so that the current generation could look back and say: this is ours, we belong here. But that sense of belonging was shaken to its foundations by the earlier revolution that overtook rural England, the enclosure movement.

Between 1760 and 1815 a quarter of the entire farmed area of the country – seven million acres – became privately owned. In many places the old cooperative way of working the land was killed off. The open-field system that had evolved post-1066 had had a place for everyone, from the lowest serf to the ambitious, look-ahead yeoman farmer. The new system sealed the transition from feudalism to capitalism. Those best placed to exploit it took control and prospered. Those less well placed became the labouring class. Those at the bottom of the pile were dispossessed, sank into poverty and over time vanished from the scene altogether. The consequence in the village was that the divisions in the hierarchy – always there but blurred by the communality of effort – became more clearly defined and, inevitably, widened.

When the medieval village was abandoned and died, there was no one around to pick up a pen and interpret this as a symptom of society's sickness. But the upheaval resulting from the enclosure of the common land was documented in detail, and then assessed by a new breed of social commentator. The concept of the changing face of the countryside was born.

In 1751 Thomas Gray published his *Elegy Written in a Country Churchyard*. It celebrated the weary plodding ploughman and his way of life and the village and the land around in such a way as to suggest that they formed some sort of appointed harmonious whole, timeless and unchanging. The truth, for many a ploughman, was that their time was up. A decade later Oliver Goldsmith wrote in *The Deserted Village*:

> *Sweet smiling village, loveliest of the lawn,*
> *Thy sports are fled and all thy charms withdrawn;*
> *Amidst thy bowers the tyrant's hand is seen,*
> *And desolation saddens all the green:*

Introduction

One only master grasps the whole domain,
And half a tillage stints thy smiling plain.
No more thy glassy brook reflects the day,
But chok'd with sedges, works its weedy way.

John Clare witnessed the legalised seizure of common land in his quiet corner of Northamptonshire and cried out in protest: 'Inclosure, thou art a curse upon the land.'

The new order swiftly became the established order. The economic inequalities cemented into increasingly rigid social distinctions. In 1873 the government produced a survey entitled *Return of Owners of Land* which revealed that one quarter of rural England was in the possession of 363 landowners, each with an estate of at least 10,000 acres. Half of them were peers of the realm. Three thousand members of the landed gentry, the squirearchy, had holdings of between 1000 and 10,000 acres. Below them came the 250,000 farmers, most of them tenants; and below them came the one million farm labourers, the vast majority living in tied cottages.

This was capitalism at work: the rich getting richer and more powerful, the middle class generally prospering and able to ride out economic lows, the labouring class anchored in poverty at the mercy of whatever squalls overtook the agricultural sector. The changing rural world acquired its standard types: the remote and infinitely arrogant landowner, the upwardly mobile and generally bullying farmer, and the poignantly pathetic archetypal landless farm labourer, known universally as Hodge.

The name, an elision of hedge and clod, was an expression of the man: slow in wits and movement, fathomlessly ignorant and credulous, dimly aware of his lowly situation but too gormless to do anything about it. The stereotype received its fullest treatment in *Hodge and his Masters* by Richard Jefferies, published in 1880, in which a life of toil on behalf of others reaches its lingering end in the degradation of the workhouse. As the critic Raymond Williams pointed out in his searching cultural analysis *The Country and the City*, Jefferies has himself been mythologised as a lifelong countryman and the descendant of generations of yeomen farmers, whereas he never worked on the land, lived mainly in suburbia and earned his living by journalism. Far from being a work of objective social reportage, *Hodge and his Masters* is a consciously political assault on a system which Jefferies saw – with considerable justification – as having relegated the most defenceless sector of the rural population to pauperism.

It took a true countryman, Thomas Hardy, to redress the balance. In an essay called 'The Dorsetshire Labourer' he invited subscribers to the Hodge caricature to come to Dorset 'where Hodge in his most unmitigated form is supposed to reside'. There, he said, they would discover for themselves that the typical Hodge 'was somehow not typical of anyone but himself'; and that for those prepared to take the trouble to know him, the 'dull, unvarying, joyless Hodge' disintegrated into 'men of many minds, infinite in difference'.

From the degradation of Hodge it was but a small step to conclude that the village – his *locus operandi* – was similarly on the slide. The crucial text in this strand of the story was George Sturt's *Change in the Village*, which came out in 1912 and recorded the decay and unravelling of the community life in Lower Bourne, then a distinct village outside Farnham in Surrey, now absorbed into Farnham's suburbs. Sturt's tone and method appear rigorously unsentimental, but implicit in his account is his own belief that this transformation had eaten away and destroyed the soul of the village, and that what was left behind was a poor thing in comparison.

Sturt's lament was taken up at intervals by other commentators in the course of the twentieth century – each recording their verdicts on the villages they had known. Almost inevitably, given our inclination to mourn what has gone, the tone of these judgments tended towards the elegiac. It was easier to conclude that the village was on its way out than to identify signs of hope and regeneration. But the last rites have proved to be premature. The village has remained obstinately alive even as, throughout its history, individual villages have decayed and become moribund.

What happened to it was that it changed so fundamentally, and moved so far from its familiar past, that the transformation could be, and frequently was, mistaken for a kind of death.

1

GROWING UP

Twyford, Berkshire

When I was a year old we moved to Twyford, a largish village in Berkshire, roughly midway between Maidenhead and Reading. My father was a Member of Parliament and needed to be in London much of the time. But with a growing family – I was the fourth son – he and my mother did not care to live there. Twyford's great asset was its railway station, twelve minutes' brisk walk from our house (my memory is of him always leaving late, always at a run, clutching bowler hat and briefcase).

Like all villages, Twyford owed its existence and particular character to its location. It had been a coaching station on the old Bath Road, and was an obvious choice for a stop on Brunel's Great Western Railway, being thirty minutes or so away from Paddington. It had no industry or speciality of its own to make it remarkable, although Waterer's celebrated Floral Mile of nurseries ran along the A4 not far away. When we moved there in 1952 it was recognisably a village of a traditional, familiar kind.

Its centre was around the intersection between the Bath Road and the road between the neighbouring villages of Hurst and Wargrave. It was the usual mixture of shops, businesses and pubs, among which the pubs – or rather their names – are clearest in the memory. The Kings Arms stood on the crossroads, with the Bell facing it from the other side of the Wargrave Road. The Station Hotel, as you might expect, was opposite the station, with the Golden Cross no more than a couple of hundred yards away on the same road. The Bull and the Duke of Wellington were on the Bath Road, with the Waggon and Horses further along towards Reading. A little way from the village centre was the Grove Hall Hotel, a red-brick pile excitingly and mysteriously destroyed by fire when I was a few years old.

There were two butchers, a bread shop which sold cakes and cream buns, a greengrocer or possibly two greengrocers, Mrs Read's sweetshop, Newberry's the newsagents and Mr Gillett's antiques shop. There was a saddler's run by Mr Seymour amid a thick, beguiling aroma of leather and polish; he was also the secretary of the local angling club and sold fishing tackle and bait, of critical interest to myself and two of my elder brothers as we were mad for fishing. There was a cycle repair shop where our punctures were mended by a man steeped in oil whose hands were, for reasons never explained to me, short of the normal complement of fingers. And there were doubtless other retail premises, milliners and haberdashers and hairdressers and suchlike, which did not impinge upon my limited consciousness.

Although Twyford was 'home' and remained so until I was into my twenties, I realised much later that we played

Twyford village centre – pre-1914 and 1960s

little part in village life. At that time the English class system still retained its rigid grip, defending the demarcation lines between sectors of society in a way that seems extraordinary now. We were of the upper middle class – my father went to Eton, my mother to Benenden – and there were very few of us in Twyford. Indeed there was only one other family like ours with parents and children of similar background, ages and outlook. Fortunately for us they owned a large house on the river that ran along the western boundary of the village, giving us unfettered access to a mile and more of good fishing water. But none of their children was in the least interested in the things that interested me – mainly fishing, cricket and football – and I did not forge strong bonds with any of them.

I had no playmate in the village apart from my brothers. A month short of my eighth birthday I was sent off to boarding school in Northamptonshire. Two of my brothers were already there; the eldest had by then graduated from prep to public school. Soon after I was eight my father was killed in a motor accident. Subsequently my mother became head-mistress of Roedean School near Brighton, but the family base continued to be our house in Twyford. In my mother's absence everything was organised by my grandmother, who lived next door.

Unlike the rest of us, she entered energetically into aspects of village life. She was, in the best sense, a busybody: pillar of the church, the Conservative Association and the WI; familiar in every shop, known to every trader and a good many villagers. She had friends there, many more than my mother, whose brief breaks from her duties on the Sussex coast were mostly spent on solitary exertions on her knees in the garden keeping weeds at bay and plants in order.

The village was growing. In the Fifties it retained its irregular but comparatively compact form, gathered around the crossroads and the approaches to it, and the station. It extended east and west along the Bath Road but remained cushioned by fields to the north and south. Inexorably these fields were swallowed up by new housing. What had been neglected, rabbit-infested meadows across the road from our back fence were annexed for a new school and an expanse of streets and closes and cul-de-sacs lined with new houses and bungalows built from that pale, bloodless brick favoured by the mass housebuilders of the Sixties. The grounds of the Grove Hall Hotel were annexed by an estate of detached and semi-detached houses and maisonettes in the same brick, relieved by cladding and panelling, with flat-roofed, swing-doored garages and neat rectangular gardens.

The new housing was occupied by newcomers who commuted to London or had jobs in Reading. As the village centre was enclosed by its swelling surround of housing, so it gradually surrendered the diversity and the distinctiveness that went with it. The Kings Arms migrated from the crossroads to anonymous red-brick premises behind. The handsome stuccoed nineteenth-century building was demolished to make way for a thoroughly nasty parade of shops. In its new home the pub faltered and failed, eventually becoming an Italian restaurant. The Bell closed as well. For a time both butchers kept going, until Franklin's and the land behind it were sold to Waitrose. The opening of the supermarket in 2000 dealt a mortal blow to the retail heart of the village. Within a few years there were no food shops left, and the vacant premises were mostly eaten up by cheap restaurants and estate agents.

This process – the bleeding out of retail diversity in response to the tightening of the supermarket grip so familiar in so many similar settlements – took many years. By the time it was completed I had long since ceased to live in Twyford. I do not remember remarking upon it as it started and gathered pace, although later I noticed aspects of it, and I recall writing a piece for the *Financial Times* lamenting the end of Franklin's and the disappearance of its incomparable sausages. But as a lad I saw very little, heard nothing and knew almost no one, until 1968, when I was seventeen.

That summer I played a few games of cricket for the village team. My eldest brother had started playing the year before, and soon the second eldest was playing as well when home from university. For the first time I met and consorted with people from the village, my village. One or two of them were true Berkshire, with the rustic burr that has long since vanished utterly. But most were incomers from elsewhere, white-collar types, united in very little other than their enthusiasm for cricket.

Nearly half a century later I am still playing cricket for the village. I have not lived there since 1972 but until last year I was still chairman of the club. Most weeks during the summer I go over to work on the square, as well as playing Sunday matches. My spiritual commitment to the club remains as strong as ever, preserving my link to the village itself.

Twyford has continued to expand, and now has a population of almost 10,000. But it is still classified as a village, with a parish rather than a town council, and it clearly still is a village, albeit one enclosed by tracts of housing estates. Its character has not changed significantly since Waitrose opened. Its great transformation, which took place in front of my largely unseeing eyes, was effected over four decades, from the 1960s to the end of the millennium.

Its home owners still commute to London on the train or drive out to the business parks around Reading. Its children go the local schools. Its people eat in the Indian, Thai and Italian restaurants and pick up takeaways from the chippy and the Chinese. The surviving pubs – the Waggon and Horses, the Duke of Wellington and the Golden Cross – show football, put on quiz nights, stage live music. Food shopping is done at Waitrose; there is nowhere else. But there are other shops to cover other needs, and an excellent independent café, recently (and quite unnecessarily) joined by a Costa coffee house. The football club thrives, the cricket club survives, the Scouts march on and there is a host of 'village activities'.

Twyford has changed entirely since the Forts moved there in 1952. The form of the village we knew then is still there, but the life we knew has long vanished. Old Twyford is concealed within New Twyford, with a new life. But it is very evidently not dead or dying or even in precarious health.

*

There are, however, plenty of English villages which have been slowly drained of their vitality. The shop has gone, the pub has gone, the school has been converted into a second home, the old cottages have been sold to weekenders and the new houses, if there are any, to commuters from elsewhere. The church is part of a group parish of eight and gets communion once a month if it's lucky. The cricket club is a fading memory and the grass on the recreation field is two feet long. The peace is the peace of the graveyard.

This village tends to be small and distant from any major centre of population. It is rural and picturesque, richly endowed with cob, old stone, thatched roofs, crooked tiles, leaning chimneys, clambering roses, bee-humming cottage gardens; heavy with what the social historian and archaeologist Richard Muir scornfully characterised as 'the sweet and cloying lavender odour found in National Trust shops'. The local yokels have long gone, displaced by the same economic forces that have shaped the wider society we have today. The fabric of the village – the cottages and fine stone houses – has probably never been in better condition than it is now, because of the wealth of the new owners. But this village will have very little in the way of new, cheaper housing; therefore very little in the way of infusion of new blood. It is in the hands of retirees and second-homers and the reclusive, security-anxious rich, all very protective of its picturesqueness and quiet, not much bothered by the matter of its vitality.

For a village to thrive, it must have the capacity to renew itself, and that means making room for new families. The chances are that it will be comparatively big – say, three or four hundred homes and a population of a thousand or more – and with manageable connections to towns and cities where there is well-paid work. It will have a primary school, with a secondary school close by, which are much more important than those pillars of village life in times past, the church and pub (although it will have those). There will be a recreation ground and sports clubs, a library, allotments. There will be clubs, groups, activities, causes.

The price these villages pay for renewal is to forfeit something of their good looks. They will have had to accept new housing, accretions of banal and homogeneous dwellings, arranged by the dead hand and impoverished vision of developers around copses and closes and views and pightles and glebes and other meaningless harkings back to bygone days; tacked on to the irregular diversity that comes with organic growth over centuries. But if the village lives, it is a price worth paying.

I have never been a city-dweller, and although I have lived for extended periods in towns, I have never felt myself to be a natural townie. I am by nature and inclination a village kind of person, and I have spent a little over half of my life in two villages: the one where I was brought up, and the one where I live now. Neither is in the least scenic nor possessed of obvious charms. But they survive, even thrive. They are not typical of villages elsewhere because each village is particular to itself. But their stories, and the stories of other villages, together make a bigger story. And this bigger story is itself a fundamental part of the story of our nation.

2

LONG AGO

Goltho, Lincolnshire

A few miles east of Lincoln on the A158 is a signpost on the right for Goltho. The place itself is insignificant, just a scattering of houses hardly even amounting to hamlet status. But there is an arresting sight off the narrow, rough lane leading to it: a tiny red-brick church standing on its own in a broad, open cornfield.

St George's was built in the sixteenth century by the family who lived nearby at Goltho Hall. It has box pews, carved altar rails, a double-decked pulpit and a handsome stone floor. It also had a mellow tiled roof until October 2013, when it was struck by a bolt of lightning and set on fire. Sheets of corrugated metal now keep out the worst of the Lincolnshire weather.

It is sad in the way ruined churches always are, the more so because the sheets of corrugated iron are ugly and brutal and the rest of the building is lovely; and perhaps because it was brought to this state not by neglect – it had a devoted

Goltho church before being struck by lightning

band of volunteers who looked after it and it was still used for occasional services – but by atrocious bad luck or what one might call an act of God. No one enters it now and there is no one to pay to have the roof restored and the damage put right. Severed from its reason for being, St George's serves no one except those whose names are faintly, if at all, discernible on the leaning gravestones outside, and their requirements are minimal.

Underneath the floor of the church are the remains of another, even more ancient place of worship. And a few yards to the south-west of the churchyard is a slight but perceptible rise in the otherwise flat ground. There are clues here, if you know what you are looking for.

Fortunately the archaeologist Guy Beresford had a good idea of what to look for when he led a celebrated excavation of this Lincolnshire field in the late 1970s. But even Beresford was, I think, surprised by the richness and diversity of the history he and his team uncovered. The resulting book, handsomely published by English Heritage and available online, opens a window on to the often obscure and fragmented story of the English village in pre-medieval and medieval times.

The detailed chronology of the settlement at Goltho is complicated and necessarily speculative. But its broad outline is clear. It came into organised existence during the Roman occupation (although pottery fragments show there was some kind of exploitation of the site before the legions arrived in AD 43). Initially it comprised thatched circular huts, palisades and pounds for animals. Later, perhaps around AD 200, a more substantial Romano-British farmstead replaced the huts, although Beresford was not able to determine the full extent of the property.

Early in the fifth century Britain ceased to be part of the disintegrating Roman empire. Around then Goltho was abandoned. The reasons are unknown, but it was a time of chronic instability and rapidly declining population, aptly dubbed the Dark Ages. When the darkness thins a few centuries later, it reveals the field at Goltho to have been resettled by a group of Saxon immigrants. Saxon incursions from the Low Countries had begun while the Romans were still in control. After the legions left, Saxons exploited the vacuum to establish pagan kingdoms over much of the more productive land of central and southern England. The scale of colonisation is not clear, and some authorities believe that the numbers involved amounted to no more than a few thousand, and that their success was more linguistic than territorial.

At Goltho several houses built with clay and wattle walls and roofs thatched in sedge, straw or rush appeared in the eighth century arranged beside some sort of street or way, each with its own ditched and fenced paddock. Between 850 and 950 these dwellings were cleared away and replaced by more substantial ones built around three sides of a courtyard, the complex enclosed by ramparts and ditches. A timber hall was added subsequently, eighty feet long and twenty wide, with a floor of trampled clay. This imposing residence was itself then rebuilt with a Romanesque roof and a raised cobbled hearth.

It was evidently a place of wealth and importance. Quite soon – certainly by the end of the tenth century – a new stave-built manor house rose on the site, accompanied by outbuildings which included a weaving shed and kitchens, all within a strengthened enclosure. But construction at Goltho was by no means finished. Soon after the Norman invasion of 1066 work began to replace the manor house with a motte-and-bailey castle, raised on a mound well above the rest of the settlement and close to where the ruined church now stands. The castle was defended by a moat and wide ramparts, and was subsequently expanded into a proper fortified homestead suitable for the lord of this manor.

And so it remained, together with between thirty and forty humbler dwellings along a road and a side street, with – in time – a church. But at some point Goltho's fortunes began to wane. The reasons are a matter for supposition; it may be that the clay soil became impoverished or too compacted for satisfactory drainage; or that plague or some other disease struck; or that the village was caught up in some localised conflict; or, perhaps most likely, it fell victim to the well-documented worsening in the climate which meant the fields could no longer feed the people. Whatever the factors, the population diminished in the course of the fourteenth century to the point at which the village became unviable. By the time it was abandoned early in the fifteenth century there were just four homesteads left.

*

What happened at Goltho was particular to Goltho, but not atypical of elsewhere across England. It used to be stated that there could be very little known about the pattern of settlement in pre-Roman Britain because of the thoroughness with which those settlements – whether extended home-steads or groups of houses forming the earliest villages – had been erased from the landscape. But the steady advance in techniques of archaeology and in the interpretation of evidence has redrawn the picture entirely. It is now clear that, long before the Romans forged their empire, much of England had achieved remarkable progress both in food production and social organisation.

Bronze Age farmers cleared much of the original forest, and their Iron Age successors continued and extended the process, bringing great tracts of land under the plough and creating grazing for very considerable herds of livestock, mainly cattle. The population in the first century BCE is now estimated to have been not much lower than its level under Roman rule – perhaps as many as four or five million. The evidence suggests strongly that the prime motive for conquest was not to extend the boundaries of empire to include an undeveloped frontier province, but to exploit an existing production source of known value.

The notion that Roman officials arrived in the wake of the legions to impose the Roman system of administration on a country speckled with extended family farmsteads each operating independently and in isolation has been sabotaged by recent research. Thousands of settlements – ranging from tiny hamlets to a handful of what archaeologists refer to as proto-towns – had sprung up in Iron Age England. Silchester, for example – long identified as a 'Roman town' – in fact boasted an urban-style street system almost a century before Aulus Plautius weighed anchor off the Kent coast with his invasion force.

The steady rise in the population through the Bronze and Iron Ages, and the corresponding increases in food production, required people and communities to work together. Laser scanning of a site on a spur of the South Downs near Chichester has revealed traces of a complex and extensive Iron Age field system which could only have been constructed by a considerable labour force, and which was one part of a much more widespread and organised system of crop cultivation.

It is now evident that the Romans did not institute any kind of agricultural or even to any great extent social revolution. They built towns, vastly expanded industrial processes such as lead mining and iron smelting, introduced a full monetary economy and imposed a central government, funded by taxation, on what had previously been a disparate tribal system. But for the great majority of the rural population, working their land as they had before, Roman rule would hardly have impinged on daily life at all. Rather than representing an emergence from prehistoric darkness into the light of civilisation, Roman Britain can now be seen as one significant stage in a long process of organic change.

The traditional sequential version of our history saw Roman occupation give way to Saxon settlement, one phase followed by another. But it was not as tidy as that. In the short term, all that happened was that the protection of the Imperial army was withdrawn, partly in response to trouble on the Continent and partly because the British contingent had been overstretched trying to deal with bands of Saxon raiders – some of whom were actually ex-Roman army soldiers seizing the main chance when they saw it.

Fraternisation and intermarriage between resident Romano-British and Saxon incomers further complicated a complicated situation. What is clear is that, over a remarkably short period, the comparatively ordered society organised by Roman officialdom disintegrated into unstable spheres of influence riven by rivalries between competing lords who were ready at all times to resolve differences by violence.

As the population declined and what had been fertile fields were reclaimed by thorn and brush, many long-standing settlements ceased to exist. Others continued in occupation but at a much reduced level. The Saxon immigrants sometimes built their wooden houses next to an existing settlement, sometimes on new sites. The best known, at Mucking in Essex, included 200 smaller structures and a significant number of more substantial dwellings – one of these, fifty feet long and much bigger than the rest, may have been the hall of a ruling thegn – which were built and rebuilt on various parts of the site from the earliest years of the Saxon incursions onwards.

It was an unstable time in an unstable world, and clear patterns of occupation are difficult to establish. Some settlement sites clearly remained in use over long periods; others were abandoned. Under pressure of war or disease or shortage of food, groups would move on to try somewhere else, fragment, disperse, form new groups; leaving little trace beyond shards of pottery and marks on the ground discernible only from the air. A sense of permanence as we understand it – belonging in a specific location in a familiar, lasting dwelling – would have been unknown. Villages there certainly were, in the sense of groups of dwellings sustaining a communal life. But how they functioned and were organised – what village life was like – remains a matter of guesswork.

*

The birth of the English village in its familiar form was bound up with the evolution of the system of agriculture known as open-field agriculture, in which the viable land available to a community was worked communally with each family having its place. That connection is generally accepted by archaeologists and historians. But how open-field farming evolved, where the model came from, where it took hold and when, whether it was adopted piecemeal or whether there was a pattern, why some parts of England embraced it and others did not, and why variations in its applications are found in some places and not in others – all these are matters for discussion and dispute which will keep the academics and their supporting faculties happily occupied into the indefinite future.

This much is agreed. The old version of the birth of Village England – that much of the country was covered by virgin woodland which was cleared in Anglo-Saxon times, that the open-field system grew from that, and that villages developed to service a new system of agriculture – was wrong. Most of the woodland was gone before the Romans arrived. After the Roman army left, the population plunged and much cultivated land was abandoned, as were its settlements. Resettlement occurred haphazardly in the early Anglo-Saxon period, and in a more organised way later on – say between AD 850 and 1000. Existing farmsteads and hamlets tended to cluster together if close enough, forming what the medieval historians call nucleated settlements, i.e. villages.

The open-field system held sway across much of the north-east, through the Midlands and down through central southern England to the Channel. Much of the north-west, East Anglia, the south-west and the south-east retained the pattern of small fields worked from scattered farmsteads and hamlets. Where open-field farming did take hold, the process was completed by about 1200. The classic pattern, of field division into furlong strips (220 yards, or a fraction over 200 metres) often replaced an earlier one of much longer strips.

However, the chain or chains of cause and effect are very often obscure, allowing the spilling of rivers of scholarly ink and a ferment of respectful disagreement. In some places the adoption of open-field farming preceded the establishment of nucleated settlements. In others it accompanied it, and in others it came later. Sometimes it proceeded swiftly, sometimes much more slowly, sometimes only partially. Variations in local conditions – such as the lightness or heaviness of the soil, or the presence or absence of extensive woodland – seem to have dictated developments. For instance, the successful cultivation of clay soil required a heavy plough, which in turn required a team of oxen to pull it, which in turn required a pooling of resources by families who did not possess enough animals on their own.

In the south-west the persistence with the old methods seems to be easily explained. The population was too small, the land too hilly and the soil too stony and thin for open-field farming to be viable. But in south-east England – Essex, for example – conditions were favourable, yet the dispersed settlement pattern persisted, and no one really knows why.

A further thorny complication is that the handy distinction between a 'nucleated' and 'non-nucleated' settlement all too often breaks down in practice, since a very large number of settlements display aspects of both categories. Some appear to have been planned around a rough grid of streets, others to have grown up randomly and organically. Furthermore, even when nucleated villages associated with open-field farming do survive, they are sometimes not in the same place as they were when the fields were laid out.

Much of this confusion arises from the long-established assumption that Domesday – that medieval marvel of central planning – listed villages. In fact it described and recorded land holdings (which is where the value for tax purposes lay). These may have been gathered into manors or estates, but were certainly not the same as a settlement and its holdings. Some estates included several villages, others – just as meticulously recorded – none at all.

Altogether the picture of 'Village England' in the immediate post-1066 period is one of almost infinite variety, which is very pleasing to the archaeologists and those whose pleasure it is to pore over tithe and manorial rolls. The great difficulty in establishing where those villages were and what they looked like arises from the limited choice of available building materials. Hovels of clay, wattle and thatch were not built to last, indeed were built not to last. That sense of the impermanence of things must have been a dominant feature of the medieval mind, colouring every aspect of life.

Where a building does survive, it is usually the church, the only one built of stone. But the positioning of the church was determined by a number of factors. St Augustine had instructed that the place should, where possible, be the same as that previously used for pagan worship. The land had to be given by the local lord, or by the community. It may have been close to, or in the heart of, the settlement; or some distance away, according to what site was available. Often a later, permanent settlement – the village – did coalesce around the church; but that does not necessarily mean it started there.

*

We may have no more than a hazy idea of where exactly the medieval village was or what it would have looked like had we stumbled upon it down some muddy, stony track. But thanks to the efforts of inquisitive and open-minded historians to make sense of the earliest written records – the manorial and court rolls – as well as more elusive sources, we now have a reasonable grasp of how it was organised.

For a start the people would not have called it a village, the word being unknown at the time. It is derived from the Middle English *vill* meaning 'town', a unit established to organise the working of the fields. Vills were grouped into tens, confusingly known as hundreds, for taxation and other administrative purposes. The vill could act as a collective of tenants, or indeed as the collective lessee of an estate.

The medieval village has left no written record. The documentation available from that period is in the form of church, manor and state records. It is extensive but inevitably lopsided. It presents its account of the workings of society through the eyes of the clergy, the landlords and their literate employees, and royal officials. It is one version, and for a long time was the only version. But the village and its people had another version, only there was no one to write it down. It has had to be deduced by clever detective work.

The official version has a society that is pyramidal in structure, with the king at the apex, owning everything. Below him were the lords, forming the aristocracy, and the Church, both given charge of lands not reserved for direct royal control. These lands were divided into estates or manors. At the top of the village section of the pyramid were the free tenants, who paid rent to the manor (indirectly to the lord or bishop or abbot or abbess) for their land, and owed service and obligations. Next – able to look up and down – was the villein: not a free man yet not a slave either; technically not allowed to own anything, but with certain time-honoured rights; the backbone of agriculture, empowered by custom and practice to take decisions on how the fields should be cultivated and to compose a jury to sit in judgment on his fellows. At the bottom, able only to look upwards, were the cottars, with the smallest dwellings – the cottages – the smallest holdings of land, the greatest burden of obligation to those above them.

The village also required its specialists, who stood slightly outside the pyramid. The two most important were the miller and the blacksmith, who were likely to have the status of free tenant or villein. There were also the officials, chief among them the reeve, who was generally drawn from the villein class and was chosen by the village to serve as the lord's general foreman. There would also be a priest, who as often as not combined the duty of conducting worship with that of farming his glebe land.

This was feudalism, a system built on obligations and rights which were partly imposed from above and partly drawn from an existing, pre-Norman pattern of land control. Its structure was mightily complex, its operation even more so. The distinctions it sought to define and preserve were very much less precise than the written records would have us believe. Some villagers were clearly freemen, villeins or cottars, but some straddled two or even all three of those divisions. Obligations varied hugely from manor to manor, region to region, village to village, as did the success the top tier enjoyed in enforcing them. Like all systems of government it developed multiple lives of its own, making it inadvisable for historians to offer sweeping generalisations about how people fared under it.

Nevertheless some important common features are worth mentioning. The ruling class did not exercise absolute power, however much it might have wished to, or asserted that it did. Broadly speaking the noble lords preferred to concentrate on important matters such as hunting, fighting, religious observances and attendance on the King, and left the mundane tasks of collecting rents and organising court judgments on land disputes and petty crime to their officials. These men over time acquired extensive knowledge of administration and law, which gave them their own authority. Drawn from the community themselves, their upward mobility enabled them to form a power base that restrained – and could even challenge – aristocratic tyranny. And the village itself jealously guarded the rights that came umbilically attached to the obligations, and learned to stand up for itself against the capricious exercise of power from elsewhere.

The application of the rigid rules of feudal status and service was haphazard. Families belonging to the lowest order quietly moved away to better themselves when they were not supposed to. Wage earners broke contracts. Villeins evaded duties to the lord or paid someone else to discharge them. Marriages were made and land transfers effected without anyone bothering to secure the necessary permission.

Settlements were formed by people acting on their own initiative in order to organise the cultivation of the land. Oligarchal tendencies inevitably prevailed: the more resourceful, enterprising, ruthless and ambitious members of the village community rose to the top and directed the others. The law was enforced in the name of the manorial court, but the rules and regulations that actually mattered in daily life were not framed by the lord but by the villagers. The class system that emerged was one in which everyone knew their place and that of their neighbours. But it was not imposed from above, nor was it identical in its particulars to the one in the next village. People had the freedom, within the feudal web, to make choices.

Every village was acutely status conscious. The class divisions were complicated and nuanced; disputes were frequent, bitter and often violent. But in the interests of survival – the only interests that mattered – the village had to be able to function cooperatively. It had to be able to accommodate human nature or it would fail.

Many medieval villages did fail. It used to be believed that there were two main factors in forcing the abandonment of established settlements. One was plague. The other was forcible eviction so that the fields could be converted into grazing for sheep, enabling rapacious and tyrannical over-lords to profit from the booming market for wool. In fact detailed research has uncovered very few examples of villages being wiped out by plague, or being seized by bailiffs and torched. Much more often a village fell into slow decay, as in the case of Goltho. There might be various reasons for this: an outbreak of plague might be one, causing a fall in population to a point at which the land could no longer be efficiently cultivated. Sometimes the village was just too small to be viable, or too close to a stronger competitor.

The medieval peasant could not afford to be sentimental about his place of birth and upbringing, or anything else. On the other hand, an investment in the village in terms of land acquired and home built would give rise to a natural prac-tical impulse to stay put. At Wharram Percy in Yorkshire, a celebrated and thoroughly excavated deserted village site, the villagers constructed longhouses ranging from 50 to 75 feet in length, with timber-framed walls and thatched roofs. Early in the thirteenth century they began to build walls from chalk blocks bonded by clay; then reverted to timber, but with stone footings. Elsewhere stone walls to shoulder height or a little above became the norm over the course of the thirteenth century, although the roofs – of poles and thatch – meant the lifespan of the dwellings was still limited.

Little by little the notion of permanence took a hold, the desire to belong and to put down roots. It was a slow process, requiring as it did a total revolution in attitude. But it made the English village as we like to think of it possible.

3

COUNTRYSIDE ENCLOSED

East Hendred, Oxfordshire

East Hendred is a particularly lovely village of mainly sixteenth- and seventeenth-century houses and cottages below the Berkshire Downs. For most of its history it was in Berkshire, but since the county boundary changed in 1974 it has been in Oxfordshire. In 1800 its resident squire, Basil Eyston, got together with two other local bigwigs, Sir John Pollen and Richard Hopkins, three more landowners designated as 'gentlemen', ten yeomen, a blacksmith, a cordwainer and a mason to petition parliament for an Act of Enclosure. It was passed the next year and three commissioners were appointed to 'divide and allot and lay in severalty the open and common fields, common meadows, common pastures, Downs and other commonable and waste lands'.

Notices to this effect were placed in newspapers and pinned to the door of the church. There is no record of any opposition, and by the end of the year the award had been made. A total of 1250 acres was divided between thirty-six

East Hendred in the 1960s

people, including the Rector of East Hendred. A few years later the remainder of the common land was similarly parcelled out.

The enclosure at East Hendred was no different in its essentials from the thousands of such awards made across the country (the first recorded was at Radipole in Dorset in 1604, the last at Elmstone Hardwicke in Gloucestershire in 1914). There were two main waves, between 1760 and 1780, and between 1790 and 1815. Altogether more than five thousand enclosure awards were made, affecting three thousand parishes and seven million acres, a quarter of the open countryside. The west of the country, from Cumberland and Westmorland (now Cumbria) down to Devon and Cornwall, was little touched by the drive to enclose, and its pursuit was patchy in Kent, Essex and East Sussex. But across much of England's most productive agricultural land it amounted to a revolution which would have immense social consequences.

The bonds that bound feudal England began to slacken in the fourteenth century. The calamity of the Black Death, which wiped out a third of the population, caused a radical rebalancing of the agricultural labour market. The landowning class, faced with the painful realisation that many – sometimes most – of their tenants had perished, and their labour and rents with them, were forced to offer inducements to get their land tilled at all. Those that refused to substitute tenancies for feudal services found their remaining able-bodied workers quite prepared to move elsewhere rather than bend the knee. Most gave way sooner or later, and the class of bondsmen was converted to one of rent-paying tenants. At the same time it suited some landowners to rent extensive holdings to one prospering, ambitious farmer and leave him to organise sub-tenancies and the actual farming as he saw fit.

The village had a single function, which was to enable the land to be worked. But as it settled in its position, it developed its own dynamic. Some of its spaces – the church, the churchyard, the roads, the green if there was one, the environs of the pond if there was one – were public. Villagers also met socially at the mill, at the bakehouse and the house where ale was sold. But privacy and independence were important. Each dwelling was separate, however closely they were clustered together. Most had a surrounding ditch and bank enclosing the outbuildings as well as the home, with a fence or hedge or wall. A gate led from the street to the front door. Visitors were received in the hall; the chamber beyond was for the family. Doors were secured with locks, as were chests where valuables were stored.

Disputes between neighbours were extremely common, and almost everyone was summoned to the manorial court at some time or other to answer for themselves. Much of the trouble stemmed from the division of the land into multitudes of narrow, unmarked strips separately owned or rented. The pages of the court rolls are filled with records of the fines imposed for encroachment. Quarrels that started in the fields easily spilled over into the village, often leading to violence. Fights and assaults were another staple of court proceedings.

But although people may not have liked each other, they had to live and work together to survive. By degrees communities took shape, and those forming them began to show a cautious confidence in the future. They put down stone foundations for their houses, raised stone walls, installed windows and even roofs of slate. Once a family had established its presence on a particular plot, it was natural for it to aspire to a bigger, better home when circumstances were favourable, either by extension or rebuilding altogether. In Foxton in Cambridgeshire, for example, the entire village of fifty houses was rebuilt between 1550 and 1620 of stone with oak-braced walls, so robustly that twenty of them are still standing today.

The great historian of the English landscape, W. G. Hoskins, dubbed this period The Great Rebuilding and ascribed to it a general impulse for home improvement across much of the country. Sadly, as so often with the identification of pleasing overarching historical themes, it turns out that there was no such movement. Rebuilding occurred haphazardly at different times in different places, dictated more than anything else by the availability of building materials. Certainly by 1500 two-storey village houses with stone walls and thatched roofs were comparatively common.

The village began to assume its familiar form. Some were built or rebuilt according to a plan, a favourite being two rows facing each other across a green with the road running by it. Much more often, though, the growth was piecemeal and organic, the dwellings put on plots as and when circumstances permitted, facing each other, side by side, at irregular angles and different heights, squeezed along winding lanes and down dark alleys, everything thrown together on to the available spaces without thought given to the shape or form or the look of it.

Such villages were the expressions of fierce individualism: each family seeking the best for itself and whatever advantage it could obtain over its neighbour. Each village was unique and often almost every building in it was unique. But because the villagers were seeking the same goals, because the building techniques and models were restricted, and above all because they had to use the same materials – the same timber from the same woods, the same stone from the same quarries, the one kind of thatch – the product of this individual striving acquired the harmony of design, texture and colour that creates the magic of the classic village scene. Weatherboarding in Kent, tile-hanging in Sussex and Surrey, brick-and-flint in the Chilterns and in Norfolk, cob and thatch in Devon and Dorset, slate in Cornwall, stone in the Cotswolds and the North – each bestows its own shared distinctiveness.

But it is easy to be deceived by the appearance of these villages. They have been there a long time, at one with their landscapes, apparently almost sprung from the soil. They are a visible connection with a life which in virtually all other respects has long since vanished. Those weathered walls and crooked roofs and gable ends are so solid and permanent. The temptation is to invest the lives of those who left them with the same qualities.

You wander around the churchyard and note the recurrence of the same names, generation after generation of them; and if there is a good history of the village, it is sometimes possible to connect those names with individual houses. And you may reasonably conclude that this indeed was village life: a triumph of continuity stretching over centuries, people finding their places, putting down roots, establishing strong and lasting bonds with the place of their birth.

But that was by no means the full story. The other side of it belongs to the names that are not on the gravestones, and that story is not so readily accessible. A similarly lopsided perspective comes from studying the manorial records, in which the same family names crop up again and again. It is understandable to concentrate on those names, because they present a reasonably coherent narrative line. But there are plenty of others whose names are mentioned in passing or not at all, because they did not hang around. Migration and mobility were constant realities, then as now.

The cosy assumptions about the continuity of country living were demolished by the Cambridge historian Peter Laslett in his 1965 study of pre-industrial society, *The World We Have Lost*. Laslett and his colleagues took the novel step of examining the parish records of two villages in Northamptonshire, Cogenhoe and Clayworth, to see what light they could shed on the demographics. They revealed a startling turnover of population. Almost half of those living in Cogenhoe in 1618 – eighty-six out of 185 – were no longer there ten years later. Sixteen had died; the rest had moved out. Over the same period ninety-four people moved into the village. In Clayworth between 1676 and 1688, 244 out of 401 named inhabitants disappeared from the roll, and 255 new names were recorded.

Laslett's methods were taken up elsewhere and extended, and similar patterns were revealed. The Norfolk church rolls for the period between 1499 and 1530 showed that just over a quarter of the males and just under half of the females in the parishes covered were aged between twenty-one and thirty when their names were recorded for the first time – i.e. they were incomers. Fewer than a quarter had been resident since birth. Records for villages in Worcestershire show that over a 200-year period from 1327, a measly 8 per cent of families remained in the same place.

In general people did not move far – fifteen or twenty miles at most. They did so for much the same reasons that they do now: to better themselves economically, to take advantage of work opportunities, to escape difficult or intolerable circumstances.

But although the cast in village life changed much more than was once realised, the structure of that life and its fixed points did not. The spiritual horizons were low and confined, and the opportunities for leisure were severely restricted. There were occasional holidays and feast days. There was attendance at church, nominally compulsory, which gave a rare chance to stand around and do nothing (pews were unknown), listen to stories from a book and socialise outside. Most villages, but not all, had a church. Very few had a dedicated ale-house. If they were lucky there might be a monthly or even weekly market.

Of the fixed points the most imperative was work. Six days a week the villagers toiled in the fields unless they were too old or sick or injured, or were on an errand appointed from on high. Work filled the hours of daylight for men, women and able-bodied children. The hours of darkness were for rest.

Village affairs were ordered by a local elite generally composed of the parson, yeomen farmers and skilled craftsmen, aided by the churchwardens and the constable – those with the confidence to speak up at meetings and the competence to take decisions. Although the manorial court limped on into the seventeenth century, the influence of the manor house and its lord over the daily lives of the people – always intermittent and variable – waned into insignificance.

The services due under the feudal system were never abolished. They merely lapsed as the effort to enforce them became more trouble than it was worth. Lords increasingly resorted to leasing out estates in their entirety, retaining the home farm to supply the needs of the manorial household. Over time the leaseholds mutated into proprietorial rights defendable in the common law courts. Tenants were able to retain a greater portion of the profits from the land, which gave them an incentive to maximise those profits. As they and their descendants became property owners, they also became buyers and sellers of land, the transactions faithfully recorded by those manorial courts which had once directed their lives.

A new social order was emerging in rural England. The changes were not planned or organised as a matter of policy. They happened in response to localised circumstances, so that often the arrangements in neighbouring manors would be entirely different. The pace of change was uncertain and uncontrolled. But broadly speaking its principal consequence was a growing divide between made-good, property-owning yeomen farmers intent on accumulating land and increasing production, and a wage-earning labouring class available for hire. Although the ancient common rights of every villager persisted, the amount of land on which they might be exercised diminished steadily. The stage was set for capitalism to establish its grip across great tracts of the English countryside.

*

A paradox of enclosure is that it has often been depicted as a wicked land grab orchestrated by the unscrupulous ruling class at the expense of an ignorant and downtrodden peasantry; yet a crucial component of our shared and cherished image of rural England – the irregular chequerboard of fields and hedges and copses – was its direct result. Once the new owners had got their hands on what had once been everyone's, their first impulse was to advertise their ownership by fencing and then hedging their fields, so that all and sundry might know what belonged to who, and where they might and might not go.

The charge that enclosure represented the robbing of the poor by the grasping rich has always been beguiling to social historians of leftish inclination. It is certainly true – as observed by Raymond Williams in *The Country and the City* – that it was 'part of a wider process in which a capitalist social system was pushed through to a position of dominance by a form of legalised seizure enacted by representatives of the beneficiary class'. It is also true that as a result of enclosure, social divisions in the countryside widened and hardened. The big landowners, the squires and the yeomen farmers pulled ahead. The small-scale tenants got a share of the enclosure spoils according to their status, but these were rarely viable, particularly if they had to bear the cost of hedging or walling. They tended to sell up and either emigrate to town or city, or become farm labourers. The poorest, often little more than squatters dependent on the common land to scrape by, sank into destitution.

But an equally compelling truth is that the state of the nation demanded the agricultural revolution of which enclosure was a part. The old, open-field communal system evolved to feed those who practised it. Constricted by its web of obligation, it offered few incentives to improve production. While England remained an overwhelmingly rural society, that did not matter. Although many periodically went hungry, very few actually starved to death. But industrialisation and urbanisation created a massive new demand for food. A way had to be found to satisfy the hungry mouths of the factory workers and their families. Farming had to become more efficient. As so often, the market found a way, and there were winners and losers.

The effect of the changes on the village varied considerably. The major holders of lands, the lords and squires, had generally preferred to live outside the village anyway. In some cases the soaring profits from farming and increased rents enabled them to commission new mansions and lay out parks, which were intended as visible expressions of new-found wealth and power. The game laws they enacted, allowing for the most savage punishments to be imposed on poachers who dared infringe on their properties were a hated extension of that power.

The made-good yeoman farmer, previously the strongest voice in village counsels, now tended to remove himself by building a new home in the middle of his expanded lands from which to direct his labourers, watch over his tenants and keep his horses for hunting. The workers themselves usually had no choice but to stay in the village, but now found themselves sharing it – not with their fellows, all bound in the same enterprise, but with shopkeepers and traders.

There had been rural paupers before enclosure, but now they were more conspicuous. Parishes had long since been required to provide relief for the destitute – a duty they often fulfilled by driving them outside the parish boundaries and keeping them there. The first attempt to organise relief on a wider scale was the so-called Speenhamland system, devised by a group of Berkshire magistrates at a meeting held at the Pelican Inn at Speenhamland near Newbury in 1798. It allowed for a means-tested supplement to the lowest wages, calculated according to the price of bread. The intention was to lessen the impact of widespread impoverishment, but the effect was to encourage employers to keep wages down in the knowledge that the extra – funded by the whole parish – would top them up. The new Poor Law of 1834 did away with Speenhamland, replacing it with the concept of the 'deserving poor', which was given bricks-and-mortar expression in that forbidding Victorian institution, the workhouse.

The main waves of enclosure were accompanied by a significant growth in the rural population, which put downward pressure on earnings. At the same time, the landowners and farmers seized the opportunities offered by mechanisation to push up yields and profits while reducing the labour force. The upshot was the bonfire of rural unrest known as the Captain Swing riots which was lit in Kent in the summer of 1830 and swept across the counties of southern England in a matter of weeks and burned itself out by Christmas.

Like the Luddites in the towns and cities, the Swing rioters saw themselves being pauperised and victimised by technological advances in which they had no stake. They burned hayricks and smashed the hated new threshing machines and issued illiterate threats to spill blood in the name of the mythical Captain Swing. As with the Luddites – named after the equally mythical General Ludd – the capitalist ruling class called out the military to enforce order by force, and then used the laws they had enacted to crush opposition and punish the troublemakers with the utmost viciousness.

For the most celebrated rural radical, William Cobbett, the tragedy arising from enclosure was not the actual division of the fields, but the expansion of individual holdings and the social elevation of their owners. 'I hold a return to small farms to be absolutely necessary to a restoration of anything like an English community,' Cobbett wrote. 'When farmers become gentlemen, their labourers become slaves.'

Poets like Goldsmith and John Clare railed against the changes. Another versifier, the splenetic social agitator Ebenezer Elliott, went further. In his *The Splendid Village*, published in 1833, Elliott's Wanderer returns to the place of his birth to find that every good thing he recalls from his childhood has been destroyed. The callous and bullying butcher's son has been appointed the lord's steward. The lawyer and the doctor compete in the splendour of their new properties. The old inn is now run by the Constable and the Bailiff, both hated and feared by the villagers in equal measure. The Common is no more and 'the very children seem afraid to smile'.

The American writer Washington Irving painted a rosier, not to say sentimentalised picture of the English countryside in his study *Rural Life in England*, published in 1819. But he still found a growing division between gentry and peasantry. Irving quoted an old squire of his acquaintance lamenting how 'our simple true-hearted peasantry have broken asunder from the higher classes and seem to think their interests are separate. They have become too knowing and begin to read newspapers and listen to ale-house politicians and talk of reform.' The squire's solution – for those like him to spend more time on their estates and for a revival of 'merrie old English games' – was as much wishful thinking as Cobbett's call for the resurrection of the small-scale farmer. The tide was running irresistibly the other way.

Reviewing East Hendred's past history from an early twentieth-century perspective, the politician and agricultural historian Lord Ernle found the pre-enclosure village united 'in a singularly close relationship. Their farming was their common enterprise, even though each individual took the produce of his holding. For good or evil, it allowed no room for the exaggerated individualism and fevered competition of modern life.' Enclosure and the new methods, Ernle judged, had justified themselves economically by their success. But the impact on the displaced and the dispossessed had been severe – 'with the break-up of the village farm,' he wrote, 'community life shrivelled at the source.'

The same has been asserted many times, with varying degrees of vehemence. But is it true? The village may no longer have been a community of farmers united in a common enterprise. But it did not cease to exist. It remained a village, therefore a community, therefore with a community life. Then as now. Common sense says so.

*

In East Hendred the ancient Church of St Augustine stands across the road from the equally ancient Hendred House, home of the lords of the manor, the Eystons, for the past 550 years and more. On the face of it the situation of the two most important and imposing buildings in the village would appear to symbolise that relationship of squire and parson so critical to the welfare of the community for so long. As it happens, the Eystons have always been Roman Catholic, and have always worshipped in their own – also very ancient – chapel at the side of the house. Even so, there is an Eyston chapel in the Anglican church and Eystons are buried in its graveyard, suggesting a cordial working relationship despite doctrinal differences.

Hendred House is unusual for a manor house in being at the heart of the village, and very unusual indeed for still being occupied by the same family that was there when Henry VI was on the throne. The Eystons have played little part on the wider national stage; only one of them, Charles – an early eighteenth-century antiquary and expert on ecclesiastical buildings – warrants an entry in the *Dictionary of National Biography*. Their low profile was undoubtedly connected with their unswerving Catholicism. The benefit for East Hendred was their availability for involvement in village life.

Speaking generally, however, the squire has largely disappeared from the rural scene. Even a hundred years ago he had become a threatened species. His imminent passing was mourned by an incurably sentimental Tory cleric, the Reverend P. H. Ditchfield, who was the Rector of Barkham in Berkshire for almost half a century, a stalwart of the Berkshire Archaeological Society and the author of a host of books with titles like *Bygone Berkshire*, *The Parson's Pleasance* and *Old English Sports and Customs*. In his *Old Village Life*, published in 1920, Ditchfield paid a nostalgic tribute: 'The old squire was an upright magistrate, a kind landlord, a liberal contributor according to his means, a friend of the poor, the unflinching protector of the oppressed, a firm opponent of the wicked, ever willing to advise, ever ready to help . . . but the race is dying out.'

A less charitable view was presented by Lord Macaulay – admittedly of the seventeenth-century incarnation: 'His chief pleasures were commonly derived from field sports and from an unrefined sensuality. His language and pronunciation were such as we would expect to hear only from the most ignorant clowns. His oaths, coarse jests and scurrilous terms of abuse were uttered with the broadest accent. His opinions . . . were the opinions of a child . . . his animosities were numerous and bitter . . . his ignorance and uncouthness, his low tastes and gross phrases would, in our time, be considered as indicating a nature and a breeding thoroughly plebeian. Yet he was essentially a patrician . . .'

The familiar figure was moulded of materials from various sources. His ancestor may have been a knight, or an esquire who waited upon a knight, or an upwardly mobile lawyer, administrator or tax collector. The squire had land enough to live more or less comfortably off the rents. He was a Justice of the Peace and sometimes undertook other unpaid duties, such as inspecting prisons, schools, the work-house or the local lunatic asylum. He hunted as if it were a religion and often served as Master of the Hunt, regarding his duty to preserve the game on his estate as sacred. He regarded himself as belonging to a particular stratum in the English social hierarchy, forming with his fellow squires a powerful force for stability — one naturally requiring the maintenance of superiority and strong control over the lower orders.

The essayist Joseph Addison, co-founder of the *Spectator*, created an enduring exemplar of the breed in the figure of Sir Roger de Coverley. He is a Worcestershire squire, a Tory and dedicated hunter of foxes, a magistrate and village benefactor. He and his family have their pew in church, at the front, and when he leaves at the end of divine service his tenants bow to him as he makes his slow and majestic pro-gress along the aisle. Every now and then he stops to inquire as to how one or other is doing, or to ask why one is absent, 'which is understood as a kind of reprimand'. He is a good man, liberal by his lights, but very jealous of his prestige. Sir Roger is particularly wary of the man on the rung of the ladder immediately below his, the yeoman farmer — 'with about a hundred a year . . . and qualified to kill a hare or a pheasant'.

The squire's obsession with riding to hounds and preserv-ing game, and the belief of so many that chasing and killing birds and animals were the greatest accomplishments of civilised life, served to distance him further from his tenants and the labouring classes. When that obsession was aided and abetted by the Game Laws, prescribing savage penalties on any poacher caught taking a precious bird or beast, that distance easily transmuted into resentment and hatred.

W. H. Hudson, a great observer and celebrant of natural history and the English countryside, deplored the influence of the squire: 'What I heartily dislike is the effect of his position (that of a giant among pygmies) on the lowly minds about him, and the servility, hypocrisy and parasitism which spring up and flourish in his wide shadow whether he likes these weeds or not. As a rule he likes them, since the poor devil has this in common with the rest of us, that he likes to stand high in the general regard.'

By the time Hudson wrote these words (in *A Shepherd's Life*, published in 1910) the sun was setting fast on the squire's heyday. For several centuries he had formed a partnership with the parson which had done much to shape village life. On the whole it can be said that he generally acted from the best intentions, as determined by his restricted horizons. He was often ignorant, dim, prejudiced, intolerant and extremely slow in seeing what was in front of his face. But he gave freely of his time and energy, and without him the village would have been poorer materially, and probably spiritually as well.

4

WHAT GOLDEN AGE?

The Bournes, Surrey

On the Ordnance Survey map a cluster of settlements is shown just south of Farnham in Surrey. The names are Upper Bourne, Middle Bourne and Lower Bourne; and for good measure the map also displays a collective, The Bournes.

But they are names only. The distinct places they were, with their distinct identities, disappeared a long time ago, swallowed up by the southerly creep of the town. This happened steadily and inexorably, but quite discreetly. What had been woodland and heathland was annexed, not by housing estates, but by large and sometimes rather splendid residences replete with external beaming, extravagant gables, high eaves and big chimneys and dormers, each standing in large gardens secluded among tall trees. They were well spread out, quiet, leafy, exclusive, now fabulously pricey.

Lower Bourne was a modest, haphazard village scattered along the brook known as the Bourne, which flowed only

Lower Bourne in 1924

after sustained rainfall. It had no long history, having been wasteland until some itinerant squatters built shacks there in the middle of the eighteenth century. It had no nucleus, no green, no squire – not even a parson until the church was built in the early 1860s. Its identity was precarious even 150 years ago, except for those who lived there, for whom it was their village.

One of those was George Sturt, an unmarried man who lived with his spinster sisters in a plain red-brick cottage standing above Old Church Lane. He was a rung or two above most of the villagers on the social ladder. His father had been a wheelwright in Farnham, and he went to the grammar school in the town, working there for a while afterwards as an assistant. In time he and his brother inherited the wheelwright business, but George Sturt was a reluctant craftsman. He found someone else to run the business while he devoted himself to studying and recording the rural life around him, just as it was being obliterated for good.

In a series of books – published under the name George Bourne, presumably a nod at the brook that lent its name to the village – he chronicled the lives of the smallholders and artisans he knew. The first, *The Bettesworth Book*, was subtitled *Talks with a Surrey Peasant*, and focussed on Fred Bettesworth – real name Fred Grover – who was the Sturts' gardener. Sturt later produced a sequel about Fred's wife Lucy. But the book for which he was best known was *Change in the Village*, which came out in 1912. In it he tried to set down dispassionately and objectively how the village functioned, how its people worked, spoke, thought, took their leisure; what it was about the place that mattered to them and enabled them to be what they were; what was valuable and irreplaceable about it.

Enclosure had come late to Lower Bourne, because there was little worth enclosing. But come it did, and Sturt – looking back half a century later – saw it as a hammer blow to the old way of life. 'It was', he wrote, 'like knocking the keystone out of an arch ... it left the people helpless against the influences that had sapped away their interests.' Being a fair-minded observer, he accepted that at the time no one objected; and that it was actually welcomed because the money the villagers got for selling their shares of the common land enabled them to buy plots and build proper cottages in place of the hovels they had lived in before.

But the charge sheet listing the evil consequences of enclosure is long. The peasant was 'shut out from his land and cut off from his resources'. For the first time he was dependent on money and had to wait for others to give him work instead of 'going for a livelihood to the impartial heath'. Competition had replaced cooperation. The villagers had become servile, their wisdom and particular skills no longer valuable or useful. The village temper had acquired 'a sort of reserve ... a want of gaiety ... a subdued air'. The children were furtive and suspicious, no longer free to play in the woods, fearful of authority. 'Today,' Sturt declared, 'we have a great mental and spiritual destitution ... we have here, not a distinct group of people, but numerous impoverished people living provisionally from hand to mouth.'

For all his sympathy and understanding, Sturt displayed a deep and arrogant condescension towards the class below him. His assumption was that he – the literate, educated one – was better able to judge what was happening to them than they were. He was determined to enlist them in his version of what Raymond Williams identified as the myth of modern England: that the transition from a rural to an industrial society represented a kind of Fall, and was the true cause of our sense of dislocation.

George Sturt loathed the modern world. He hated what had happened to Farnham. He hated the gentrification, the spread of villadom, the disappearance of the countryside under bricks and mortar, the march of technological advance. He convinced himself that the villagers of Lower Bourne had possessed a set of ancient virtues rooted in the soil they worked. They had 'the country touch . . . the village character was genial, steadfast, self-respecting . . . they had a great fund of strength, a great stability.' They made the best of it and 'met their troubles calmly'. They were not resentful of their poverty because 'they have never learned to look upon the distribution of property that has left them so impoverished as anything other than an inevitable dispensation of Providence.'

This was not all. The peasant's relationship with the countryside was instinctive and intimate – 'he was part of it and it was part of him'. There was an unwritten code, 'and where it flourished it ultimately led to gracefulness of living and love of what is kindly and comely.'

No awareness of individualism is permitted to colour Sturt's obituary on his village. No one speaks for himself or herself. There is no voice to say: I was glad to build my house, I was glad to escape the poverty and isolation, I was glad to work for a wage, I was glad for the chance to better myself, I was glad not to have to toil all day on my plot in the wind and the rain and come back and sit in the dark in my comfortless, damp habitation and contemplate the prospect that this would be my lot until the end of my days.

It is true that he did not portray village life as being in the least idyllic. He dutifully catalogued the drunkenness, cruelty, incidents of 'infamous vice', degrading poverty, ill health, dirt, primitive living conditions, the lack of refinement and mental stimulation and the rest of it. So why do we not hear from those – and they must have existed among Lower Bourne's 500 or so inhabitants – who wished to exchange that life for another? The reason is that to do so would have been to risk compromising the message. And the message was that they were better off as they were, even if they were too ignorant to realise it.

*

Soon after the publication of *Change in the Village* came the conflict that would turn rural life upside down. In the year of its outbreak, 1914, a reforming and socially progressive politician called Ernest Bennett produced a little book called *Problems of Village Life*. Bennett examined the living conditions in the village of Potterne, near Devizes in Wiltshire. It comprised one- and two-bedroom tied cottages in a 'vile and deplorable state'. Forty-four dwellings shared the use of three WCs. Rheumatism, pleurisy, bronchitis and pneumonia were rife. Two-thirds of the children suffered from malnutrition.

Where George Sturt saw a community 'taking pride in their skill and hardihood', Bennett found an 'absolute mechanical existence ... the villagers go to bed at eight o'clock to save on oil and candles ... the careworn faces of the women, the sullen endurance of their husbands, the dreary respectability of the farmer ... there is so little to refine the mind or cheer the soul in rural England.' To Ernest Bennett, Sturt's noble peasant was 'the poorly paid English labourer, the social product of centuries of repression and neglect'.

There was no shortage of evidence to support Bennett's version. Much of it was gathered by H. Rider Haggard – of *King Solomon's Mines* fame – who spent most of the years 1901 and 1902 visiting farms and rural settlements across southern England and recorded his findings in two massive volumes entitled *Rural England*. Rider Haggard found the agricultural depression which had taken hold in the 1870s – blamed on rising imports of cheap food from abroad – maintaining its grip. The young men and women, he reported, were leaving the villages for the towns, leaving 'the dullards, the vicious and the wastrels behind'. Parts of rural England were becoming 'almost as lonesome as the veld of Africa'. The farm labourer was at the very bottom of the social scale. 'Feeling this, and having no hope for the future ... he does not even take the trouble to master his business. He will not learn the old finer arts of husbandry; too often he does as little as he can, and does that little ill.'

An estimated quarter of a million farm labouring jobs were lost, and for those who stayed on the land, wages were severely depressed. It is hardly surprising that when the Great War began there was a great collective movement to join up and get away from the land. The names of those who did not return are recorded on memorial crosses and plaques on village greens and in churches throughout the country. Those who survived came back to a rural England that would soon be in the throes of convulsive change.

Overall, one in eight fighting men was killed in the 1914–18 war. But the death rate among the sons of the rural elite, the class of major landowners, was much higher – one in five. Many a proud estate owner, with family roots deep in the soil, no longer had a male heir to shoulder the responsibilities. Steep rises in land and inheritance taxes compounded the problems. Finding and retaining servants in the old way became impossible. Mansions fell into disrepair and were sold off or demolished. Between 1918 and 1922, 7 million acres of agricultural land – a quarter of England's total – changed hands.

In the village the established order was tottering. The two figures that had traditionally dominated proceedings – the squire and the parson – were receding into the background. Many villages had never had a squire anyway, but almost all had a priest – albeit often a poor, harassed curate. But the official religion had been in decline for a long time, its authority eroded by widespread indifference and the assaults of non-conformism; it is estimated that as early as 1870 no more than 30 per cent of the rural working population were regularly attending church.

Forelock-tugging, cap-doffing and deference in general were in retreat post-1918. The extension of the franchise and the growth of trade unionism and radical politics had long since constrained the political power of the ruling class. Elected councils – parish, district and county – had brought a degree of democratisation, even if in practice these bodies were, more often than not, dominated by the established interests. Perhaps more important, the experience of war – men fighting and dying together, sharing the terror and the suffering – had nibbled away at rigid and apparently immutable class divisions. Officers and the ranks had, to a degree, learned to look at each other in a different way, which made a return to the old servility difficult to swallow.

Furthermore the physical and spiritual isolation of many rural communities was eroding fast. Men who had shed blood and lost comrades on foreign battlefields were not content to shut themselves away back in the village of their birth just because their fathers and grandfathers had done so. Motor cars and buses and the humble bicycle introduced intoxicating visions of freedom and opportunities for amusement and excitement. The cinema and the wireless opened windows into undreamed-of worlds.

The fabric of the village was also changing. The 'Homes Fit for Heroes' campaign and the 1919 Housing Act led to the birth of council housing. To eyes accustomed to old stone and cob and thatch, these stark blocks of brick tacked on to the edge of the village or carelessly deposited on an empty space were unsettling. But they offered comforts – hot running water, for one thing – unheard of in the traditional tied cottage. Although the old cottage-based craft industries like weaving and bootmaking had long since vanished in the face of factory competition, new retail outlets – the cycle repair shop, the tea room, the machine workshop, even the petrol station – joined the village shop to give a commercial heartbeat.

By 1900 almost all villages had a school, which were now controlled by the new county councils instead of being dependent on local benefactors. Post-1918 the school was increasingly joined by the village hall, which has remained the key pillar of village life ever since.

The village hall was a very different animal from the reading room or institute of the late Victorian era, provided by some high-minded local philanthropist – often tee-total and with strong religious convictions – in an effort to counter the pernicious influence of the ale-house. In Lower Bourne George Sturt had been instrumental in establishing an Entertainment Club. With his characteristic honesty, he admitted that after a successful start it petered out. The songs the people knew were sung so often that everyone became bored with them. The night school foundered in the face of indifference and ignorance. In Sturt's words, the club 'began to depend on the few members with a smattering of middle-class attainments . . . they gave themselves airs of superiority to the crowd, and that was fatal.' It could not compete with the pub, being unable – in his words – 'to lend itself to the easy intercourse that tired men enjoy at the public-house'.

The impulse behind the movement for village halls was the desire to leave a lasting memorial to those who – as Lawrence Weaver, one of its leaders, put it – 'gave their lives so that the sanctity of their villages, no less than the safety of the nation, might be kept whole and undefiled'. This some-times caused trouble with the rural elite who argued that the funds raised should be spent on traditional memorial crosses and plaques and stained-glass windows. At Northchapel in

Sussex a bitter rift opened between campaigners for a village hall and a clique led by the rector and the well-known playwright Sir Arthur Pinero, which wanted a memorial in the church.

A more forward-looking example was set at Balcombe, another village in Sussex, by the local bigwigs, Lord and Lady Denman. They funded the transformation of the existing working men's club into the Victory Hall, able to seat 500 people. The upper walls of the hall were decorated with frescoes by another progressive aristocrat, Neville Lytton, the Earl of Lytton. One depicted the war in which he and 200 Balcombe men had fought. Another, entitled *Peace and Hope for the Future*, shows local craftsmen at work on the hall amid scenes of dancing and music-making; with Lady Denman herself discussing the plans for the hall with her clerk of the works.

At that time this remarkable woman had served five years as the first president of the National Federation of Women's Institutes. Trudie Denman, as she was known, devoted much of her life and energy to good works in war and peace, among which her devotion to the WI was just one. The WI movement, originally imported from Canada, assumed a critical importance in village life which it has never lost. It is impossible to conceive of the village hall – that focal point in the life of so many settlements – without the meetings and the contribution of the WI. In many cases the WI led the way in getting halls built – as in Wolvercote in Oxfordshire, where the ladies started fund-raising, then persuaded the Duke of Marlborough to donate a site, then secured a loan and grant from the National Council of Social Service to fund the building. By 1938 the NCSS had helped establish more than 400 village halls across the country.

The get-up-and-get-something-done attitude of the WI was one response to the catastrophe of war. Another was an extended exercise in soul-searching by certain intellectuals, who wrestled with the burning question: what had gone wrong with humankind that such horrors could happen? A powerful strand of thought was that as a nation we had taken a spiritual wrong turn by embracing urbanisation and mechanisation, materialism and the consumer society. We had turned our backs on the 'true' England, the England of our forefathers.

And where was that England to be found? The answer was obvious: in our fields and along our hedgerows, in our woods of oak and beech, in our villages – timeless communities where bonds stretching back centuries had been forged; bonds based not on notions of equality or the rivalries of competition, but on the ancient virtues of trust, respect and obligation. A way must be found to restore that Old England of Alfred and Queen Bess before it was too late.

The search had actually begun before the Great War. In 1911 Cecil Sharp founded the English Folk Dance Society, having spent several years on a self-appointed mission to rescue England's great store of folk music and dance from oblivion. Sharp worked tirelessly tracking down, annotating and publishing the traditional music in the unswerving conviction that it represented 'the faithful expression in musical idiom of the qualities and characteristics of the nation'. Exactly what these qualities were and how they manifested themselves were not precisely defined. It was enough that

they belonged to some pre-industrial idyll of peace and harmony rooted in the English countryside.

Like many visionaries, Sharp was distinctly odd and
extremely intolerant of views that deviated from his own.
Later commentators have accused him of appropriating and
then gentrifying the musical traditions of the rural working
class, and patronising the practitioners. This version ignored
his close collaboration with a host of authentic musicians
and dancers, his heroic rescue of a great body of music and
dance that would otherwise have been lost, and his liberating
influence on a generation of English composers including
Vaughan Williams and Benjamin Britten.

Nevertheless, the awkward truth was that, while the tunes
and the jigs could be saved from destruction, no amount of
high-minded endeavour could restore them to the position
in rural life they had once filled. As one of Sharp's follow-
ers in the Lake District noted, no more than a quarter of
her dance group were born and bred locally – 'the farming
community always gave us a wide berth . . . the English Folk
Dancing Society always appealed to an often rather mobile
intelligentsia.'

Post-1918 a distinct back-to-the-land movement developed, with a strong mystical, quasi-religious tinge to it.
One of its most eloquent spokesmen was H. J. Massingham,
London born and reared, Oxford educated, a countryman
by adoption. Massingham's central theme was that by sacrificing its peasant agricultural society, England had lost its
soul. In book after book and paper after paper he ranted and
railed against the modern world, and the destruction of the
old order and the established religion. His ideal society was

founded on the parish – he scorned towns and cities – which itself was founded on the trinity of church, houses and fields, corresponding to God–Man–Earth. The squire and the parson, in manor and rectory, topped the structure; below were the yeomen, craftsmen and peasants in farmsteads, workshops and cottages.

Writing in 1952, the last year of his life, H. J. Massingham reviewed the fate of his rural types in an article entitled 'Village Bedrock'. The peasantry had vanished or had been 'degraded into a landless proletariat'. The yeoman – the 'aristocrat of the peasantry' – had turned into an individualist tenant farmer. The craftsman had become a museum piece, the squire and parson no more than figureheads. All five classes had been uprooted in 'the process called Progress' and the real England had been abandoned wilfully and wickedly.

Another, more popular version of its fate was that it had actually survived the 1914–18 war and subsequent upheavals intact – if only you knew where to find it. This version was peddled by H. V. Morton in his phenomenally popular *In Search of England* and was inspired, so its author claimed, by his memories while he was serving in Palestine: 'a village street at dusk with a smell of wood smoke lying in still air . . . I remembered how the church bells ring at home and how the sun leaves a dull red bar down in the west and against it the elms grow blacker minute by minute . . .'

Morton's search begins with an encounter in Berkshire with a bowl-turner – the last in England – who tells him in deeply rustic tones that making bowls is better than making money and that money is trouble. At every turn thereafter a living representative of Old England appears in rude homespun apparel to utter earthy philosophical truths and express contentment with an unchanging order in which towns, cities, machines and politics do not belong. It is an exercise in myth-making of the crassest kind, and it comes as no surprise to discover that Morton – a vicious anti-Semite and Little Englander of the worst kind – made most of it up. But it sold in mountains because – like Batsford's celebrated British Heritage series of guides – it fed a notion of England and Englishness which retained huge sentimental attraction.

Morton, naturally, travelled by car. The paradox was that the new mobility allied with the marketing of the countryside through the booming genre of travel guide inevitably tarnished the very beauties depicted in sunlit prose and carefully composed photographic images (with never a car or a pylon or a modern building to be seen). The rise of tripperism, the creeping spread of suburbia and the bungalow, the addition of plain, functional council housing to many villages, the disease of ribbon development – all were seen as symptoms of an assault on rural England in which the pleasure-seeker, the holidaymaker, the cyclist and the railway excursionist were the foot soldiers.

A counter offensive, orchestrated by the Council for the Preservation of Rural England, enlisted writers and campaigners to denounce these evils. J. B. Priestley's judgment in 1939 was typical: 'It took centuries of workmanship and loving craftsmanship to create the England that was renowned for its charm and delicate beauty. In twenty years we have completely ruined half that beauty.' Another well-known journalist and commentator, Beverley Nichols, lamented 'the desertion of the countryside . . . every other village is an advertisement of the fact that we are not only a nation of shopkeepers but a nation of usurious vandals.'

Occasionally a sceptical voice was raised questioning the paradisial version of rural life promoted by H. V. Morton and the covers of the Batsford guides. One dissenter was J. Robertson Scott, founder and long-serving editor of the *Countryman* magazine. In his sarcastically titled *England's Green and Pleasant Land*, Scott set out to expose the conditions in which agricultural workers actually lived and to demolish cherished myths about the old order. The squire-archy, Scott declared, were the 'flotsam of feudalism . . . short on brains and public spirit'. As for the other great pillar of the village community, the church, Scott regarded it as dead or dying, partly because many parsons lacked ability and character and partly because people were no longer inclined to believe what was read, sung or said.

The journalist Ivor Brown delivered an equally vigorous counterblast to the sentimental pastoralist in his book *The Heart of England*, published in 1935. 'The picturesque façade of the traditional English cottage,' Brown wrote, 'is too often the mask of a rural slum.' He mocked the 'rhapsodist' for finding 'the stout heart of England beating in the rural pub' which in many cases was 'a tawdry beer-house dispensing tepid swipes in dirty glasses in a fly-blown bar.' The squires gave 'little enough value for lazy privileged lives', the parson was there 'pinching and scraping and keeping up a respectable air . . . but the villager fights shy of him.'

Few, if any, of these competing accounts of rural England were written by men who worked the land or oversaw the pulling of the plough. They were the work of journalists and professional writers, each with an axe to grind, each convinced that his insights were superior to the next man's, all presuming to know what the working man and his family were experiencing and what was going through their minds. Generally speaking the working man himself and those around him were occupied doing what their forefathers had done, which was endeavouring to make a living and a life against the odds. Few had the time or inclination to share their thoughts with a wider public.

One shining exception was Fred Kitchen's *Brother to the Ox*, accurately subtitled *The Autobiography of a Farm Labourer* and published in 1939. Kitchen's notably good-tempered and plain-speaking record of his hard times as boy and man in south Yorkshire was rightly praised for its determinedly unsentimental, anti-pastoral content and tone. Kitchen did not try to distil any great moral from his story, beyond that times change and we change with them.

When war broke out again in 1939, much of the countryside of England looked very similar to the way it had in 1914. The boundaries of the fields were the same as after enclosure. Sheep grazed the uplands, cattle the lower pastures, and the horse did the work on the arable land. The bond between the village and the land may well have been weakened, but it was unbroken; and the primary purpose of the village was to service the land.

Village England had, broadly speaking, survived one World War intact. It would not survive another.

5

Common Stream

Foxton, Cambridgeshire

There is nothing unusual about Foxton except how much is known about it. It is south-west of Cambridge, and just to the south-east of the A10 Cambridge–Royston road. The railway between Cambridge and London intersects the A10 just north of the village, and there is a station there, which makes Foxton a desirable commuter settlement.

It is shaped like the Greek letter *lambda*, with the upward stem ending at the station and formed by the strip of housing either side of Station Road. At the bottom is a junction with a minor road leading west towards Shepreth and east and then north-east towards Fowlmere. The old houses of Foxton are positioned along the lower part of Station Road, and both ways along the minor road, with the fine old church set back near the junction. A succession of housing estates built from the 1960s onwards have swelled the lower part of Foxton; since 1950 its population has doubled to around 1200.

Two views of old Foxton

In 1949 a schoolmaster bought one of Foxton's ancient dwellings, a thatched cottage on the western side of The Green, on the road to Shepreth. Rowland Parker was the son of a Lincolnshire farmer. Before the outbreak of war in 1939, he had taught French at a school in Cambridge, and after serving with the Royal Artillery during the conflict he returned to his teaching post. Part of his cottage in Foxton dated back to medieval times, and Parker became curious about its history. One Nicholas Pepperton had rebuilt it in 1501, and it had been expanded and extensively altered in 1583 by a later occupant, Thomas Campion. A subsequent Campion added an extra chamber upstairs; although the place was lived in by several different families after that, the cottage remained pretty much unchanged until 1960, when Parker and his wife added a new kitchen.

By then his curiosity about its past had deepened and intensified considerably. He wondered why the ceilings were so low, and who had embedded a sheep's jawbone in the chimney breast and why there should have been an 18-inch drop into the main bedroom. He wanted to know who these people were, and how they had lived. So Parker started looking for answers.

He set about trawling through the thousands of records of the manorial court that had had jurisdiction over Foxton. They ran from the early fourteenth century through to the late seventeenth century, when the manorial system of administration finally gave up the ghost. From manorial rolls he turned to wills and inventories, parish records, the papers of bishops and archdeacons. It took Rowland Parker years, but in the end he had the story of his house.

He wrote it and called it *Cottage on the Green* and had 500 copies printed at his own expense which were snapped up in no time at all.

By now Parker had become incurably infected with the history bug. In gathering the material about his own dwelling, he had sifted his way through a mountain relating to the other houses of Foxton and the families who had built and lived in them. His obvious next move was to write the history of the whole village. In this he was assisted by the fortuitous discovery near Shepreth of the site of an extensive Roman villa. Although nothing of it remained above ground, excavation revealed the ground plan and produced enough mundane evidence of daily life – chiefly from the midden – to enable a speculative account of its occupation. 'The Roman villa came into the picture, adding a thousand years to the story,' Parker recalled in his characteristically laconic way.

Several more years of research, writing and rewriting followed. The final result was a remarkable book to which Parker gave the memorable title *The Common Stream*. The inspiration for the name came from the humble brook – itself unnamed – that the people of the village had dug sometime after the Roman occupation to make viable the place they had chosen to settle.

In writing *The Common Stream*, Rowland Parker did a great deal more than just write the history of Foxton, one more worthy parish record to add to the thousands. He conjured something unique – as he put it, 'not just the history of my village; the history of any village.' It was published in 1975 and was an immediate bestseller. Although its author is not even noticed by Wikipedia, the book is a classic and will remain so – its status recognised by Eland Publishing, which has recently produced a handsome new edition. Scholarly, wise and elegantly written, it is a key chronicle of English rural life. In my view it stands up there with Ronald Blythe's *Akenfield* and Laurie Lee's *Cider with Rosie*.

The claim Rowland Parker made for it – as the story of *the* village, not just this one – was a bold one, and strictly speaking false, since every village is different. But in a deeper sense it is splendidly justified. 'This is no chronicle of kings and prelates and nobles,' he wrote in the introduction. 'It is the story of the Common Man, of the ordinary men and women who in their countless thousands have trudged through life and then departed from it, leaving little trace.'

Little trace, but some; and it was in uncovering and teasing out and making sense of those traces that Rowland Parker displayed his mastery as a historian of unusual distinction. His range was extraordinarily limited, but he penetrated to an extraordinary depth. These humble Cambridgeshire peasants and yeomen farmers, limited in their spheres of activity to the struggle for survival and advancement, achieve a kind of dramatic reincarnation as a result of his tireless hunting through the ancient records – in their industry and resourcefulness, their quarrelsomeness, their rivalries and litigations, their acts of meanness and generosity, their striving to make something of themselves.

Inevitably much of the pre-medieval narrative is guesswork of an informed and intelligent kind. 'Where I have not written what actually did happen,' Parker explained, 'I have written what I firmly believe, and have good reason to believe, could have happened.' His reconstruction begins with the arrival of those he calls The People by the Brook, the first settlement, the rearing of livestock and growing of crops and catching of fish in the reedy meres. The Romans arrived, the area was colonised, and work began on building a residence for an important officer of the Roman army. Parker had little to go on, and some of his conjectures may seem fanciful enough; from the absence of broken toys among the excavated fragments of pottery, for instance, he deduced that the commander and his presumed wife had no children; from the presence of large quantities of the shells of oysters – prized by Romans as promotors of virility and fertility – he guessed that they wanted them badly.

At some point the villa was ransacked, burned and destroyed. Parker's version of events – for which there is no direct evidence whatever – is that it was attacked in the course of the revolt led by the Iceni queen Boudicca, and that the Roman army officer and his wife were killed. He speculates that their bodies were burned by the villagers who then dismantled the villa down to its foundations and levelled the site in the hope of convincing the legionaries when they arrived intent on retribution that it had never existed.

If so, the ruse does not appear to have worked. At least some of the village huts were burned, and the site was abandoned for a time before being partially reoccupied. Roman rule was certainly reimposed after the revolt, and the Roman system of administration restored – for a time. Then it crumbled entirely. New settlers spread across southern England including Fenland, and new settlements arose. 'It was, I believe,' Parker wrote, 'the most momentous thing that ever happened to England – the Common Man's England, and nothing that has happened since has succeeded in undoing what was then done.'

At some point in this murky post-Roman period – Parker asserts that it was in the sixth century – a settlement took shape where old Foxton now stands. To enable it to function – which meant providing its own water supply – the settlers dug a channel between two existing streams flowing to the south-west and the north-east. It was over a mile long, and although it was no more than four feet deep and in many places could easily be jumped over, it provided Foxton with its water for over a thousand years. The shape of the settlement was determined by the course of the Brook; every dwelling had access to it. Its well-being was crucial, and maintaining it in good order was the prime communal responsibility until well into the nineteenth century.

From the digging of the Brook and the establishment of the proto-Foxton, Parker took what he referred to as 'a leap across the remaining dark centuries' to AD 1000. By then Foxton and its boundaries had been accorded official recognition in charter. It was registered as the property of the nunnery of Chatteris which had been founded towards the end of the tenth century in the Fens about thirty miles to the north. After 1066 half of the estate was given away to one of William the Conqueror's intimate circle of Norman backers, Geoffrey de Mandeville. The remainder, including Foxton, was retained by the Abbess of Chatteris. By 1200 she had acquired the so-called 'view of frankpledge' over Foxton which – in theory anyway – gave her word the force of law.

But in practice her word counted for very little and she

hardly impinged on the lives of the folk of Foxton. They tilled their holdings along the village brook. They lived in single-room habitations of timber, wattle and daub, roofed with straw or reeds. Their inanimate possessions were few: stools, benches, tables, platters, bowls, cups, earthenware cooking pots. They ate coarse bread, gruel, pease, eggs, cheese, a few vegetables, an occasional piece of mutton or bacon, a very occasional chicken or rabbit. They dressed in homespun wool garments and tanned animal skins. They drank water or a fermented brew of water and barley which they called ale. They had to use the village mill to grind their corn. They had to go to church on Sundays. If they became involved in a dispute – which most did, sooner or later – or if they were accused of a crime, they had to attend the manorial court for judgment.

By 1250 every family in Foxton had a surname. Everyone paid rents and fines. Everyone made payments: to get married, to be buried, to conclude an agreement with a neighbour, to bring a case to court, to attend the court hearing, to be exempt from attending the court hearing, to bequeath property. The one inescapable event in life that was not subject to a charge was being born.

The special quality of Rowland Parker's *The Common Stream* lies in its wealth of mundane detail, in the very ordinariness of the life revealed. I do not want to steal Parker's thunder, so I will give just one example, illustrating the matter of peasant mobility in the medieval period. In Foxton we have one Thomas Pate attending on the manorial court in 1317 to argue that his elder brother John should be denied a holding of land because fifteen years before he had come to the court 'and paid the Lady (the Abbess of Chatteris) five shillings to go where he pleased'. The custom – which according to Thomas 'has been in use since time out of memory' – was that such an arrangement meant permanent exclusion from any land holding in the manor. Parker points out that the principal tenants could have bent the system to allow John Pate back in – but they chose not to, possibly because of personal antagonism, but more likely because land was scarce and they wanted more for themselves.

The absence of fraternal affection manifested by Thomas Pate was entirely typical of the village. It existed in a state of continuous low-level strife: brother against brother, husband against wife and vice versa, father against son and vice versa, neighbour against neighbour. Boundary disputes arising from encroachments of one kind or another were the main source of trouble, filling the pages of the manorial court records. An extraordinary map reproduced in Rowland Parker's *Cottage on the Green* helps explain why quarrels were so common and why working lives were so arduous. It shows the distribution of the land holdings of Nicholas Campion, who at one time lived in Parker's cottage. His forty-five slender strips were scattered literally all over the parish, scarcely any of them next to another and some up to two-and-a-half miles apart. Not until enclosure in 1826 did this incredibly burdensome and inefficient kaleidoscope of holdings begin to evolve into something more rational and productive.

For a long time the condition of the Brook continued to be the measure of how the village itself was doing. The records for 1500 show that Foxton was being run by a small, self-appointed committee. This organised the weekly market and imposed sanctions on those who stepped out of line. Ale-keepers, the butcher and the baker were regularly fined for overcharging and fiddling the weight of merchandise. The maintenance of the Brook, which provided all the village's water and kept the mill-wheel turning, was the key communal duty. The butcher was fined for letting his dunghill drain into it. A fine of twelve pence was slapped on anyone who failed to help in the cleaning and scouring of the watercourse; and twenty pence on anyone caught washing clothes in it. A warning was issued that anyone releasing the contents of their gutters or cesspits before 8 p.m. would be fined. Even ducks and geese were banned from Foxton's precious watercourse.

But over time its useful life came to an end. The farmers who took advantage of enclosure to consolidate and augment their farms dug boreholes and ponds to provide their own supplies of water. Communal upkeep of the Brook gradually lapsed and its water became foul. In 1873 the Reverend William Selwyn, a Canon of Ely Cathedral who had taken up residence at Foxton House, paid for deep wells with pumps to be sunk on The Green and at the end of Mortimer's Lane for general use. The water was good and reliable, and the Brook became no more than a convenient ditch for dumping rubbish, and gradually filled in. Today it has pretty much disappeared except in one or two places – most evidently in front of the houses on The Green – where it retains a ghostly afterlife as a waterless dip crossed by miniature footbridges.

*

In August 1885 a field of barley half a mile from Foxton railway station was being cut by men with scythes. There were twenty-four of them. At the end of a long day thirty acres of barley lay in swathes, ready at a later date to be turned, raked, heaped and taken by cart to the barn for threshing and eventual delivery to the maltster.

In August 1970 Rowland Parker watched the same field being cut by the farmer and two men using a combine harvester and two tractors with trailers. At the end of their considerably shorter day only swathes of straw were left behind. Sixty tons of malting barley were in the barn ready for collection.

Parker calculated that the first day's harvest required 560 man hours of labour for a yield of fifteen tons of barley; the second thirty hours for four times the yield. He guessed the same exercise in the 1930s, when he was a boy, would have required 330 man hours and yielded thirty tons of barley.

Parker also provided revealing figures for the composition of the village itself. In 1901 it had a population of 426 living in seventy-two houses. Eight were farmers and forty-five were farm workers. By 1941 the population had risen to 490 and the number of houses to 123; there were seven farmers and thirty farm workers. In 1974 1200 people lived in Foxton, in 380 houses. There were six farmers and six farm workers.

The figures tell the story of England's twentieth-century rural revolution. The detail differs from place to place, but the essentials are the same. Farming has not died. The same fields that were tilled at the time of the Norman invasion are still being tilled, but by machines, not men with horses. In

1945 a million people made their livings from working the land. In the 1990s the number was below 100,000.

The link between the village and the land was broken for good. But the village evidently did not die. Foxton almost tripled in size, and it was not alone. Rowland Parker explained what happened with exemplary clarity: 'By an ironic twist of circumstances the one-time supposed "superiority" of the town has been reversed and many people now prefer to live in the country. It is cheaper, healthier, quieter, cleaner and more pleasant. It is all that, but the real reason, of course, is that, thanks to the motor car, one can now live in the country and work in the town so having the best of both worlds.'

The middle-class takeover of the village proceeded steadily in most parts of the country. Between 1951 and 1981 the rural population grew from 8.4 to 11.4 million, from less than a fifth of the nation's total to a quarter, and the trend has continued. The village ceased to be a working community focussed on farming and became a place of residence and – increasingly – leisure.

The agricultural workforce was not forcibly displaced. It just largely ceased to exist. Centuries ago a social upheaval on that scale would, as likely as not, have led to the village being abandoned and left to rot. But the reverse happened. The cottages of the peasants were bought up, repaired, modernised and given a new lease of life. Between 1946 and 1951 186,000 new council houses were built in rural areas. They generally lacked the charm of the old village houses and cottages, and their designers made minimal effort to achieve any kind of aesthetic harmony of past and present, but they were decent enough to live in. As the demand for country living grew so did the availability of new private housing – often banal and downright ugly, but nonetheless places where ordinary people could make good lives.

Far from wasting away, the village expanded and prospered. According to Rowland Parker's daughter Jane – who still lives in the Cottage on the Green – he welcomed the expansion of Foxton on the grounds that it needed to grow in order to renew and sustain itself. He loved the place deeply, but he was no sentimental pastoralist. He acknowledged that 'community spirit' was less evident in modern Foxton, while pointing out that it actually depended on a community of interest *and* an element of compulsion. He suspected that it was dormant, not dead; that if a real danger threatened the village – his example was a plan to put a motorway through it – it would burst back into life, with the incomers, the new villagers, leading the way.

At the same time, Parker observed, 'village life' – in the sense of everyone knowing everyone, of making entertainment, of housewives being tied to the home all day, of speaking the local dialect and distrusting anyone who didn't, of using an outdoors privy and going to bed to save on coal and lamp oil, of washing in cold water and eating cold fat bacon for breakfast, of finding your own way across the fields and along deserted lanes and enjoying it, particularly when courting – that was dead, for good. 'There is no point in talking about "village life" and "town life"', Parker wrote. 'There is just life.'

*

To me, an outsider passing through, the old village of Foxton – of thatched, rendered cottages and mellow brick houses – seemed to have been almost overwhelmed by the housing developments of the 1960s and later. I wandered around some of these new accretions of architecturally commonplace and charmless estate homes, chatting to anyone who was prepared to chat to me. And I learned again an important lesson: that aesthetic distinction – the look of a place, its prettiness or picturesqueness or heritage status, call it what you will – matters very much less to the people who live in a village than whether it works for them, whether it is alive and kicking.

Foxton people like Foxton. They like it for having an old church which they can go to if they feel like it, and a scattering of old houses and a long history that someone has taken the trouble to write up. They like it because it has pleasant countryside around. They like it because they can get into Cambridge easily enough. They like it because they have been able to afford to live there, generally in one of those mundane, mass-built brick boxes that connoisseurs of pretty villages stick their noses up at.

They like it for having a smart new primary school for their kids to go to, and a smart new village hall – both funded from the proceeds of planning permission for a new development of thoroughly insipid early twenty-first-century detached homes just west of the splendid recreation ground. They like it for having a pub, the White Horse, and a decent village shop. They like it because it is friendly, peaceful and unpretentious.

In September 2015 Foxton Cricket Club achieved

something remarkable, reaching the final of the national Village Cup at Lords. A fleet of coaches brought 500 supporters to the Home of Cricket in London to cheer on their team against three-time winners of the trophy, Woodhouse Grange from Yorkshire. In the end the Cambridgeshire side were beaten by nineteen runs, but it was still a day of enormous pride for the village and its cricket club which – due to the passion and dedication of a small band of volunteers – had lifted itself from mediocrity to being the best in the county.

Generally speaking, Foxton is doing well, and not just at cricket. But on occasions dark clouds still threaten. Over the years it has grown step by step to a size at which it functions nicely: roughly five hundred homes, a population of 1200. Its village plan allows for small-scale additional developments of up to fifteen homes within the current form – the so-called 'village envelope'. It is the view of the great majority of the people of Foxton, of its parish council, of its district and county councillors, and of the South Cambridgeshire District Council as a whole that any significant expansion into the surrounding countryside would threaten the village's integrity as well as opening the way to further unrestrained building. It is also my view, for what that's worth.

But the pressure for more homes is as intense in Cambridgeshire as anywhere in the country. A year ago Gladman, the best-known speculative land developer in the country, lodged an appeal against the refusal of South Cambridgeshire District Council to permit the building of ninety-five homes on what used to be a turf farm beside the Shepreth Road, beyond the western fringe of Foxton. Companies like Gladman do not have a view about the viability of villages or any interest in what happens to them. Their job is simply to secure planning permission by whatever means are available and to sell the land to a housebuilder for the highest price they can get.

In the event they lost the appeal, and for the time being Foxton can breathe more easily. But the hunger of land for housing will not go away. There will be more battles to come, which the village will have to fight and win if it is to retain the integrity and character that have made it what it is over the past two thousand years.

Rowland Parker ended the last full chapter of *The Common Stream* by observing the children of the village walking home from school: 'These children are healthier, better fed, better clothed, better educated, better behaved, prettier and – did they but know it – happier than any generation of children that ever before walked the village street. For us of the older generation, the past is past and we do not regret it. For them – the future.' Those words were written forty years ago, fifteen years before the death of this wise and humane man. They still hold true, and should be studied by anyone tempted to wring their hands over the state of the English village.

6

THE CURSE OF THE QUAINT

Bibury, Gloucestershire

On the inside cover of a recent version of the UK passport, the guff about Her Britannic Majesty's Secretary of State requesting and requiring free passage for the bearer is framed by the Queen's coat of arms and three curious emblems. Two are of oak leaves, one with a blue butterfly on it. The third, eccentrically coloured in royal blue, is of Arlington Row, a terrace of ancient cottages in the Cotswold village of Bibury.

Whoever chose it offered a telling insight into their image of the country we live in. It could have been Windsor Castle, St Paul's, the White Cliffs, even Stonehenge. But the committee – one assumes it was a committee – selected an irregular line of modest cottages built from Cotswold stone standing back from a millstream with a marshy river meadow beyond.

This, the image declares, is England. The cottages are small, therefore quaint and homely, therefore intended for ordinary people. They are evidently old, and England is very

Arlington Row, Bibury, in the 1950s

old. They are the work of craftsmen, and there was a time when we had craftsmen. They are irregular, therefore individual, and we pride ourselves on our individuality. They are conspicuously lacking in grandeur; and although we can do grandeur better than anyone when we must, we are generally not that impressed by it.

There is more to it than that. The cottages clearly belong in a larger village scene. And England – the true England – is a country of villages. The sentimental image of the village and its place in the landscape chimes with Stanley Baldwin's celebrated paean to rural life: 'The tinkle of the hammer on the anvil of the country smithy, the corncrake on a dewy morning, the sound of the scythe against the whetstone and the sight of the plough-team coming over the brow of the hill, the sight that has been seen in England since England was a land . . .'

It is immaterial that by the time Baldwin delivered these stirring words (1924) the plough-team, blacksmith, scythe and whetstone were already in or on their way to the countryside museum, and that more intensive farming methods had already triggered a collapse in corncrake numbers that would see it vanish almost entirely from the English countryside. Rather like John Major and his much-derided celebration of the England of warm beer, invincible green suburbs, dog lovers and the fillers-in of pools coupons, Baldwin was articulating a shared apprehension of common identity none the less potent for being divorced from reality. At its heart was the belief in – or a longing to believe in – continuity and permanence, a solid core of Englishness rooted in our past and the events that shaped us, in our landscape, in our communities.

Putting Arlington Row in the passport sealed its fate. Once lived in by working people engaged in the struggles of daily life, Bibury has become a living museum and one of the unmissable tourist sights of England. Every day of the year coaches heave their way into the village to discharge shoals of visitors to gawp at the pale stone houses and richly bloomed cottage gardens, the trout-filled Coln running by the road, the little bridges and cobbled yards. All of them find their way sooner or later to Arlington Row where they grin into their cameras, with the ancient gables, eaves, dormers and fat, slightly crooked chimneys behind.

Arlington Row has achieved – or been reduced to – global heritage status. When a retired dentist who lives opposite the cottages dared to park his yellow Vauxhall Corsa so that it intruded on the universal selfie, he found himself on the receiving end of a firestorm of online abuse for spoiling the view.

*

I would hazard a bet that very few of the hundreds of thousands of tourists who descend on Bibury each year ever stumble across the village cricket ground, known as the Bat Field. Yet it is a treasure beyond compare; I have seen many lovely cricket grounds in my time, and played on some of them, but none lovelier than this one.

It is reached by a track off the road to Cirencester which winds between fields and along the edge of a wood to a gate. Beyond the gate and the fence is the ground, oval in shape, with a smart pavilion at one end built of dark wood, with a veranda for sitting out on a warm evening to watch the final overs as the sun sinks behind mid-wicket (or cover, depending on which end is bowling and whether the batsman is left- or right-handed).

The Bat Field has many glories: its hidden-away situation, the rolling fields around, the hanging woods that plunge down behind the pavilion with the high chimneys of Bibury Court beyond and below. But the chief of them – certainly in the opinion of the club stalwarts who look after everything – is the square in the middle of the oval on which the wickets are cut. It is billiard-table flat, close cut, the grass tightly woven into one firm carpet, the whole glowing with the care and – yes – love lavished on it.

But there is a sharp poignancy here. There is a fine pavilion and there are benches and nets and rollers and mowers and all the accoutrements of village cricket at its most idyllic. But Bibury cannot put out a proper team any more, and the ground is used on Saturdays by a league side from Lechlade. The Bibury team – such as it is – play short-format twenty-over matches on Sundays only, and not every Sunday at that. There are simply not enough able-bodied and willing cricketers left in the village to keep the old tradition going.

That may not sound much of a tragedy to a non-cricketer. But to Terry and Brian, Bibury cricketers from boyhood, dropping out of the league and giving up on traditional Sunday friendlies because there are not enough blokes left who want to play is tantamount to the dawning of a new age of barbarism. They are now well past playing, but the care of the square remains a sacred duty to them and the collapse of cricket is a source of great sadness. And it is part of a wider picture, in which the village where they have spent their lives has been sucked of its lifeblood to a point where they hardly recognise what it is any more.

Terry came to Bibury with his family more than seventy years ago, when he was four, and he played cricket for the club for more than fifty years. When I asked him how many wickets he had taken, he replied: 'Thousands.' Registering scepticism in my raised eyebrows, he said: 'I had a hundred five seasons in a row, and a hundred-and-fifty in one of 'em', and I stopped looking sceptical. He and Brian, who was more of a batsman, were there week in, week out, regular as the pavilion clock – 'We had a helluva side in the Sixties, won just about everything going.' Terry had to pack it in 2007 after a major operation, by which time Brian had already hung up his bat and pads and the club was on the slide. 'Every week was the same – we'd be begging, borrowing and stealing players wherever we could find them.' But the village had changed too much.

The two chums spoke with one voice, on this matter anyway, chipping in to complete sentences in the same way they sorted out the mowing and rolling. 'They're not much good now, those that do play. We both went to the grammar school at Northend – not there now, is it? – and the history master taught us names and dates and battles and that, and how to stay in line against a quick bowler by keeping a bat handle against your arse.' Bibury used to drink in the Swan, the fine old coaching inn facing the old stone bridge that takes the road over the River Coln into the village's other half, Arlington. 'Wo, what evenings we had there, eh! Cor, do you remember old . . .?' And the memories came crowding in.

The Swan is now part of the Cotswold Inns and Hotels group, marketing the Cotswold brand to the rest of the world. The snug bar where great deeds with bat and ball were celebrated and relived season after season has long gone, and what was the village pub has become a processing centre for the coachloads of tourists who are decanted into Bibury each day. Terry and Brian haven't been into either of the licensed premises – the Catherine Wheel is up the hill on the Arlington side – for five years and more. There are some locals like them left – old so-and-so who ran the football club for all those years, old so-and-so who's still doing his garden most days looking pretty chipper – but now they only get together for funerals in Bibury's extraordinarily lovely church.

The village's great house, Bibury Court, is behind the church, separated from the graveyard by a high stone wall. It was built in the 1630s by Sir Thomas Sackville, a younger son of the immensely wealthy Earl of Dorset. The Sackvilles lived there on and off for a few generations, but thereafter ownership changed hands several times, and Bibury never enjoyed a close and constant relationship with a squire. In 1926 the house – which is Grade I listed and very fine – together with a much-reduced land holding was bought by a rich and distinguished lawyer, Sir Orme Clarke, whose family also had estates in Norfolk. He was married to a Roosevelt, so there was no shortage of funds for restoring the place to its former glory. Sir Orme died in 1949 but Lady Clarke lived on well into the 1960s; Terry recalls that at Christmas her chauffeur would drive her around the village in the big car filled with presents for the children, which he handed out while she remained in the back seat, hatted and gloved.

That's how it used to be. The quality did not have to do anything much, except know their place, which was above everyone else's, and show their faces every now and then. They did, however, have to hang on to the big house and live in a certain style. The failure of so many of these families to manage their money prudently – and in particular to provide for death duties – was the usual cause of their downfall. So it was with the Clarkes. Sir Orme's heir, Sir Humphrey Clarke, died in 1973, and death duties forced the sale of the house, which became a hotel. The sixth baronet. Sir Toby, continued to live in Bibury in the somewhat reduced setting of Church House until a brace of expensive divorces elbowed him out altogether.

Even as a hotel Bibury Court remained one of the cornerstones of village life. The bar was well used, people had Sunday lunch there, the annual fete was held in the grounds each August bank holiday. But when I visited Bibury in May 2015 the relationship had gone off like sour milk. The hotel had been bought in 2008 by the founder of the Shipton Mill flour business, John Lister. He poured money into upgrading it, seeking to make it more than just smart. But the guests failed to materialise, the refurbishment stalled and the village was made to feel unwelcome there – or came to feel that way, which amounts to the same thing.

A small change sealed the disenchantment. The gate between the churchyard and Bibury Court, through which generations of the gentry and parsons had freely passed one way or the other, had a coded security lock fixed to it. Since then bad feeling has festered. Efforts to rebrand Bibury Court as a wedding and special events venue misfired, and permission has been sought to turn it back into a country house, apparently with the aim of selling it.

*

Sometime in the 1890s a wealthy young man in pursuit of an ideal of country living became the tenant of Ablington Manor, a grand late Elizabethan house in a hamlet a mile or so upstream from Bibury. Joseph Arthur Gibbs was not a countryman by birth, but once installed at Ablington Manor he embraced country life and the duties of a country squire with great enthusiasm. He hunted, he shot, he fished the glass-clear waters of the Coln for its brown trout, he tramped the wolds, he quaffed ale in country inns and engaged the good folk in conversation, he took voluminous notes about the churches and stately and less stately homes.

He wrote a book about it all, which he called *A Cotswold Village*. It was published in 1898 and was a considerable success. The fourth edition came out in 1901, by which time its author had died of heart failure at the pathetically early age of thirty-one. His mother, a member of the Hallam family which included Tennyson's poet friend Arthur Hallam, referred in her foreword to the book to her son's 'taste for literary work and deep poetical feeling', which probably accounted for the abundance of quotations from the poets – Gray, Horace, Burns, Chaucer and many others – with which the pages of *A Cotswold Village* are peppered.

It has remained in print, off and on, ever since it first appeared, invariably referred to as 'a classic' and praised for the truthful and realistic picture it paints of rural life in Gloucestershire at the turn of the nineteenth century. This reputation is not deserved, and will not – I guarantee – survive a close reading of the text by any sensible person.

In fairness to Gibbs, he was very young when he wrote it, and it is burdened with the faults of youth: self-consciously literary, overwritten, sentimental, prone to archaisms ('list' for 'listen', 'I would fain', etc.), superficial, gushing, arch, disorganised. It is worth looking at, not for what it records of the Cotswold village – which is actually very little – but for what it reveals about the attitudes of the class Gibbs represented, as well as of those who would bestow the status of classic on it.

He was warmly praised for his portraits of the village people – particularly the local gamekeeper and fount of local lore, whom he dubs 'Tom Peregrine'. 'He was,' Gibbs wrote, 'so delightfully mysterious ... he became part and parcel with the trees and the fields and all living things ... he would talk all day about any subject under the sun: politics, art, Roman antiquities, literature ...' Tom Peregrine heads a parade of rustic stereotypes: the farmers, 'on the whole an excellent type of what John Bull ought to be'; the parson, 'quite a character ... an excellent man in every way ... ruling his parish with a rod of iron he is loved and respected'; the miller, 'a man worthy to sit among kings'; the village politician, 'many a pleasant chat have we enjoyed in his snug cottage'; and so on.

As for the people in general, Gibbs finds them 'healthy, bright, clean and old-fashioned ... simple, honest, God-fearing folk who mind their own business.' The farm labourers are, predictably, 'somewhat lacking in acuteness and sensibility', with 'a marked characteristic of inertia', but they have 'a sense of humour and love of merriment that is quite astonishing'. After a short time at Ablington Manor, the new squire – the role Gibbs consciously assumed – was 'glad to find so much good feeling existing among all classes . . . this was a contented and happy village.'

They were, however, difficult times for agriculture: 'Time was when the uplands of Gloucestershire were almost entirely under the plough . . . now, alas, farms are to be had for the asking rent-free but nobody will take them.' But then again, 'the labourer is better off than he has ever been' and 'the farmers seem to be more liberal in bad times than good.' After this searching social analysis, off the young squire gallops on another ride after the fox, or a spot of woodcock shooting, or an evening casting a fly for a trout, or a comical game of cricket for the neighbouring Winsom Eleven, 'delightful old-fashioned people . . . quaint and simple folk.'

'The whole country,' Gibbs exclaims at one point, 'reminds me of the days of Merrie England, so quaint and rural are the scenes.' The words reminded me, irresistibly, of the glorious climax of Kingsley Amis's comic masterpiece *Lucky Jim*, in which the inebriated Jim Dixon delivers his lecture on the subject of Merrie England and the immortal words 'the point about Merrie England is that it was about the most unMerrie period in our history.'

A Cotswold Village is interesting as a prime specimen of rustic myth-making. The fate of the Cotswolds has been to fulfil in the public perception a shared image of the ideal rural life. As a result it has evolved from the working agricultural landscape of Arthur Gibbs's day into a kind of pastoral dreamworld. The descriptive vocabulary applied to it has, in the process, been distilled into a residue of clichés endlessly recycled by the tourist guides and marketers of heritage – and, of course, the estate agents who offer those honey-coloured stone treasures as second-home boltholes at prices the few remaining Cotswold farm labourers could not hope to earn in a lifetime.

*

After peering over the high wall in front of Arthur Gibbs's Ablington Manor – now owned by a retired scrap dealer – I cycled in his tracks for a while along the quiet lanes to Winsom, Coln Rogers, Coln St Dennis and Fossebridge, following the river up towards its source. Gibbs found in all these villages 'the good old honest labouring folk', watched over by 'the village parsons – good pious men'. But he was anxious for their future. Their populations were declining as work got scarcer, and he looked forward with foreboding to a century hence, when the Cotswold country would become 'a huge open plain ... and these old villages will contain scarcely a single inhabitant.'

He was not entirely wide of the mark. There is no open plain and the walls whose decay he predicted have never been in such a state of perfect repair. The lovely old houses stand behind their sculpted hedges, beside their swept gravel drives, with their close-mown emerald lawns framed by fan-trained apple trees and vigorously espaliered plums. But on a midweek morning, there was scarcely an inhabitant to be seen – the only people around were the hired hands on sit-on mowers with earmuffs on and blokes from building firms in Cirencester working on barn conversions. There was not a school, not a shop, not a pub – just grave-silent old churches with Arthur Gibbs's good, honest, toiling labouring folk at rest in the ground outside.

The favoured names of these houses toll like a funeral bell. There is not a Mill House where the mill-wheel turns, an Old Forge where the blacksmith's hammer is heard, an Old Bakehouse where bread is made, an Old Schoolhouse with a desk or blackboard in it, a Glebe Cottage with any glebe left – not even an Old Rectory with a rector inside. But there is beauty, almost a surfeit of it. The fields, the woods, the streams, the rise and fall of the wolds, the hidden places suddenly revealed, the walls and houses and barns and gardens – all come together in a composition that is not merely ravishing in its own right, but overwhelmingly suggestive of that idea of the old, simple, pre-Fall rural England that clings on in our hearts. But it is a sham, a deathly silent sham, and after marvelling at the perfection of it as I pedalled past, I could not help wondering: what is it for?

Arthur Gibbs can probably be credited with initiating the canonisation of the Cotswolds as 'the quintessence of England'. The seeds he sowed were then watered and nourished by that generation of topographical and countryside writers – including H. V. Morton and H. J. Massingham – which came to the fore between the World Wars. Unwittingly they promoted an unresolvable conflict between celebrating a region for its charms and retaining the old ways of life. They gave the impression of having stumbled across a survival of the pre-industrial Golden Age just as the Modern Age was poised to sweep it all away. In effect they extended an invitation to all and sundry to jump on a charabanc or motor car or bike to come and take a look. But they carefully concealed their own part in the process of destruction.

Massingham in particular could be venomously snobbish about the lower class of Cotswold tourist. One extraordinary passage refers to the 'human sparrows from the Midlands towns' digging up bluebells and stripping hazel trees, and congratulates the farmer for shooting out the tyres of 'these cits while they were away grubbing and smashing'. Popular Cotswold destinations were viewed with contempt – particularly Broadway, described by Massingham as being 'hateful . . . it reeks of "Ye Olde"'. The countryside writer John Moore likened the village to a harlot 'who not only charges you an exorbitant fee but seizes the opportunity to pick your pocket'.

Bibury has long been one of those favoured destinations. William Morris's comment about it – 'surely the prettiest village in England' – is quoted in every brochure and leaflet and tourist puff, so that it comes to sound more like a curse than a compliment. Yet it is gorgeous. This is partly because of the building materials, the rough, weathered stone roof slates and stone walls, the mullioned windows and door surrounds, the gabled frontages and dormers and ashlar chimney stacks – that feeling of the houses and cottages having somehow been drawn from the earth; partly because it is full of surprises, unexpected corners leading to little lanes that open up new views and angles; partly because of its setting, the rolling fields and meadows and hanging woods above, the river through it.

There are a few imposing single buildings: the church, Bibury Court, Arlington Mill. But most of Bibury is modest and unpretentious. Wandering about, you glimpse cottages behind other cottages, embraced by steep irregular gardens where roses ramble and apple, pear and plum trees hang with fruit in season and raised beds keep compost heaps company; the dwellings jumbled about but at one with each other, expressions of the way the village grew and what it was for. Once it was just another working place in the country where they wove cloth, ground corn, worked the fields and helped themselves to the stone from the quarry at the top of the hill to build their homes.

It is now something else entirely. The locals are a shrinking, ageing rump. The old houses are taken by incomers and weekenders. The Swan, where the floor of the public bar was awash with spilled ale on cricket nights, is chintz and carpet and allegedly fine dining, its car park solid with coaches. Every day the coaches come, clogging roads intended for carts and horses, discharging flood tides of visitors to ebb and flow through the village's arteries. They surge down the road by the river, pour over the footbridge, swill around the lane in front of Arlington Row, circle around the church, gaze through the gates of Bibury Court, fan up the hill through Arlington and around its green, then down again past Arlington Mill and the Bibury Trout Farm back to where the coaches wait, the air around them thick with diesel fumes.

Bibury does not offer much in the way of 'olde-worlde' shopping – not one antiques shop or proper heritage shop, for instance. But the photo opportunities more than compensate:

Arlington Row, of course, the low wall along the river, the footbridge, a great selection of quaint old doors and stone gateposts and low walls enclosing cottage gardens to pose in front of. The resident population have had to learn to share their village with the daily invasion of curious, mainly foreign humanity, although the manoeuvrings of the coaches as they jockey for position and the occasional pressing of faces and camera lenses against kitchen windows do cause resentment. There are those who maintain that the village survives as a village despite the onslaught; and those, mainly old-timers, who shake their heads and tell you that Bibury sold its soul a long time ago.

It has its church and village hall and its CoE primary school. Apart from the Swan it has a pub on the Arlington side as well, the Catherine Wheel, although it is a little smart to qualify as a village boozer. It lost its shop some years ago but the Trout Farm – which was established more than a hundred years ago by the owner of Arlington Mill, Arthur Severn, to stock the local chalk streams – has a shop selling the basics of life as well as the fish. The Trout Farm also has a café, and there are one or two other teashops about the place.

Like other Cotswold villages, Bibury is perhaps too perfect for its own good. It was designated a Conservation Area in the early 1970s, which means its buildings are watched over and protected as carefully as the treasures of the British Museum. Cotswold District Council permits no deviation from its core doctrine: 'It is crucial that any new building follows its traditional architectural character using traditional building materials.' So no wood, no glass, no brick, no – horror of horrors! – concrete, no sharp angles; nothing to suggest that architecture might still be a living art revealing new possibilities.

The effect is that there has been no significant building in the historic heart of the village for decades; and rigid restrictions are imposed on repairs, refurbishments and minor alterations which elsewhere are waved through without any requirement for planning permission. For instance, the paints permitted for outside doors and windows are limited to a small range of genteel pastels: Crushed Aloes, Moorland, Lizard, Hopsack, Buttermilk, Willow, Antelope, Orion, Chive. The names tell the story.

The only sizeable additions to the village in the past half century have been well up the hill on the Arlington side, where the Cotswold character was diluted long ago by nineteenth-century villas and the like. In the early 1970s a cluster of nine one-bedroom cottages for elderly people, known as The Quarry, was built out of something resembling the local stone in colour, but cut smooth and regular and distinctly non-authentic. The grip of conservation orthodoxy has tightened since then – witness Arlington Fields, a development of Housing Association homes at the extremity of the settlement, which were finished and handed over to local families in 2015.

These are prime examples of the 'Cotswold style' as appointed by the district council: regular frontages in stone or pale wash, steep pitched roofs with ridge tiles and coping, wooden windows and stone surrounds, plain front doors. The stone is *bona fide*, the colours appropriate, the overall effect perfectly pleasant if somewhat bland, and unavoidably compromised by the provision of car parking spaces as laid down by council standards (twenty-five for eleven houses), which means that the area of tarmac with white lines greatly exceeds that of the small rectangular gardens.

*

It so happened that the Annual Parish Meeting was being held the evening I was in Bibury, so I went along. It took place in a side room at the village hall while Pilates or Zumba or something more strenuous went on in the main part. There were three members of the public – four if you include me – and six members of the parish council under the chairmanship of a local lady farmer, soft-voiced but firm, and adept at keeping things moving without letting anyone think that their contribution was not valued.

The items for discussion were no more exciting than at any of the thousands of parish meetings across the country (and I have been to a few in my time). Grass-cutting opposite the Catherine Wheel was going well. The parking of coaches remained a problem but the designation of two bays opposite the Trout Farm had helped. Someone from FWAG – the Farming and Wildlife Advisory Group – was making progress with a report on flooding. The precept, the parish's share of the council tax, was going up to £10,000 to pay for flood prevention measures.

The discussions became more animated for a while on the subject of a pair of plant boxes which had been installed by my cricketing friend Terry outside his house at the top of the approach to Bibury Court to make it impossible for coaches to get past. The councillors did not like the boxes. They were suburban, even – Heaven forfend! – a touch 'Milton Keynes'.

But there was nothing much to be done about them as the road was private and therefore beyond the long arm of the parish council or even the Highways Department.

Conscious of not having had any dinner and wishing urgently to repair the omission, I slipped away as the focus of discussion switched to the reluctance of the district council to provide drawings on paper to enable informed consideration of planning applications. Before leaving Bibury the next afternoon I went back to the Bat Field, cycling slowly along the track through the fringe of the wood above Bibury Court. It was a delicious May day. The beeches and oaks were in new leaf, and the ripening summer wheat waved across the fields. The cricket square glowed emerald green, its edges as sharp and straight as if cut with a knife against a ruler held against the longer, lusher grass of the outfield. The roller stood at the ready near the pavilion, and I knew that in the shed, securely padlocked, was Terry's pride and joy, the Lloyds Paladin cylinder mower with which he sculpted the lines up and down the square.

I fell asleep on the springy turf in the shade of a big oak near the gate and woke up thinking about cricket.

7

SEA SHANTY

Robin Hood's Bay, North Yorkshire

The closure of the Scarborough–Whitby railway line half a century ago is still mourned by rail enthusiasts; and quite understandably, as it must have been one of the great stretches on the whole national network. But all was not lost when Beeching's axe fell. The line was acquired by Scarborough Borough Council, and although the track was removed, the cinder bed on which the sleepers had been laid was left. In time what had been a wonderful train ride became a wonderful cycle ride, the Cinder Track.

The attractions of the section immediately north of Scarborough are discreet, even low-key. The track cuts through green countryside and leafy woods. The sea is never far away but it remains out of sight, and there are no more than occasional glimpses of the clifftops. For long stretches the path is hemmed in by trees, the branches meeting overhead in a casual intimacy that would never have been tolerated when the locomotives were chuffing through. The

Robin Hood's Bay from the air

cinders make an easy cycling surface, the inclines are gentle and the curves gradual. The cyclist is able – or this cyclist was able – to slide into a contemplative, contented state of mind, so that the miles slip by almost unnoticed.

The one slightly taxing ascent is up to Ravenscar, where an imposing hotel is perched above dark, shaly cliffs, the one survivor from an impetuous and ill-fated plan in late Victorian times to transform this exposed clifftop hamlet into a swanky seaside resort. At Ravenscar the cycle path abruptly becomes grand, dramatic, even epic. Landscape and seascape come together as Robin Hood's Bay shows itself: framed in the distance by the sharp outline of the headland known as Bay Ness, a crescent of steep-sloping brown cliffs with a chequerboard of green fields splashed with gorse and broom inland, a great sweep of water a mile-and-a-half across creased by white lines of slow, purposeful waves.

Seen at high tide under a blue sky on a summer's day it all looks benign enough. But the ebbing tide reveals an extraordinary shoreline. Dark tongues of hard shale are exposed with channels between where softer rock has eroded. These tongues – known as scaurs or scars – curve away from the shore like the corrugations on a sea shell. Along the southern half of the bay they are at a fairly acute angle with the beach. Further north, around where the village of Robin Hood's Bay spills down a cleft in the cliffs, the angles are wider, so that the scars thrust out into the sea. As the tide recedes further, the channels between the scars empty. Plateaus of bedrock, pitted with holes and tiny pools, stand up from the lower rock base. Massive boulders, seemingly distributed at random, rest on these platforms.

In calm weather the waves chase each other playfully across the fissured rockscape. But even then they come at varying angles and speeds, colliding as they break over the scars. In a storm on a low or ebbing tide the bay becomes a churning battleground of competing forces of water, surging this way and that in a roar of spray and foam. And if that storm is blowing from the east, thrusting big rollers from the open sea to smash across the scars, then to be out there in an open boat is to face the utmost peril.

Viewed from Ravenscar the village of Robin Hood's Bay appears as a cheerful and incongruous red against the green of the woods and meadows clasping it from behind. In fact it is only the pantiled roofs that are red. The walls of the cottages and the few more substantial buildings are constructed from rough brown slabs of sandstone hewn from compacted deposits of the same rock that gives the cliffs and the shore their dark, stern hue.

Space was always the scarcest and most precious commodity in Baytown – or just Bay – as the village is known. There is the one road in and out (there was another 200 years ago but it was smashed away by the sea). It is called New Road, and it makes for an alarming and brake-squealing descent on a bike. On either side the cottages and crooked little houses are squeezed side by side, front to back and apparently almost on top of each other around a warren of tiny cobbled streets, passages, flights of steps and miniature squares – 'perched like the nests of seagulls among the cliffs', as a Victorian travel guide put it.

It is invariably referred to as a 'fishing village' or 'former fishing village' and a long time ago that, indeed, was its prime function. There were almost no gardens and every level bit of land that did not have a dwelling or a shed on it was filled with lobster pots, buoys, coils of rope and other fishing gear, or blocks for cutting and cleaning fish. Every post and fence supported netting or more rope, every shed was crammed with more equipment, and there were hurricane lamps on hooks for lighting the tables on which the nets were repaired and the lines with their weights and hundreds of hooks were carefully coiled so they could be taken to the boats in the darkness and loaded.

The bottom of New Road opens out to face the sea, with the Bay Hotel on one side and the old coastguard house on the other, and the slipway in front. Looking out you wonder how this could ever have been a fishing village. There are no protective seawalls, no harbour, no quayside with deep water beside, nowhere for boats to be safe from a storm and a rising sea. They were simply pulled up out of harm's way at the end of each day's fishing, and launched again the next, heaved down over the rock and shingle and thrust out into the waves. The designated channel was known in that terse Yorkshire way as The Landing. It was the task of the helmsman on an incoming boat to locate it, and woe betide any that failed. On either side the rocks waited, and in a storm in failing light the posts marking the way were hard to spot. Many were the boats smashed to pieces, and many the Robin Hood's Bay fishermen drowned within hailing distance of the shore.

There had been boats and Bay men facing that peril back in Tudor times, but the heyday of Baytown came early in the nineteenth century when, for a short while, it rivalled Whitby and Scarborough in importance for landing fish. At the high point as many as forty-five boats and 130 fishermen were working the inshore waters out of Baytown. The boats were cobles, generally thirty to forty feet long. They had a high bow, a raised stern with undercut transom so they could be landed stern first, and a long tiller which operated a heavy rudder that acted as a centreboard to balance the craft. The cobles were rowed, although a sail was stored and raised when conditions were favourable. Pots were set for lobster, drift nets for salmon and baited hooks for cod, haddock and anything else that came along. When the boats came in at dusk the village turned out. The boys helped bring the boats in and unload the catch, and then the women and girls set about sorting it, cleaning and then barrelling the fish. There was a part for everyone; when a man got too old for pulling the coble oars he could still be useful putting out the crab and lobster pots.

Although fishing was the mainstay of the Bay economy, an important secondary prop was the alum works along the clifftop towards Ravenscar. Alum crystals were widely used in the dyeing and tanning industries in the eighteenth and nineteenth centuries, and its extraction from the shale deposits required heating in water, which required coal. Potash from kelp was used in another process, and ammonia from human urine in another – and all these materials were more easily delivered by sea to the foot of the cliffs than by land. At times as many as fifty men were employed at the alum works, and up to twelve boats on delivering materials and taking away the finished product.

So Baytown prospered, but as it did so, the fishing families thought to prosper more, which is the way economics works. That had to mean bigger boats, and that storm-blasted strip of shore in front of the village could not deal with bigger boats. Although mid-nineteenth-century Baytown was full of resident seafaring men, most were by then working on vessels registered and kept in Whitby to the north, where there was a secure harbour. Alan Storm, a descendant from one of the principal fishing dynasties, compiled an exhaustive study entitled *Family and Marine Community: Robin Hood's Bay c.1653–c.1867* charting the course of Baytown history. His researches revealed that most of the ships registered in the names of Baytown families were actually engaged in transporting cargo rather than fishing. The younger men from the village were sailors rather than fishermen, generally working far away as deckhands.

Jacob Storm, who was born in 1837, stated in his memoir of Bay life that around 1850 there were seventeen cobles fishing out of Baytown as well as two luggers and a yawl. The fishing was, he said, 'prosecuted with vigour'. But the drain of men to merchant shipping meant that by the end of the century there was just one family still at it: one of the numerous branches of the Storm tree, this one comprising Thomas Smith Storm (known as 'Argy') and his sons Thomas, William, Oliver and Reuben (all of whom served at one time or other as coxswain of the Bay lifeboat). By then the opening of the Scarborough–Whitby railway line had introduced a new role for the village. Visitors from faraway Scarborough and even York discovered the village perched above the North Sea and pronounced it quaint and delightful. Baytown was becoming a holiday destination.

*

For my sixtieth birthday a few years back a dear friend, Padraic Fallon – now dead – gave me a book I had never heard of by a writer I had never heard of. On the inside cover he wrote: 'To Tom Fort, a good man with words and a man of good heart', which would be a nice way to be remembered. When I asked him about it, he just said that everyone in his family had read it and so should anyone who loved the sea and fishing.

The first sentence of Leo Walmsley's *Three Fevers* reads: 'It was treacherous weather, even for a Bramblewick December.' That's the way to start a story – you cannot help but read on, and I did. It did not take me long to reach the end, for it is a shortish novel (250 modest-sized pages).

It is the story of two fishing families and the north-east Yorkshire village where they live and fish. The Three Fevers of the title are the compulsions that overtake them successively: for catching cod, then lobster and finally salmon. The fevers are stoked by the rivalry between the Fosdycks – the resident Bramblewick family, going back to the time of the Dissolution of the Monasteries – and the Lunns, who are incomers. The Fosdycks, ageing and traditionalist, fish the old way, slow and safe. The Lunns have an engine on their boat, and are risk-takers. The families fear and hate each other, but they are also trapped in a web of mutual dependence. Each needs the other to help manhandle its boat in and out, and when danger threatens, each must turn to the other as the only source of assistance.

More than that, they are bound together in their challenge to the sea. The action is narrated by an unnamed outsider who fishes with the Lunns. It revolves around the individual fishermen and their womenfolk, the business of fishing, the terrifying peril the sea can conjure at the drop of a lobster pot, and the way the two crews meet and face down that challenge. It is very simply told and all the more powerful for that. The descriptions of the storms and the rage of a sea that is their provider as well as their mortal enemy are heart-poundingly exciting. More than that I will not say – as my friend Padraic said to me, if you are interested in the sea and the story of those who lived from it, read it.

Having finished it I became curious about Leo Walmsley. It turned out that Bramblewick was Robin Hood's Bay and that the story of *Three Fevers* came from the story of Baytown's last two fishing families. The Fosdycks were the Storms, the Lunns were the Dukes, migrants from Flamborough. The narrator – not a popular man in the village – was Walmsley himself.

The Walmsleys were themselves incomers, from Shipley. Leo's father, Ulric, was an artist who moved to Baytown with his wife Jeannie and their four children in 1894, when Leo – the youngest – was two. Ulric Walmsley spent the rest of his long life there, making a living and little more from selling his watercolours of the area, teaching and photography, and as a sign-writer. His wife was a devout Methodist, the effect of which was to turn her youngest child off religion for life. Leo also found the narrow, inward-looking life of the village unsympathetic; it is noticeable that in his autobiographical books he makes little mention of his parents and none at all of his siblings.

As a child he was an outsider, but he found an escape and consolation along the Bay shore and on its waters: fishing, hunting for fossils, examining and classifying the creatures of the pools and fringes. At the age of twenty he got a part-time job as curator of the marine laboratory recently established at Robin Hood's Bay by the distinguished Professor of Zoology at Leeds University, Walter Garstang. Walmsley was paid five shillings a week and was left to determine his own working hours, which he combined with teaching at a local school. In 1913 he had an article about the geology of the Bay published in the *Whitby Gazette*. A year later he enlisted in the Royal Army Medical Corps, transferring later to the Royal Flying Corps. He served with distinction as an observer during the East Africa Campaign and was awarded the Military Cross.

In 1928, having embarked with little success on the life of a writer, Walmsley returned to Baytown to live with his first wife, Elsie. By then the Storms and the Dukes were still fishing commercially, and no one else. The majority of the Bay folk evidently did not care for him or his bohemian ways or the manner of his talk. But he made friends with the Dukes and went fishing with them often enough to acquire the solid background material he needed to write *Three Fevers*. It was published in 1931, by which time Walmsley's first marriage had broken down and he had moved to a creek near Fowey in Cornwall. It was enthusiastically reviewed – J. B. Priestley said 'it is done with extraordinary assurance and conviction . . . and is grandly alive' – and the sale of the rights to a film of it, called *Turn of the Tide*, enabled Walmsley to return to his home territory with his second wife. He built a house a couple of miles inland from Baytown and wrote three more Bramblewick tales, none of which repeated the success of *Three Fevers*.

After a period living in Wales, Walmsley's second wife left him, taking their children with her. In 1945 he came back to Baytown again for a while, before retreating to Cornwall. He married a third time, had a daughter and died at Fowey in 1966. In all, this unusual and – reading between the lines – difficult man wrote twenty or so novels, guide books and memoirs. The last, *Angler's Moon*, is an engaging medley of recollections, many of them from his Baytown days.

Walmsley classified the Bramblewick stories as 'autobiographical novels'. Of *Three Fevers* he wrote: 'All I had done by way of invention was to increase the rivalry between the two families to a feud – the old-timers against the foreigners.' The entire narrative is concentrated on them – 'The book had no plot,' Walmsley said, 'and the sea itself was the protagonist.' Although the dwellings of the Lunns are carefully realised, there is no overall impression of the village itself or what anyone else was doing. In fact, by 1928, when Walmsley spent his fishing season there, most of the old cottages were already holiday homes. By 1935, when *Turn of the Tide* was filmed on location, the last Storms had retired from fishing and the Lunns had decamped to Whitby and bought a small trawler.

*

The sea is no longer the protagonist in the story of Baytown. Its role is limited to providing the setting, the beauty of which is undimmed, and a playground in fine weather for boaters, recreational anglers and the occasional brave swimmer. The gulleys between the scars and the rock pools are invaded and netted and picked over by holidaymakers on summer days, without a thought given to the appalling hazard these weed-draped spits of rock once presented.

I have never been to a place whose maritime past – for so long its reason for being – has been so thoroughly erased. Even along the Devon and Cornwall coast, where former fishing villages have all been swallowed up by the holiday industry, there is often an inshore crabber or two left to provide an authentic link with the long ago. But in Baytown the history is all that is left, lovingly cherished but ever more remote.

In the winter months the village shuts down almost entirely, except at Christmas and over New Year, when the lights blaze from the rented cottages and second homes and music is heard. Everything is very carefully and smartly maintained. The 'authentic features' inside the cottages are proudly on display among the smart hobs and flat-screen TVs and heated airing cupboards where the duvets and duck-down pillows are stored. The tiny terraces where the fishing gear was stacked have pot plants and trestle tables and ornate cast-iron seats and little beds of flowers. The sheds where the bait was cut and lines of a thousand hooks were assembled have been converted into that priceless extra bedroom. Roses climb over porches, whitewash gleams, the alleyways are swept. There is not a fish scale to be seen, but you may find craft shops, art shops, antique shops, knick-knack shops, a secondhand bookshop, any number of coffee shops and faintly fancy bistros.

But before anyone waxes indignant about second-homers conspiring to drive out the locals through superior spending power, it's worth examining the history of Baytown closely.

The process of turning it into a holiday village began a long time ago, once its time as a significant centre for fishing was over. There was no alternative economic lifeline – the alum extraction towards Ravenscar had petered out in the mid-nineteenth century. Some families stayed in Bay and the fishermen went off to Whitby and thence to sea. But many moved away, leaving their spray and salt-ravaged stone dwellings empty. Had they not been bought up and looked after, they would have decayed beyond repair. The investment of part-time Baytowners – some of them owners of the same holiday homes going back several generations – have saved the village from ruin. They have also wielded sufficient clout to compel the authorities to maintain and enhance the defences against the sea – most significantly the new concrete seawall installed in the early 1970s and now approaching the end of its useful life. Baytown has become far too valuable as a tourist draw to be allowed to slide into the sea, which might well have happened otherwise.

It is true that it has long since ceased to function as a village in any meaningful sense. However, the village bearing the name Robin Hood's Bay has not perished – it has merely moved a little way away. The present version is not at all quaint or picturesque, and it has nothing in the way of old history. But it is alive, which counts for something.

It is to be found at the top of the road leading down to Baytown, on what has always been known as Bay Bank. Following the opening of the railway in 1885, plots were offered for sale on what was grandly designated Mount Pleasant – 'splendid sites close to the sea for the erection of superior Villa Residences or High Class Boarding or Lodging

Houses.' No one could call the buildings that resulted beautiful. They were large, red-brick, abundantly provided with bay windows, dormers, gables, tiled floors, front doors with panels of coloured glass in lozenges and other late Victorian decorative features. They had big rooms and big gardens from which the steady stream of visitors could look down on the claustrophobic huddle of Baytown.

The opening of the resplendent Victoria Hotel in 1897 further enhanced the appeal of the new settlement, sometimes referred to locally as Top of Bay. Many of the original houses did become lodging houses (and are still run as B&Bs today). But others became the homes of master mariners from Baytown who were more than happy to exchange their cramped quarters down the hill for modern comforts and extra space. There was no shortage of room up there; the settlement could expand as it wished. Over time the big, ugly villas were joined by 1930s semis, 1950s bungalows and 1970s houses as it spread along the clifftop and inland.

The connection between Bay Bank and the Bay itself is tenuous. The primary school and the village hall are both named after Fylingdales rather than Robin Hood's Bay – Fylingdales being the parish, which covers a large area of moorland and is more usually associated with the RAF radar and early-warning station which is many miles inland. In contrast the bowling and tennis clubs – near the dark and forbidding late Victorian Church of St Stephen – proudly invoke the name of Robin Hood's Bay.

However it is designated, this shapeless nondescript mishmash of late Victorian and twentieth-century housing – in look and character far removed from the sweet, old cottages of Baytown – is where the heart of a community beats. Children flock to the school from all around. From inside the village hall I could hear cries and thuds and music advertising a vigorous aerobics session; there is a full programme of bingo and domino drives and other more sedate entertainments. Outside the Grosvenor, a sprawling Victorian roadside pub, posters announced a Tuesday night gig by blues legend Steve Phillips and the Rough Diamonds. The crown bowling green was quiet mid-morning, but come evening the bowls would be purring their way across the velvet turf.

I went to visit one of the bowling club's faithful regulars, still playing in her nineties. She lives in a spacious bungalow near enough the cliff edge to have a fine view of the Bay from her smartly tended and luxuriantly shrubbed and hedged garden, but far enough away not to be in danger of slipping over. It was built in the 1950s by her father, whose firm was responsible for a number of other similar dwellings in Top of Bay. She moved up from Baytown with her husband, who was one of seventeen children from an old village family. They were not one of the fishing dynasties, but did almost everything else, from running a farm and the butcher's shop to delivering the bottled gas.

She remembered Leo Walmsley, not with affection. There was an old story about a fight involving him in which one of her husband's brothers or cousins had been blinded in one eye. 'The family didn't have much favour for him,' she said unforgivingly. 'And he made a lot of that book up anyway. It was as well for him that he went off somewhere else.'

I asked her why she had moved from Baytown. She waved a mottled hand around her conservatory. 'Why do you think?

A lot of young families moved out when they got the chance. Some went to the new council houses at Fylingthorpe because they were modern and you could park a car outside. You couldn't have that in Bay.'

She hardly ever went down there any more, except when her son came over from Scarborough and they took a stroll for old time's sake. 'There's almost no one left I'd know,' she said. She didn't seem sad about it, and certainly not bitter about what had happened to Baytown. 'It's the way of things,' she said.

Later I pedalled back along the Cinder Track then cut down a steep hill to Mill Beck and followed it to Boggle Hole where a handsome stone youth hostel stands within sound of the sea. I looked south to Ravenscar – in *Three Fevers* 'that headland whose foundations of rugged iron-stone reached out seawards like the forepaws of an immense sculptured lion.' In the final scene of the novel, the two Lunn sons, Marney and John, take the coble out on their own, leaving their father, Henry, nursing a poisoned thumb. It is a day in late summer and their target is Spinney Hole, below the cliffs of High Butts (Ravenscar), where the salmon and sea trout come in on a high tide to feed in the channels behind the scars. The method is to fix the nets across the mouths of the channels then drive the fish out on the ebb, beating the water with a pole.

Inevitably a storm blows out of the south-east, the most deadly quarter. Mist creeps across the moorland, and the barometer drops like a stone as the wind picks up. Bolts of lightning split the sky and the rain falls in sheets. The rising seas are running straight across the way into The Landing, threatening to drive any boat attempting to get in on to the rocks. The Fosdyck boat makes it in the nick of time, but there is no sign of the Lunn boys. Henry Lunn and the nameless narrator make their way in haste along the shore to Spinney Hole, where they find a fresh salmon with a Lunn gaff stuck in it. But there is no answer to their cries from the roaring blackness in front of them.

Back at Bramblewick the Fosdycks are preparing to launch the lifeboat, in the full knowledge that they will be risking their lives to save those of their enemies. But all thoughts of the bad blood between them are put aside in the common cause against the sea. Then, through the fog, they all hear the sound of oars from beyond The Landing. The Lunn boat beaches and the sons step ashore into a blast of rage from their father. In the bottom of the boat are twelve salmon, thirty-three seatrout and a dozen cod. The peril over, the family at once get down to discussing the three weeks of the salmon fishing left, and the prospects for the cod beyond that.

It was a different world then.

8

IDYLL

Chelsfield, Greater London

London's suburban spill to the south-east is halted with surprising suddenness less than a dozen miles from Canary Wharf. Orpington is unashamed suburbia. But cycle a little way east from Orpington railway station into Avalon Road and take a right turn into Chelsfield Lane and you are in the English countryside. Even at my cycling speed the change was abrupt. One moment I was passing bungalows and pairs of semis behind paved forecourts and street lamps; the next I was between unkempt hedges with fields of ripening rape beyond and woodland in the distance. Administratively, this is Greater London these days (more precisely, the Borough of Bromley), but in character it remains rural Kent.

I pedalled along slightly disbelievingly, hearing birdsong instead of traffic noise. The lane curved a little to the left past a couple of 1960s houses. Then I was in the village of Chelsfield, the low grey Victorian school on one side, the pub – the Five Bells – on the other.

Chelsfield in the Second World War

The Five Bells, Chelsfield, 1860s

It is a very small village. At the crooked crossroads in the middle of it one lane goes off left into more open countryside. The one opposite goes past the village hall and the cricket ground on one side, and Chelsfield Hospital on the other, towards the hamlet of Maypole. The road to the right, in front of the pub, takes you past some old cottages and out of the village. There are fields either side as you go, but the rustic peace is soon invaded by the insistent growl of traffic along the Orpington bypass.

This road, built in the 1920s, was the great injury done to Chelsfield in the name of progress. It cleaved the parish in half, cutting the village off from its fine old Church of St Martin of Tours. To reach it, worshippers for the past ninety years have had to cross the bypass, an undertaking that has become increasingly hazardous with time and increased use (I say this with feeling having been knocked off my bike doing it, and having been very lucky to have escaped with cuts and bruises and a sprained ankle).

Although the church is (and always has been) a fair distance from the village of Chelsfield – and thanks to the bypass feels as if it belonged somewhere else altogether – we are far from having finished with the name of Chelsfield having reached it. Church Road continues in a south-westerly direction. There are fields and then, on the left, a golf course; and on the right a handsome dark-red farmhouse with the curious name of Julian's Brimstone. From there the land to the west dips down, revealing Chelsfield Park, a fine example of how responsible and civilised housing developers approached the business of building a housing estate long ago.

The land, almost 200 acres of it, had formed part of the

estate of the Victorian squire of Chelsfield, William Waring. In 1920 it was sold by his son, Arthur Waring, to a company called Homesteads Ltd., with offices in the Strand. They set about creating a settlement that would both be a pleasure to live in and the height of convenience for commuting from Chelsfield railway station – handily placed at the northern edge – to central London. The plots were spacious, averaging two-thirds of an acre each, big enough for a small-scale agricultural smallholding as well as a house. The homes were detached, but modest in size, built in an unpretentious style characteristic of the time, with exposed beams and dormers and lots of little arts-and-crafts touches. Existing mature trees were retained where possible, and new trees were planted, to ensure a bosky, semi-rural feel. A recreation ground and sports club were provided, as well as a refreshment pavilion. Crucially the company imposed covenants on each plot stipulating that no more than one dwelling would be permitted on it.

Chelsfield Park was pretty much completed by the late 1930s. Subsequently the area to the north and west of the railway station was comprehensively built over as well, although in a more piecemeal fashion. But the land to the east, around the original village, was not touched and has not been touched by the developer's hand. Perhaps as an act of reparation for being sundered from its church, old Chelsfield has been protected in its rustic setting instead of being swallowed up by Orpington.

So there are three Chelsfields: the nondescript sprawl attached to the station; leafy Chelsfield Park; and the village.

*

One day in March 1921 a little girl, seven years old, alighted at Chelsfield station with her elder sister, her mother and her father to begin their new life. Then, as now, there was a footpath along the edge of the field behind the station that led to Church Road. Then, as now, it gave a clear view across to the cluster of trees part hiding Chelsfield Church and to the countryside beyond. Much later in her life, the girl stated that it was this prospect that first ignited the love of nature and the open air that ran like a stream through the books she would write.

The family made their way on foot to Church Road, then along it to the top of Chelsfield Hill. Today this looks down on to the A21 link with the M25, but then the view was of woods and fields. 'Half-way down the steep hill,' the girl remembered seventy years later, 'a cart track led off which ended in a south-facing field heavily hedged. These hedges yielded more joy, for under them grew sheets of blue violets and later little spangles of white stitchwort whose seedpods could be popped with great satisfaction.' Beyond was a wood where 'wood pigeons clattered from the oak trees, blackbirds fled squawking from the bramble bushes, tits collected the swinging caterpillars from their gossamer threads . . .'

Their home was at the top of the hill. It was one of the first in what would become Chelsfield Park, a bungalow, newly built of asbestos sheets on a timber frame. It stood well back from the road in a double plot; the girl's father later sold off half the land for another house. The family kept chickens and goats and grew vegetables. Opposite their gate was a pond: 'In early spring it was awash with frog spawn . . . there was one large tree, probably a crab apple or wild cherry, which we could climb . . . a flutter of squabbling little tabby sparrows came to drink and splash in the shallows and we were entranced.'

She had been born in Norwood and spent the first years of her life in the south London suburb of Hither Green. She and her mother had both been stricken with the Spanish flu after the end of the 1914–18 war, and her father, an insurance agent, decided the family needed country air. 'At Chelsfield,' she wrote, 'I came into my own and I have never ceased to be grateful.'

She was just old enough to go to the school in the village. It was a walk of over a mile. It took her past the low wall in front of the yard beside Julian's Brimstone, from which the geese would sometimes emerge to chase her, past the gates leading to the big house, Court Lodge, past a row of limes, and another of elms, and into the village with the fire station on the right opposite a cottage where a German couple lived, very quietly no doubt. She passed the three shops and the Five Bells and turned left at the crossroads and there was the school, much as it is today.

The headmaster, Robert Clark, had arrived a year earlier. He was thirty years old, full of the enthusiasm of youth, and proved to be an inspiration to the girl. He lent her books and she became familiar with Dickens and the other classics. He introduced gardening as a school subject and threw himself into the life of the village. In the church choir he deployed a bass voice 'almost as velvety smooth as Paul Robeson's'. Thanks in large part to him, she experienced a happiness which remained with her for the rest of her very long life – 'the place fitted me as snugly as a cocoon and lapped me in warmth, security and friendship. I thrived as never before.'

But her time at Chelsfield Village School was all too short-lived. After three years she won a scholarship to the girls' grammar school in Bromley. From an early age she had had the writing itch, and wanted to become a journalist. But her father discouraged her so she went into teaching instead. She worked at various primary schools in suburban London, married another teacher, then moved to Witney in Oxfordshire. After the Second World War she combined supply teaching with bringing up her daughter and – increasingly – writing. She was a regular contributor to *Punch*, specialising in sketches of everyday country life, and produced many scripts for the BBC's Schools Service. The literary editor at *Punch*, H. F. Ellis, said she was his favourite – 'she has no arrogance . . . she writes about what she knows and never goes beyond it.'

In 1953 Sir Robert Lusty, a director of the publishing house Michael Joseph, read an article of hers in the *Times Literary Supplement* and admired it sufficiently to suggest to her that she might have a book in her. The result was *Village School*, which she regarded as fiction and expected to come out under her own married name, Dora Saint (her father's name was Arthur Shafe). But Lusty had a better idea. He persuaded her that it should be dressed up as non-fiction, with the appearance of being a memoir by a spinster schoolteacher called Miss Read (Read was her mother's maiden name). The trick worked nicely and the assumed identity stuck for the thirty-odd books that followed over the years.

Village School was set in a place called Fairacre (her sub-sequent stories were divided between it and Thrush Green, which is situated in the Cotswolds and is directly drawn from her time living in Witney). Geographically and physically Fairacre is nebulously realised; Miss Read's daughter said it comprised elements from Chelsfield and Chieveley, near Newbury, where she lived later, as well as other villages she knew from her supply-teaching days.

But the school of the first Miss Read book is the one she had known and loved as a child. By an unusual stroke of imaginative transference, she casts herself – not as the girl pupil – but as Mr Clark in female form: wise, tolerant, firm, a spreader of enlightenment and delight. How curious it is that the experience of those three years should have been so intense, the memories so indelibly stamped, that she should have wanted and been able to work on them in such a way so long afterwards.

Miss Read's talent, a slender but very distinctive one, was to be inside her village, to portray it from within. Her char-acters – the school cleaner, the vicar, the bossy postmistress, Mr Willet the school caretaker and sexton at St Patrick's Church, Mr Mann the local ornithologist, Mr Annett the choirmaster – are drawn with unobtrusive, unsentimental skill. Her novels are not really novels at all, but collections of loosely connected stories in which the regular cast sometimes act as sources or witnesses, and at others as a kind of Greek chorus, commentating on incidents of curious or unexpected behaviour.

In general the events are suitably mundane: a fallen elm, a leaking skylight, a jumble sale, a harvest festival service, the making of a Christmas pudding. One exception was the running story in *Storm in the Village*, of how the villagers of Fairacre suspend their differences and put their usual concerns aside to unite in opposition to a plan for a housing estate on Hundred Acre Field to accommodate the families of employees of the Atomic Energy Authority. But it was unusual for Miss Read to permit the world outside Fairacre to intrude when there was so much going on within to keep her pen busy. As she wrote in the fifth of the Fairacre chronicles, *Over the Gate*: 'With what avidity I listen to my neighbours' accounts of tales of long ago and with what unfailing curiosity I observe the happenings of today ... the story of the village goes back a long, long way; and it still goes on ... Can you wonder that we are never dull in Fairacre?'

Elsewhere she refers to the village as timeless and unchanging – this is why her fans loved Miss Read, because she gave them the impossible and made it seem real. Her Fairacre recalled for them a place and time which had somehow regained and retained the simplicity and innocence that the modern world had annihilated. In Fairacre there was love but no sex. There were differences of opinion but no hatred, setbacks but no disasters, going short but no poverty. Children might be rough, but there was no bullying. People might be down in the dumps but there was no clinical depression. The harsh, ugly, incomprehensible aspect of life was kept at bay – a sleight of hand that also protected the residents from ageing or becoming decrepit, and ensured that time did not really move at all.

Miss Read was extremely popular in her day, but that day seems to be over. Her work really belonged to the same era as that in which crime fiction still featured upper-class pipe-puffing amateur sleuths who solved intricate mysteries through ingenious deduction, usually assisted by a dim-witted sidekick and even dimmer-witted, heavy-footed but scrupulously honest police officers. The toff sleuth eventually made way for the detective-as-police-officer, invariably divorced or with his marriage on the rocks, hopeless at relationships (because of the job) but irresistible to women, disdainful of the rules of procedure. Every murderer became a serial killer and every murder involved torture and dismemberment instead of genteel strangulation or a single shot through the heart.

The contemporary equivalent of Miss Read's Fairacre Chronicles is J. K. Rowling's *The Casual Vacancy*, a 500-page epic in which the vacancy in question – on the parish council in a town in the West Country (never mind that towns have town councils not parish councils) – sets off a perfect storm of murder, rape, sexual abuse, drug-taking, porn-watching and other miscellaneous nastiness. The author, who lives in Edinburgh, maintained that her reason for writing the book was to explore 'real issues' affecting 'real people'. While it is certainly true that not one of her gallery of social misfits and monsters would have been allowed over the parish boundary into Fairacre, the question of who gives the truer picture of village life – Miss Read or the creator of Harry Potter – remains open.

*

My first port of call in Chelsfield was at the school, where the headteacher kindly invited me into her office to tell me what a happy place it was. On a shelf were the logbooks from the time Dora Shafe had been a pupil and I browsed through these while the head dealt with a tortuous narrative of misbehaviour coaxed from three sheepish and crestfallen lads, one of whom had cut his hand and was trying to explain why he had hidden in the toilets taking the playground basketball with him.

The 1921 summer term, I discovered, had opened on a positive note with 'the scholars' celebrating Empire Day by singing 'Flag of Britain' and 'The Recessional'. At the beginning of June attendance was 100 out of 115. But many of the children were required to contribute to keeping their families financially afloat, hence the logbook entry: 'Fruit picking has commenced.' On 17 June the school closed for three weeks for the 'Fruiting Holiday', which may have been a holiday for Dora and the other children of professional salary-earners, but was anything but for many of her schoolmates.

School reopened on 25 July then closed again on 2 September, the time for hop-picking. The following year, 1922, the attendance in June was assessed as 'very poor' and the logbook for the 19th noted: 'Certain growers have started fruit-picking.' Three days later the school closed until late July. Attendances through the winter months were generally patchy owing to the incidence of measles, whooping cough, scarlet fever, influenza and other illnesses, and the difficulty of getting the children in from the outlying hamlets and farms when there was snow on the ground. The brief entries in the regular handwriting – Mr Clark's or the school secretary's? – suggest a harsher context of economic struggle, toil and unwholesome living conditions than Miss Read ever allowed to intrude into her village idyll.

That context now seems infinitely remote. The agricultural society that dictated the school year was dismantled long ago. The notion of children having to pick hops and fruit instead of doing their lessons seems to belong more to Victorian times than the century we have recently left behind. The diseases that ravaged school ranks have been largely eliminated, and absenteeism is likely to land parents in court. Miss Read herself went back to the school in 1975 to write an article about it for the *Sunday Telegraph*. She was reassured to find the building largely unchanged, the shed where it used to be, the lime trees still flourishing. The children, she noted, were more interested in learning than in her day, the teachers were quieter and the whole school was more tranquil. 'It was this domestic atmosphere which I so clearly remembered and so feared to find gone which impressed me most during this return visit,' she wrote.

She would still find it today. But what might surprise her would be the demographics, a word she would have disdained. None of the children come from the village itself, the headteacher told me, because there are almost no young families; and those that there are send their children to private school. Much the same applies to Chelsfield Park, where the stratospheric inflation of house prices means that incoming families buying houses must be rich, and rich families favour private education. There are long-established families both in the village of Chelsfield and in Chelsfield Park, but their child-rearing days were long ago. Because it is a sweet little school in a good area, Chelsfield Primary pulls in children from the Chelsfield around the station and well beyond. But the umbilical connection between school and village has been broken for good.

I cycled out along the road the little girl had walked each school day, over the bypass and past the church. Dora's mother died in 1937. Her father remarried and continued to live in the bungalow at the top of Chelsfield Hill until his death in 1968. The local historian and expert on Miss Read, Patrick Hellicar, told me that there was no evidence of her having been a dutiful or regular visitor to Chelsfield after she left to pursue a career in teaching. Her parents do not figure prominently in her two volumes of autobiography, nor does her sister, which perhaps suggests that the intensity of belonging she felt at school may not have been matched at home.

The fate of the family home, Bramleigh, is typical of the fate that has been gradually overtaking Chelsfield Park as a whole. It lasted until 2014, when it was demolished and replaced by – I can do no better than quote the estate agent's brochure – 'an imposing and spacious 5 bedroom house offering a superior specification.' The brochure characterises the house as 'opulent', though some observers – faced with the frontage of red brick, tile cladding, beaming and leaded windows with dark-brown frames, kept company by double garage and paved drive behind the inevitable security gates – might search for another adjective.

Two million pounds would have secured Bramleigh, with its cinema/games room, Stoneham kitchen units, its underfloor heating and its 'sophisticated perimeter alarm system'. A little way down the hill is Edelweiss, belonging to the same architectural genre as Bramleigh, but with the addition of 'indoor pool complex' plus marble stairs, limestone fireplace, galleried landing and 'multi-room audio-visual system with surround sound' plus CCTV – hence a price tag of £2.5 million.

All over Chelsfield Park the original unassuming houses built by Homesteads Ltd. have been or are being bulldozed to make way for mansions routinely advertised as stunning, wonderful, contemporary, magnificent, beautifully crafted, luxurious, exclusive, exceptional, perfectly suited to family life and so on. The one-dwelling covenants on the plots have prevented wholesale redevelopment, but have made it worthwhile for developers to pay £1 million for a perfectly decent and pleasant three-bedroom house, knock it down and replace it with a six-bedroom monster. Some of the plots are on to their third rebuilding inside eighty years.

In 2001 the Chelsfield Park Residents' Association produced a Millennium booklet commemorating the history of the settlement. It is easy to detect the community spirit that once prevailed. Car ownership in the 1930s was limited, and the salaried commuters forged friendships walking to and from the station in suits and bowler hats, carrying their umbrellas and – in bad weather – wearing wellington boots that they left in the booking office to await the return walk. Some Chelsfield Parkers kept chickens and ran smallholdings, and had eggs and produce for sale. There was cricket and football on the recreation ground, and the tennis enthusiasts got together to build hard courts. There was a drama club and a swimming club. Most families were of the same social class and shared the same interests and were eager to come together.

Today there is a handful of second- and third-generation Chelsfield Parkers left. But the survivors are elderly, and the old community of interest and the spirit it fostered have withered away. The families that have moved in come from all over the economically advanced world, and the one thing they have in common is wealth. Their children go to private schools, and when at home they generally retreat inside their high walls and CCTV-monitored security gates to pursue their private, sealed-off lives.

*

In the early evening I made a point of attending Chelsfield village hall's AGM, hoping as ever to stumble across scandal, drama or at least a decent feud. No such luck. The meeting, attended by twenty or so villagers, was over inside half an hour. The bookings secretary was congratulated on his excellent performance in securing bookings. The retiring chairman was congratulated for his work upgrading the kitchen. The retiring secretary and the retiring treasurer were congratulated for their sterling contributions over many years. The replacements in all these posts were warmly welcomed. The only debate was at the beginning, and arose over who should sit where: a very English debate, because English people always want to sit at the back.

Outside the hall — a rather sweet and modest wood-and-brick affair which was a Coronation initiative and replaced the previous reading room — I had a chat with Chelsfield's exceptionally friendly and talkative rector. A career bank worker and manager until being made redundant when he was nearly fifty, he had come to Chelsfield after a stint in charge of a tough parish at Accrington in Lancashire. Chelsfield presented a different kind of challenge: a very long-serving rector of staunchly conservative leanings had been replaced by a reforming rector whose new ways had provoked discord and strife and led to an early departure.

My genial acquaintance told me that his task had been to steady the ship. Changes were needed but they had to be gradual. How gradual, I asked? He laughed. Well, we still use the 1660 Prayer Book, he said. We have Evensong with anthems and Choral Matins and Choral Eucharist. He laughed some more. 'I'm trying to bring in a Family Service,' he said. 'That would be a start. We all know things have to change, but the change needs to be managed diplomatically.' I asked him how he liked his job. His face lit up. 'He's just the best boss, the Lord is. I am so lucky.'

I went to the Five Bells in search of food. At lunchtime the place had been busy with passing trade but at 7.15 in the evening it was very quiet and I discovered to my dismay that they did lunch but not dinner. However, the landlord came to my rescue with a ham-and-tomato sandwich to keep my couple of pints of Harvey's Sussex Best Bitter company. In the gloaming I cycled up Church Road for the last time. The Chelsfield Ladies Group was having a meeting in the Brass Crosby Room behind the church (so named after a Chelsfield dignitary who was Lord Mayor of London in 1770) which I was anxious not to miss. By a splendid fluke it featured a talk about Miss Read and her local connections by Mr Hellicar, and although I was clearly neither a lady nor from Chelsfield I was made most welcome. The chairman told me the group had previously been called the Young Wives until the label had ceased to be wholly appropriate. She looked around the gathering. 'We're flagging,' she admitted. 'It's so difficult to recruit new members these days.'

Mr Hellicar's talk was absolutely first-rate and very expertly illustrated, and I would like to record my gratitude to him for making his material available to me subsequently, as I had to leave a little before the end to get home. As I pedalled back to Orpington railway station along the path beside the bypass, it occurred to me how much Miss Read would have liked the Chelsfield Ladies Group and how much at home she would have been with them. She would have enjoyed the prayers before the talk and would have nodded approvingly as the chairman thanked those who had made the posies for Mothering Sunday and done the flowers for Easter.

The meeting was a taste of an England which has never received much attention and which is now quietly disappearing. Miss Read herself did not claim that she had 'a message'. 'I think people like to look back,' she said, 'not because everything was better in the past but because often they were happy then.'

9

PARSON POWER

Eversley, Hampshire

Eversley is at the north-eastern edge of Hampshire, where the winding River Blackwater forms the boundary with Berkshire. Although classified as a single village for administrative purposes, it actually comprises three distinct components, all named on the Ordnance Survey map: Eversley, Eversley Centre and Eversley Cross. Plain Eversley is very insubstantial – coming over the river from the direction of Reading you are through it in the blink of an eye. Eversley Centre is next, presumably so designated because the school and village hall are there and because it is halfway between Eversley and Eversley Cross, where the two pubs and the village shop are to be found. The topography of Eversley is further complicated by the situation of its lovely, spacious church, which is somewhere else altogether, standing with its enormous rectory and a couple of other substantial houses well away from all three related settlements.

The land around is flattish, well wooded, pleasant enough

but for the pounding of traffic along the A327 leading from Reading to the suburban sprawl to the east embracing Yateley, Blackwater, Sandhurst, Farnborough and Frimley. There are fields between the copses, and paddocks with horses, and plenty of characterless new private housing developments. It is prosperous, mundane commuter-country. But this was once a desperate part of the country.

When the new curate was appointed in 1842, his parish was a byword for poverty, neglect and ignorance. It was a wild tract of land, much of it unreclaimed heath. The fields, waterlogged by floods from the Blackwater, were poor, able to support no more than a meagre population of illiterate, downtrodden peasants, poachers, hedgers, ditchers, labourers and Gypsies, eking out subsistence livings in a scattering of damp and insanitary cottages. There was no school and the only source of education for the children was the village cobbler, who – according to the curate's wife – operated in the parish clerk's room where 'cobbling shoes, teaching and caning went together'.

At the church, communion was celebrated three times a year, attended by a handful of communicants. The font was a cracked basin, the alms were collected in a wooden saucer. The churchyard was used to bury the dead and to graze sheep when grass was in short supply elsewhere. When the new curate proposed monthly communion, Eversley's churchwardens told him he would have to provide the wine himself.

His name was Charles Kingsley, remembered today principally for his children's story *The Water Babies*, but renowned in his own lifetime as a poet, novelist, historian and essayist. He was the son of a clergyman, Cambridge educated, a gentleman

Charles Kingsley's home in Eversley, with the church behind

with some private means, high-minded, radical in his thinking, passionate by nature, somewhat neurotic and afflicted by
a stammer which he learned to live with but never control,
addicted to tobacco, stern-featured, loving and much loved.

When Kingsley came to live permanently in Eversley –
having been promoted to be its rector – he was twenty-five,
newly married and ready for a mission. He yearned to put
his fierce faith into practice, convinced that it could raise
people to a higher level however humble their station in
society. He found the right challenge in this almost literally
God-forsaken parish. And despite his achievements in other
spheres, Eversley remained his focus and took his best efforts
and energies.

There was no source of help or charity for his parishioners, apart from what he and his wife could provide. Kingsley
arranged funds for small loans, made it possible for families to
get shoes and coal, and organised help for young mothers. He
presided over Penny Readings, at which the men and boys
contributed a penny a head while the women and girls came
free. In winter there were reading classes at the Rectory; in
the spring and summer he held writing classes for girls in the
coach house. A reading room was opened, equipped with
bagatelle and other games; displaying an understanding and
tolerance unusual among the clergy, Kingsley arranged for a
cask of beer to be included in the facilities.

'The people,' Fanny Kingsley wrote, 'were kindly, civil
and grateful for notice. Kingsley was daily with them in their
cottages . . . until he was personally intimate with every soul
in the parish. It was from his house-to-house visiting still
more than his church services that he acquired his power. If

a man or child were suffering or dying he would go five or six times a day, and night as well as day, for his own heart's sake as well as their soul's sake . . . For years he seldom dined out, never during the winter months, and he seldom left the parish except for a few days at a time.'

*

Charles Kingsley was an exceptional specimen of the figure that was at the heart of the life of the village for the best part of a thousand years. The man of God has not always been worthy of his calling, nor has he always been fondly represented. But there can be no doubt about his importance, and that of the church where he officiated.

'The clergy,' John Wycliffe protested in the fourteenth century, 'haunt taverns out of all measure and stir men to drunkenness, idleness and cursed swearing and chiding and fighting . . , and sometimes neither have eye nor tongue nor head nor foot to help themselves for drunkenness.' Chaucer's version of the medieval 'poure parson' is very different; he was 'of holy thought and work, preached the Gospel gladly, taught his flock devotedly . . .'

> . . . he wayted after no pompe nor reverence
> Nor made himself spiced in conscience
> But Christes love and his apostles twelve
> He taught and first he folwed it himself.

There were good ones and bad ones and many in between, and it was ever thus. In the day of Wycliffe and Chaucer the priest's social status was not much higher than that of his working parishioners. Like them he laboured in the fields, returning at the end of the day to a hovel much like theirs. He may have had a smattering of learning, but not enough to compose a sermon or read out the Scriptures. But his very presence enabled him to be a source of comfort when there were precious few others available. He knew the right words at times of crisis, to ease passage into and out of an uncertain world. He might even – if he could be believed – hold the key to another, better world. Furthermore he was the custodian of the one building of permanent stature in the village; the one place where the people could gather for a chat, to hear a story and let their minds wander, free for the moment from the burden of toil.

Little by little his social status improved. Instead of working the land himself, he found someone else to do it and pay him rent. His tithes, once laboriously collected by cart in the form of grain, were commuted to cash. He discovered that a little learning answered better than none, and his reputation grew with his education. He took more of a part in village affairs, sometimes acting as a spokesman in disputes with the manor. Of course there were plenty of priestly fornicators, drunkards, layabouts, ignoramuses and abusers of their office, and they did huge damage to the Church's standing. But there were also plenty of 'poure parsons' who stayed true to their vows and served their people well.

The Reformation of the sixteenth century assisted the status of the clergy considerably. Sparked in large part by revulsion and anger at the corrupt and venal state into which the English branch of the Church of Rome had sunk, it made for a cleaner, leaner organisation. The priest could now have a wife if he wanted one, and a family: strong incentives to better himself. The country's emergence from feudalism into primitive capitalism created a wealth not seen before. Better educated, better housed, better rewarded, the country priest could aspire to raise himself to another level. Enclosure and the accompanying mechanical revolution nourished steep increases in tithes and the rents from glebe lands, propelling him towards that prospect considered most agreeable in English eyes, that of being accepted as a gentleman.

By the start of the nineteenth century it had become quite normal for the younger sons of squires, knights, even lords to take holy orders. This was the rural England made familiar by Jane Austen and later by Trollope, in which the rector might meet his bishop at the palace, or the squire in his mansion, on level terms. These men, educated at Oxford or Cambridge, generally employed curates to do the donkey-work. They sent their sons to the great public schools, built large and handsome rectories, rode to hounds and – in alliance with the squire – played a significant part in directing the affairs of the village. Even the impoverished clergy – such as Mr Crawley, the perpetual curate of Hogglestock in Trollope's *The Last Chronicle of Barset* – had their degrees and their Latin and Greek; indeed Mr Crawley's intellectual powers intimidated his friend Mr Arabin, Dean of Barchester, and were too much altogether for Bishop Proudie.

The parson's influence in the village was pervasive, if not universally appreciated. He was the driving force behind the provision of education – first through charity schools, then Sunday schools and finally village schools. He often funded the school himself, and invariably ensured that he controlled it by appointing the staff and regularly appearing himself. In *Lark Rise to Candleford* Flora Thompson gave a vivid impression of the vicar, who arrived at school each day at 10 a.m. to teach Scripture:

> He was a parson of the old school; a commanding figure, tall and stout, with white hair, ruddy cheeks and an aristocratically beaked nose, and he was as far as possible removed by birth, education and worldly circumstances from the lambs of his flock. He spoke to them from a great height, physical, mental and spiritual. 'To order myself lowly and reverently before my betters' was the clause he underlined in the Church Catechism ... As a man he was kindly disposed – a giver of blankets and coal at Christmas and of soup and milk puddings to the sick.

Thompson was recalling a poor and isolated rural community in north Oxfordshire in the 1870s, but her parson would have been familiar in thousands of villages across the country through most of the century. A few were committed social reformers – like Charles Kingsley, or the wit and humourist Sydney Smith, who in an earlier age had had the nerve to speak up for the poacher and denounce the savagery of the Game Laws, uttering the extraordinary heresy that 'the happiness of the common people, whatever gentlemen may say, might every now and then be considered'. But the great majority of the country clergy, having achieved the status of gentry, embraced the brand of complacent autocratic Toryism that went with it. This parson might be a generous benefactor to his parishioners, but he believed unquestion-ingly that the order of society was divinely appointed and that any change to it should be resisted. Wealth and privilege, he considered, carried obligations, but these did not extend to correcting inequalities.

The parson's social ascent gradually removed him from close intimacy with his humbler parishioners. He was some-one to be reckoned with, but not often loved, and often not much respected either. When the position of the Anglican Church came under assault from non-conformism, the gen-tleman rector found himself short of support. His authority was steadily eroded in the period up to 1914, and thereafter he has steadily retreated to the margins of village life. He – and now she – survives, as does his or her church; and often they do great things for the village. But that era when parson, hand in glove with squire, directed the affairs of the village seems remote indeed.

*

Rewind to post-feudal England, and it was the priest and the lord or squire who held power over the village. But the actual day-to-day administration was largely left to others. For a long time the manorial court was the chief engine keeping the wheels rolling. But gradually and haphazardly, without any direction from above, an additional local power base emerged. It began life as the annual parish meeting at Easter-time, to which villagers were summoned by the ringing of the mote-bell, and was generally held in the vestry of the church, hence the name 'vestry committee'. This evolved into a kind of diminutive parliament which took upon itself all manner of duties that the manorial court was not fit to exercise. These included appointing officers – churchwardens, the constable, the overseer of the poor, the surveyor of the highways. These offices were unpaid, but could be declined only in exceptional circumstances, or by paying an indemnity.

The crucial period in the transfer of power from manor court to vestry was the second half of the sixteenth century. In 1557 vestries were empowered by the Parliament at Westminster to take charge and levy rates for the upkeep of roads, and to collect and maintain weapons for the local militias. Between 1598 and 1601 a series of acts placed the burden of poor relief on them. A national system of local government was taking shape, with vestries at its heart.

Dealing with the poor was the most onerous of the responsibilities. The village overseer organised the payment of relief and was also supposed to find work and accommodation for the homeless, and apprenticeships for the young. In practice he came to see his primary role as keeping a lid on the problem, and his methods could be brutal. There was an obvious incentive to keep vagrants and the destitute out of the parish altogether so they would not be a burden on the rate. The customary method was with whip or stick. The resident poor were sometimes required to wear a badge of coloured cloth at their shoulders to distinguish them from itinerant mendicants, thus stigmatising them as parasites in the eyes of the village workforce.

Inevitably the vestry developed into an oligarchic model of control. The largest group in the village – the cottagers and labourers who had no land apart from their share of the common and the gardens next to their dwellings – worked for wages, paid no rates and were progressively excluded from any share in decision-making. This left the men of property and substance – the squire, if there was one, the parson, freehold farmers, craftsmen – to run things. Over time the open, public aspect of the vestry's operation withered. A self-appointed and self-perpetuating executive, acting in private if not in secret, took control. In theory they were answerable to the wider community, but as they did not have constitutions and their powers were not strictly defined by statute, the extent of their accountability was up to them.

In 1835 there were more than 15,000 vestries across England. Their portfolio of responsibilities had expanded; it now included looking after the church and burial grounds, workhouses, charities, market crosses, village pumps and pounds, stocks and prisons, as well as keeping the peace, dealing with vagrancy, mending the roads and poor relief. But in the end the vestries were overwhelmed by the last of these. Between 1795 and 1802 the amount paid out to the poor in England (and Wales) doubled to £4 million and it doubled again by 1817. The vestries were not empowered to raise the sums needed, and as the numbers of the destitute multiplied, parishes resorted to increasingly desperate measures to shift them somewhere else. Eventually the state intervened, and in 1834 the vestries were relieved of the responsibility. Subsequently the establishment of public boards to handle other specific issues – such as health and sanitation – over much wider areas than mere parishes rapidly eroded vestry power. The 1894 Local Government Act sealed the process by setting up elected parish and district councils. The vestries wandered on for a time, restricted to church matters only, eventually metamorphosing into the parochial church councils we still have today.

*

The notion that the village as a social organism was in trouble as it entered the twentieth century was articulated by George Sturt and others before the outbreak of war in 1914, and was taken up again when the hostilities were over. The challenge was to engineer a new purpose and direction for it, in keeping with the changing times. In a book called *The English Village: The Origin and Decay of Its Community*, Harold Peake, a distinguished archaeologist and expert on pastoralism, argued that a settlement needed a population of at least a thousand to support its essential services, such as shops, doctor, school, club and so on. Peake, writing in the early 1920s, envisaged colonies of craftsmen and women – weavers, potters, cabinet-makers and the like – supporting the agricultural way of life. His image of village life is touchingly naïve: 'All the members of our village should realise that they are members of one and the same community. The agriculturist and the craftsman, and the artisan and the professional man, would meet on common ground at the village club ...'

Post-1945 a new generation of trained planners went forth armed with the provisions of the 1946 Town and Country Planning Act to direct the building of a new England after the devastation of war. One was Thomas Sharp, author of a highly influential book about town planning and another – probably less influential – called *The Anatomy of the Village*. Sharp's guiding principle was 'conscious simplicity . . . informed, orderly, utilitarian, charming'. He deplored shapeless, ad hoc additions – 'our new villages and rebuilt villages cannot in the future have the artless and unsophisticated simplicity of the natural growing villages in the past.' They must be shaped and planned as units, by experts (presumably such as himself). New homes must be 'in harmony' with traditional cottages but not ape them. Sharp favoured small terraces of brick cottages with flat roofs and without gardens, arranged to shut off views of the surrounding countryside so that they provided 'a kind of psychological refuge'.

Thomas Sharp's approach was modernistic and autocratic. It assumed that the superior intelligence and awareness of the trained planner would hold sway over the views of bureaucrats, builders, preservationists and other interested parties. But to the great English geographer W. G. Hoskins, the professional planner was a malign and sinister figure responsible for untold damage to the countryside – 'black-hatted officers of THIS and THAT', he characterised them scornfully. In *The Making of the English Landscape*, Hoskins deployed his pioneering techniques of fieldwork – unpeeling the past through minute investigation of the land – to support his ferocious hostility to the England of his own time. 'Since the year 1914,' Hoskins wrote, 'every single change in the English landscape has either uglified or destroyed its meaning or both.' He railed against the 'barbaric England of the scientists, the military men and the politicians: let us turn away and contemplate the past before all is lost to the vandals.'

Hoskins subscribed fully to the myth of England's fall so acutely analysed by Raymond Williams. The argument was that by switching from a rural to an industrial society we had lost our way and created the conditions for all our misery and disorder. To illustrate its central fallacy Williams used the metaphor of an escalator. By analysing the testimony of writers on rural themes, he was able to show that wherever the commentator was on it – from the sixteenth century to the present – the Arcadia or Utopia or Golden Age was always located imprecisely in the past.

At the centre of the mythic vision was the village: time-less, stable, useful, at one with the landscape, sprung from the soil, organic, secure, interdependent, the true commu-nity. Raymond Williams had grown up in a village near Abergavenny in rural Wales. 'I see the idealisation of set-tlement in its literary-historical version,' he wrote in *The Country and the City*, 'as an insolent indifference to most people's needs . . . I know why people have to move, why so many in my own family moved.'

But when it came to shaping public perception the Hoskins version proved more persuasive. The revolution that was visibly sweeping the countryside – the industrialisation of agriculture and the annexation of the village by middle-class out-commuters – seemed to give potent support to the thesis of loss and destruction over gain and development. It became an orthodoxy that the countryside was in crisis and the village had been dealt a mortal blow. That strand has generally held the upper hand since Hoskins' book first appeared in 1955. Leftish-inclined academics and researchers have periodically emerged from university sociology faculties to investigate individual 'rural communities' and discovered what everyone knew all along: that farming no longer mattered, that soaring property prices had put housing beyond the reach of locals, that long-established families resented the incomers and felt excluded from their place, that the cherished 'sense of community' had been eroded. And so forth.

In the mid-1970s a young Cambridgeshire farmer, Robin Page, produced a book called *The Decline of an English Village* which was an extended bellow of rage against the agrarian revolution. 'It is,' Page wrote, 'a story of rural customs disappearing, of people being dispossessed, of communities losing their land, their beliefs, their traditions – losing themselves.' Page looked back at his Golden Age – presumably in the 1950s – when 'the sights and sounds of everyday life led to feelings of well-being and security.' There were pike, roach, dace and sticklebacks in the brook, Bert the postman delivered the mail with a nod and a smile, everyone knew everyone, everyone had a friendly word for everyone. Then progress arrived. The smithy was replaced by more council houses and the grass verges by concrete. The bakery gave way to a self-service store. Houses were built on Kings Grove – 'the bulldozers and diggers moved in as the young rooks cried greedily for food.'

The ruination accelerated. Hedges were grubbed up, the rabbit warren was destroyed, trees were felled. Grazing cows made way for arable monoculture. Machines ruled where mushrooms once grew. The brook was dredged and the willows along it were cut down. The village lost its bobby on his bike, and the rag-and-bone man called no more. Locals were priced out of housing, the pub acquired a jukebox and one-armed bandit, old people were given meals-on-wheels and 'if they became too much trouble they were sent away by busy relatives.'

In the course of thirty years, Page reflected, 'the heart of the village has died, with its soul hanging on, but only just ... village life, country life, have taken second and third place to the superficial goals of progress, efficiency and development.' With his country burr, whiskered ruddy face and heavy-limbed farmer's way, Page was a natural media personality. Crook in hand, he presented *One Man and His Dog* on BBC television and was a regular panellist until his John Bull views came to be regarded as unpalatable by the high-ups. He also became a columnist for the *Daily Telegraph*.

For the best part of fifty years, Robin Page was given licence to pound his *Telegraph* lectern. Over that time, his themes and views changed little, nor his targets: agribusiness, the EU, planners, politicians, the BBC, the RSPB, lady vicars, immigration, the anti-hunting lobby, townies, global-warming alarmists, republicans. He must have been popular with readers to have kept going so long – his column was finally dropped in July 2016. The joke, of course, is that they – or the country-dwellers among them – are the very people responsible for the fall from grace Page so loudly bemoans: incomers, second-homers, out-commuters and the rest.

The single voice you hear from Robin Page is his own. In contrast, the whole purpose of Ronald Blythe's famous work of oral history, *Akenfield*, was to permit a diverse range of voices to speak. Many of the same themes are covered – the passing of the old ways, the changing face of the village, the assault of intensive farming – but the tone both of Blythe himself and his villagers is notably unrancorous. His purpose was to record the experiences and articulate the feelings of a species of countrymen and women at a time – the book was first published in 1969 – when the world they knew was on the verge of disappearing for good. But he does not stand in judgment. He was acutely aware of the restrictive nature of the old village life – 'it was very hard to get away, to do anything or be yourself, and people worked and worked until they died.'

Fraser Harrison, a writer not as well known as he should be, pursued this point in his book *Strange Land: The Countryside – Myth and Reality*. Harrison identified the qualities ascribed to traditional village life – close ties with family, neighbours and workmates, the habit of helping others, the shared understanding of a specific area of countryside, a particular culture – contrasting them with the perceived 'dislocation, brutality and degeneration' of urban life. He perceptively analysed the danger of taking these qualities out of their context and celebrating them in the abstract. 'They should be recognised as products of poverty and repression,' he wrote. 'They were the positive aspects of a practice of survival which included such negative features as ignorance, superstition, suffocating parochialism and gross deprivation at every level, not only of physical needs but social, intellectual and political needs.'

The point is very well made. Yes, of course there has been loss. There must be when one way of life, long in the shaping and rich in texture, gives way to another. But it is perverse and absurd to harp on about the negatives and ignore the positives. And it is more absurd still to pretend that 'something could have been done about it', and to blame politicians or planners for 'allowing it to happen', as if there had ever been a choice in the matter.

But the temptation to romanticise the past is very powerful. In the case of the village, that sentimental idealisation brushes out the rudeness and cruelty, the discomfort and ill health, the financial, spiritual and intellectual poverty, the constricted horizons and absence of amusements. It ignores the conspicuous truth that country people lived that way not from choice but for the lack of it. They were forced into constant close proximity with others whether they liked it or not.

One consequence of what Raymond Williams identified as 'the mutuality of the oppressed' was the high level of feuding, fighting and bitter litigation between villagers. It is often claimed by the nostalgists that villages today are riven by divisions between cliques, and resentment from 'old' villagers towards incomers. Of course there are bones of contention – overbearing leylandii hedges, encroaching fences, shared accesses, dogs barking, late-night partying and the like. But open disputes are unusual and violence between neighbours rare enough to warrant national media attention. Contrast this to the busy work of the scribes to the medieval manorial courts and the clerks to the vestry committees laboriously recording the flowing stream of conflict between members of the village community.

Some of the hostility to the post-1945 village stemmed from misplaced sentimental pastoralism, some from political dislike of the property-owning middle class, some from an elitist disdain for the new housing. A report entitled *The Future of the Village* produced in the 1970s by the Council of the Protection of Rural England bemoaned the indisputable truth that 'the vast majority of new buildings in villages are not designed by architects and often represent the cheapest form of building available.' The *Architects' Journal* devoted an issue in 1978 to 'The Village: A Matter of Life or Death', lashing the failure of the powers that be. Village planning, the journal said, was a shambles, and the problem of unbalanced communities should no longer be tolerated. The proposed solution turned out to be the usual mixture of waffle, wishful thinking and pious intention: better coordination in allocating public resources, better public transport, more power to parish councils, less deprivation, a review of local government, more research, etc,, etc.

The sense of something precious having been lost or accidentally destroyed is often focussed on that elusive quality 'community spirit' and its good friend 'village life'. The lazy assumption is that these were tied to the link between village and land, and that when that died so did they. In his book *The Lost Village* – published in 2008 – Richard Askwith set off around the country with the apparent intention of stitching together an extended obituary on the village of old – 'that miniature self-contained ecosystem in which past and present were all tangled up and people, buildings and vegetation shared one reasonably coherent collective story.' In Gilbert White's Selborne Askwith finds it 'hard to feel any sense of the old rural England'. East Coker, in Somerset, is 'all about money'. In Tollard Royal, hidden within Cranborne Chase, he is scowled at by blonde women on horseback. On the Cornish coast he listens to the fishermen's choir in Polperro, but there is not a fisherman among them.

Then, quite suddenly, Askwith executes a crunching gear change. It occurs to him that 'there is something deeply complacent about the premise that the passing of the old rural ways was something to be mourned.' For a corrective view he drops in on Ronald Blythe, who tells him that life is better now but that somehow people were more content when it was worse. He finds that some villagers are having success in fostering 'community spirit' and that these tend to be the very incomers whose arrival was construed as the death blow. In the end, back in his own village in Northamptonshire, he muses: 'It hadn't vanished – not yet. It wasn't perfect but there was life in the old creation yet, and I could, if I chose, have a share in it.'

*

Up to the great watershed of the 1914–18 war, the squire, parson, administrative elite, craftsmen, shopkeepers and labour force were the animate foundation stones of village life. The inanimate were the houses and cottages, the shops and workshops, the church, the pub, the school. Around the village were the fields that sustained it. Within were the other familiar physical features: the green, the pond, the well and so forth. This was the village world: self-sufficient to a considerable degree, self-contained to a considerable degree, tied together by bonds that had lasted so long they may have seemed eternal, distinct.

Towards the end of this period another force, which filtered down from the development of a national enthusiasm
for organised sport, began to make itself felt at village level.
The village sports club — usually cricket or football or both —
has received little attention from the earnest academics of
the sociology and human geography departments. But it has
played, and continues to play, a potent, if fluctuating, role in
the assertion of village identity.

10

This Sporting Life

North Moreton, Oxfordshire

North Moreton sits low in the fields across from the great squat towers of Didcot Power Station. It is separated from South Moreton by a railway line and half a mile of open ground. It is untidily arranged around the junction between the lane from South Moreton and two forks of a minor road which join the main road between Didcot and Wallingford a little way to the north. It has an old and very beautiful stone-and-flint church and a number of old, beamy thatched cottages mixed up with the usual nondescript assortment of early, middle and late twentieth-century red-brick housing. Unlike South Moreton it has no shop or school. But it does have a pub, with the eccentric name The Bear At Home. And behind the pub is a cricket ground.

Moreton Cricket Club – it caters for both the Moretons – was founded in 1858 by the then vicar, the Reverend William Barff. He was an Oxford man, sympathetic to the reforming Oxford Movement, who rightly regarded the game as having

North Moreton around 1950

a moral value and the capacity to bring the village together. He also hoped that having a cricket team might wean the villagers away from their habitual heavy drinking and bad language. Although Barff did not play the game himself, his successor, William Young, did; and so did Young's curate, Arthur Winter, who was a Cambridge Blue and played a few games for Middlesex. The fixture list in those early days was limited to a few local villages and schools and Oxford colleges, but the club put down strong roots.

In 1960 Gerald Howat – a schoolmaster by profession and historian by inclination – came to live in the Old Schoolhouse in North Moreton, which is opposite the church. The next year he made his debut for Moreton CC as wicketkeeper and middle-order bat. He retired forty-four years later at the age of seventy-seven after having a heart attack. He told a journalist from the *Oxford Times* that but for his illness he would have carried on – 'I have to say that I was still worth my place keeping wicket,' he said.

By then Howat had made his reputation as one of cricket's most accomplished and distinguished writers. Biographies of the incomparable West Indian all-rounder Learie Constantine, and two of the greatest England batsmen, Walter Hammond and Len Hutton, set new standards for careful research and elegance of prose. In 1980 Howat produced *Village Cricket*, which celebrated the unique place of the game in the stories of so many villages and the lives of their people.

Howat knew at first-hand how a cricket club could contribute to a village's sense of itself and pride in its individual character. A constant theme of village cricket is the rivalry between neighbouring clubs: memories and stories of close encounters going back over decades, ready at any moment to spark sharp words and even questionable actions. Sport – and cricket in particular, because of the close identification between village and club – has been able to define and sustain a village's image of itself in a way few other social forces can.

But Gerald Howat was also acutely aware of the incurable tendency of cricket-lovers to relapse into sepia-tinted sentimentality when contemplating the village game. He himself was careful to steer clear of the minefield of associated clichés: sound of leather on willow, smell of cut grass, the creaking of the old roller, the assembly of ancient stalwarts on gnarled benches peering at the action and chewing over past heroics, the chime of church bells, the sinking of the sun behind the beech trees as the off-spinner twirls his tempting offers ever higher and slower. Other writers were less discriminating.

In 1930 the playwright R. C. Sherriff followed up his extraordinary success with his Great War drama *Journey's End* with a very different – and very much less successful – rustic comedy revolving around village cricket. The plot was banality itself: Mr Butler, an entrepreneur of vulgar stamp, has managed to acquire the cricket ground in the Hampshire village of Badger's Green and is proposing to cover it in an assortment of horrors, including bungalows, Japanese tea garden, a cinema, a dance hall and a 'park for charabancs'. The village rises up in revolt. Through various twists and turns the plot reaches a denouement in which the fate of the ground will be decided by the outcome of the match between Badger's End and their bitter local rivals,

Hagholt. Mr Butler is somehow roped in to play and makes the two runs needed off the last ball to humble Hagholt. He wakes up to the understanding that cricket is an eternal and essential part of national life, and that an attack on it is an attack on Englishness itself. The green is saved and the cast rejoice that 'the glorious "chock" of ball against bat' will be heard for evermore.

As player, long-serving secretary and finally president of Moreton CC Gerald Howat was alert to the gulf between this nostalgia-misted version of village cricket and the reality. But he also rejoiced, in his dry and understated way, in the contribution made to village life by a thriving cricket club and a well-maintained and visibly cherished ground. 'There is a pastoral charm about village cricket,' he wrote in a rare rose-tinted passage, 'which is timeless. It has a touch of Paradise. Men and women in the outposts of Empire have dreamt of less . . .'

Howat died only two years after his retirement, but his name lives on attached to the low wooden pavilion where the men – and women, boys and girls – of Moreton gather and prepare for battle as he did for all those years. I visited on a Saturday afternoon, hoping to see a match in progress, but it turned out that at weekends Moreton CC play only Sunday friendlies and are not in a Saturday league. But cricket in the village is far from fading away: they play Wednesday and Thursday evening fixtures most weeks, and have teams in the Ladies Thames Valley league and the Oxfordshire Women's Midweek League, as well as two teams of youngsters in the development leagues.

The pavilion has an authentic veranda along the front with

benches commemorating stalwarts of old. That slight but insistent smell of sweaty socks and jockstraps – familiar to me from almost fifty years of playing village cricket – lingers inside, along with the odd pad and glove and batting helmet lying around. On the walls are faded photographs of Moreton Elevens of old, and pages from scorebooks recording extraordinary feats. These are the annals of Moreton men – whether actually from the village or not – bound together by ties of friendship and blood, and love for that square in the middle with the short boundary on the pavilion side.

In The Bear At Home I chatted for a while with Sam the barman, a strapping lad who bowls left-arm and biffs it around a bit in the late order. He'd been recruited by Gerald Howat as a boy and now played three times most weeks. The pub did the teas for the friendlies and provided baguettes and chips for the midweek matches at £5 a go. Much of the cricket was T20 bang-bang stuff in coloured kit – 'Gerald hated all that,' Sam said cheerfully. 'He was a real traditionalist.' Maybe he was, but he would have liked what Sam said next: 'To be honest, without the cricket there wouldn't be a lot going on around here.'

*

The past has gone, and with it the sustaining alliance between the working people of the village and the fields and woods around. The old structure of the village society, generations of the same families in the same houses performing the same functions in the same relationship to each other, has been demolished. The local yokels have gone, dispersed by the same economic forces that have shaped the wider society we have today. They will not return. A villager born and bred is a threatened species today; one living in the same dwelling as his grandparents an extreme rarity.

A village may still have a firm, regular heartbeat, but the source of that vitality is very different from what it once was. In the old days everyone was part of village life whether they liked it or not. They were bound by a web of interdependence. Today there is no such web, and many are excluded. They may live within the parish boundaries or 'village envelope' or 'settlement area' or whatever planning term is applicable. But they are newcomers, living on the edge because that is where the new housing tends to go, working somewhere else, driving one of their several cars wherever they wish to go.

It may be that they have no desire to integrate, to be 'part of the community'. Not everyone does. Or it may be that they do, but are not sure how to go about it. This age of mobility is not congenial to the putting down of roots and the making of social ties. The new estate is organised so that no one need know their neighbour. The houses and gardens are arranged to protect 'privacy', and because everyone drives everywhere the shared space is mostly reserved for parking cars.

In times past the question of getting into village life did not really arise; but if it had, the main routes would have been the church and the public house. Both these institutions have tended to withdraw to the margins (although in many cases they do remain vitally important). The key pumps for forcing blood through the village's arteries are generally the school and the village hall. So for the incomer the easiest way into village life is to have a child and send him or her to the school. By then the mother may well have encountered other mothers through National Childbirth Trust pre-natal classes, and subsequently through the playgroup. The routine of drop-off and pick-up promotes chat, leading to coffee mornings devoted to the consuming subjects of infant sleeping and feeding patterns, speed of growth, symptoms of precocity and so forth.

Unless the mother is unwilling, or a complete social misfit, she finds herself drawn into the network. Can you help on the produce stall at the spring fair? Join the sponsored walk? Do assisted reading? The path reveals itself: Cubs, Brownies, health walks, choir, boys' football, judo, cleaning the church, history society, WI, village magazine, the action group campaigning against greedy developers, dog walkers, nature walkers, anti-dogshit activists. The list is endless.

Once you investigate, you find the village gently humming with activity. The guiding principle is that if you show an interest you are in, because all these worthy bodies are in constant and usually urgent need of new blood. There is a risk – before you know where you are, new commitments are being thrust upon you from all sides, and the phone is ringing to remind you of commitments you would prefer to forget. Your calendar becomes speckled with the times and dates of events and meetings, eating your time like a combine harvester devouring a field of summer wheat.

The village has learned to live without the squire. It could probably survive without the parson and the church, although it does not have to. It helps to have a pub, but this is not as crucial as it used to be. It needs a good village shop which is a post office as well, and if it has more than one shop it is doing well. It needs a successful school and a thriving village hall; and a recreation ground where cricket and football are played, and taught by grown-ups to the boys and girls. It needs infusions of new blood if it is not to atrophy. That means it has to be able to grow, which in turn means it has to make room for new homes.

Some villages tick all these boxes and more, and are in blooming health. Some meet enough of these needs to stay alive and look to the future with hope. Some are fighting to keep the shop open and the school going and the pub from going under, and are in trouble. And there are some that have lost most or all of the essentials, and – like a fading battery – have relapsed into the hushed quiet of the retirement home.

11

ANCIENT RECORDS

Myddle, Shropshire

Around the year 1700 a well-to-do Shropshire farmer with time on his hands sat down and did something that had not been done before and has not really been done since. His name was Richard Gough and he lived in the hamlet of Newton-on-the-Hill, which is a mile or so from the village of Myddle and a few miles north of Shrewsbury. He was then in his sixties (and would reach the ripe old age of eighty-nine), and was the fifth Richard Gough to live and farm there. This made his one of the 'antient and respectable families' of the district; and with his active farming days behind him, he decided to set down the stories of those families and of the place where they lived and worked and died.

After a few years Richard Gough came to the end of his account, which he called *Antiquities and Memoirs of the Parish of Myddle*. The notion of having it published does not seem to have entered his head; it was done for his personal

Antiquityes
and
Memoyres
of the Parish of ye
Myddle
ye Written by
Richd Gough
Anno Ætat suæ 66

Anno Dni
1700

The original title page of Gough's *History of Myddle*

satisfaction only. The manuscript came into the possession of a branch of the family that inherited the farm and remained with them until it was finally published in full in 1875.

Gough was evidently an educated man but he was not a historian in a conventional sense. Perhaps because he was writing for his own amusement and no one else's, he made little attempt to organise his material into a coherent narrative. It has the feel of work taken up and put down according to the whim of the moment, and then put away and returned to at intervals. This probably accounts for it not being as well known as it should be. At its best, Gough's *History* is a rival for the diaries compiled by his contemporary in distant London, Samuel Pepys.

It begins very much in the manner of a conventional seventeenth-century antiquarian work, by describing the extent and geography of the parish, its churches and chapels and their rectors and priests, the manor, parks, warrens, meres and pastures, the rents and leases, the castle (in ruins even then), and the lords and earls and assorted bigwigs. This section ends with a series of disjointed jottings about Myddle's modest contribution to King Charles's cause in the Civil War ('Richard Chaloner of Myddle ... this bastard was partly maintained by the parish and being a big lad went to Shrewsbury and there listed and went to Edgehill and was never heard of afterwards in this country ... ').

The unique value of Gough's *History* is in its second part which he entitled *Observations Concerning the Seates in Myddle Church and the Families to Which They Belong*. His inspiration was to draw a plan of the pews in the church, identify the families that had established the right to sit and kneel in them, and write down everything he could remember or find out about them, which was a lot.

Divine service was the only regular occasion at which the whole parish gathered. The practice of securing pews had grown up after the Reformation, with the gentry leading the grab. The order of social precedence was strictly observed: the quality at the front, the yeoman farmers and skilled craftsmen behind, the labourers at the back. Interestingly, the right to a particular pew was not attached to a family but to a property (although in many cases this came to the same thing). Property determined status, and in this way the social structure of the district – who was above, on the same level as, and below whom – achieved a formal and familiar expression.

Richard Gough's scheme was very simple. He began with the pews on the north side of the church, working back from the one nearest the pulpit, then dealt with the larger block down the middle, then with those down the south side. But although the scheme was methodical in concept, the treatment of each pew-holder is anything but. It begins with the family at their prayers in church. Gough then follows them outside wherever the trail leads him: where they live, where they lived before, the marriages, the deaths, the births, the waxings and wanings of fortunes, the mishaps, accidents, rumours, scandals, triumphs and disasters. Forbears and siblings appear, cousins and the cousins of cousins, discarded suitors, drinking companions, ne'er-do-wells, neighbours, business partners. Only when the material relating to the family with this pew is exhausted does he return to the church and address the next pew. And even then, having moved on, should he recall a detail about the previous lot, he puts it down there and then, rather than go back to insert it where it belongs.

The effect can be confusing, to put it mildly. Here is the authentic flavour of Gough's method:

There was one Richard Acherley, a younger brother of that ancient and substantial family of the Acherleys of Stanwardine in the fields. He was a tanner and had his tan-house in Stanwardine in the fields but lived (as a tenant) at Wycherley Hall. He purchased lands in Marton of David Owen and one Twilord. I suppose that these two had married co-heiresses for I find no mention of but one house of the lands and that stood on a sandy bank on this side of Mr Acherley's new barns. Richard Acherley had issue, Thomas Acherley, to whom he gave these lands in Marton. This Thomas was a tanner and dwelt in Marton and held Mr Lloyd Pierce his house there and dwelt in it and suffered the other two to go to decay. He built a tan-house which is now standing by the old mill brook. He had two sons – Thomas, the second of that name, and Richard – he also had two daughters. After the death of his first wife he married the widow of Nicholas Gough of Wolverley, a very wealthy widow. He went to live with her at Wolverley and gave his lands in Marton to his eldest son, Thomas, who married Elinor, the sister of Roger Griffiths, an eminent alderman in Shrewsbury; and this Roger Griffiths likewise married Mary, the oldest sister of Thomas Acherley. The youngest daughter was married to one Simcoks, a mercer in Whitchurch. Richard, the younger son, was married at Wolverley and died about middle age . . .

I hope everyone has been able to follow that? No? Well, I'm afraid we are still only halfway through the single paragraph devoted to the affairs of the Acherleys. It then returns to Thomas, the second tanner, and details his various land purchases and leases, his branching out into dealing in timber, the inheritances of his offspring and their marriages, and the convoluted manner in which the lands at Marton eventually reverted to another branch of the family altogether.

Nothing is left out. In his preamble to the narrative of the pews, Gough defended himself against a charge he could probably see coming: 'If any man blame me for that I have declared the vicious lives or actions of their ancestors, let him take care to avoid such evil course that he leave not a blemish on his name when he is dead and let him know that I have written nothing out of malice.'

Perhaps not, but of course it is the 'vicious lives and actions' that spice the story of Myddle. We meet George Reve, a Cheshire dairyman, 'a bragging, boasting vainglorious person'; Richard Clecton, 'an untowardly person' who married Annie, the daughter of William Tyler, 'a woman as infamous as himself' and 'soon out ran his wife and left his wife big with child'; Thomas Jukes, 'a bauling (*sic*), bold confident person' who 'often kept company with his betters but showed them no more respect than if they had been his equals or inferiors'; John Gossage, 'a drunken, debauched person . . . he married a widow . . . bedded with her one night, in the morning he cursed her for a whore and turned her off and came near her no more'; William Tyler himself, 'a tailor but altogether unseemly for such a calling for he was a big, tall, corpulent person, but not so big in body as bad in conditions ... he was a great comrade of John Gossage, of whom I have spoken before ...'

Such circles are often completed in Gough's world, where everyone knew everyone and he knew them all. Deals are made, debts contracted, land exchanged, marriages entered into and exited, houses built and lived in and left to decay, friendships forged, enmities sustained. Much of it is the small beer of daily life. But some men and women put themselves beyond the pale. The Wenlocke brothers were 'night-walkers and robbed orchards and gardens and stole hay'. A lusty son of Clarke attacked a bailiff seeking payment for a debt with a spade and 'cloave out his brains'. Hugh Elks and some companions, with Elks's dog, broke into a neighbour's house when the neighbour was at church and were surprised at their work by a servant girl who was making cheese. Elks cut her throat and the gang fled, leaving the dog which was later found 'almost bursted' with eating the cheese.

The women could be as bad. A choice example was Elizabeth, daughter of Griffith ap Reece of Newton, 'a young wanton widow' who married Onslow but 'she soon grew into dislike of him and was willing to be shot of him.' She formed a conspiracy with two other dissatisfied Myddle wives to poison their husbands one night, 'but only Onslow died, the other two escaped very hardly. This wicked act was soon blazed abroad and Elizabeth escaped to Wales.' She somehow escaped the gallows and returned to marry John

Owen, 'the worst thief in the parish', who was hanged in Shrewsbury for his many crimes.

A recurring theme is habitual heavy drinking. Professor David Hey – who edited Gough's *History* for publication by Penguin in 1982 as well as writing an illuminating book entitled *An English Rural Community: Myddle under the Tudors and Stuarts* – made the point that this weakness for drink appears rather at odds with the Protestant work ethic observed by most Myddle people. On the other hand it was the one sure solace in lives otherwise ruled by toil, and it was readily available. So Thomas Downton's wife 'went daily to the alehouse ... her husband paid £10 a time for alehouse scores.' What David Higley of Balderton 'got by hard labour he spent idly in the alehouse'. The effect could be ruinous, as with Thomas Hayward, who 'had little quietness at home which caused him to frequent public houses ... he sold and consumed all his estate and was afterwards maintained in charity by his eldest son ...'

Occasionally the wider world impinges on Gough's corner of north Shropshire, mainly in connection with the Civil War. He dutifully records these occurrences but his real interest is in his own circle, that backbone of England formed by yeomen farmers such as himself, the husbandmen, and the craftsmen and skilled workers. The gentry intrude little, and the agricultural labouring class hardly at all (they did not qualify for pew rights). He gives an extraordinarily vital picture of a society in a constant state of flux – some going up, some down, some struggling to maintain their position, some giving up the struggle, some soaring aloft. And within it are his people, real people, with their virtues and failings, vividly displaying themselves, the way they walked and talked, their habits, peculiarities and aspirations.

Gough's greatest attention is given, naturally enough, to his own family, of the ninth pew on the south side of the north aisle. His account of the several generations, their marriages, births, deaths, acquisitions, occasional scandals (one Gough daughter, Katherine, 'proved a wanton, light woman to her ruin and disgrace') occupies a substantial portion of the text. Gough does not boast about himself or the family. But his quiet, strong pride in the position they have secured is apparent.

Overall it is the sense of community that comes out so powerfully from the *History*. It belonged, not to the village of Myddle, but to the parish centred on Myddle. There were six other settlements, of which Gough's own, Newton-on-the-Hill, was a mile away and others up to two miles away. There was evidently constant contact between them all; witness the degree of inter-marriage. They moved around to work and visit, and considered it no great upheaval to relocate altogether. They all knew each other and knew a great deal about each other, although it's doubtful if any knew as much as Richard Gough.

*

So who will speak for Myddle now?

It is a striking paradox that we should know more about how this society functioned 350 years ago than anyone would be able to reveal today. Were Richard Gough still with us, living up at Newton-on-the-Hill, still coming to worship at Myddle Church, with his farm perhaps being run by a son, what could he write down that would tell them in 2365 how everything was?

He could describe his house and land and record what the farm produced, but as no one apart from his son and perhaps one other would be working on it, there would not be much material there. He could name his neighbours, but would he know them intimately? Perhaps; but it is certain that he and they would not be bound into a shared life and interdependence as they were in 1660. At church he would know the other worshippers and something about them. But the pews that announced who was who and where they were in the pecking order are mostly empty now, and you can sit where you like, and anyway the building he knew was demolished twenty years after his death and replaced.

The society he knew so intimately did not last much longer than the church. According to Professor David Hey, many of the smaller holdings were amalgamated during the eighteenth century, and there was a large-scale conversion of pasture to arable. The sector of middle-ranking farmers and husbandmen was eroded, and many of the family names recorded by Gough simply vanished. By the time of the Tithe Award of 1838 – the next detailed account of who owned what – the community had become polarised between the few prosperous farmers and the mass of the agricultural labourers.

However, the nature of the business – farming supported by crafts and trades – did not change radically until well into the twentieth century. The Ordnance Survey map of 1929 shows Myddle as a slender, irregular settlement strung out along an east–west axis created by its one through road.

The two big farms of the village – Alford Farm and Castle Farm – are positioned either side. By 1954 the village had hardly expanded at all. But the 1982 map shows new housing as having sprouted down and around Myddle Hill, to the east, and along the road past the church leading out to the west. Since then Alford farmhouse has gone and the land around it has been annexed by housing estates, although Castle Farm survives intact.

The most recent substantial addition to Myddle is Wellcroft, a typically meaningless developer name for a fist-shaped cluster of large red-brick detached houses just west of the Rectory. By the mediocre standards of contemporary house design, Wellcroft is inoffensive. It is certainly a cut above the new rectory, a dismal 1960s brick box which stands in a large garden across from the church and next to the rather splendid Old Rectory, presumably discarded by the ecclesiastical authorities because it was too grand and expensive to maintain. At the other end of the village, behind the village hall, is Eagle Farm, a representative specimen of 1980s housebuilding: detached red-brick with touches of bogus beaming, dung-coloured woodwork, double garages with dung-coloured doors, patches of pallid lawn, little gardens squeezed by high fences. In comparison the thirty-odd dwellings comprising Alford Grange and Alford Gardens are innocuous, even pleasant.

The Myddle of Gough's day has been comprehensively erased. To find a relic of it, I pedalled a little way out of the village to the west and down a quiet lane until I reached a thatched cottage on the left. The original building dates from 1581, and although now called The Oaks, was previously known as Hanmer's Cottage. Of Abraham Hanmer disappointingly little is told in Gough's *History* beyond that he was 'a litigious person among his neighbours'; that he married Katherine Emry, whose father had been a tenant in the cottage; and that 'hee had noe children and therefore he took this Daniell, a bastard of his brother Thomas and brought him up as his child.'

I was welcomed there by a very sweet and chatty elderly couple. He had been a master thatcher, and she – a native of Myddle and a direct descendant of the Hanmers – had run a driving school in Shrewsbury. As a girl, she said, the great presence in her life had been her grandfather. In addition to squeezing what he could from his smallholding, he had been the village barber, cycle repair man and cobbler. 'Everyone knew everyone then, and everyone helped everyone else,' she said sadly. It was a familiar refrain. But the two of them were contented enough in their little old house, and they kept up old contacts in the village by going down once a month for the Friendship Club lunch. The one cloud in their sky was the uncertainty over the future of their little bit of countryside. A developer had tried to get permission for houses on the field opposite, and although they had been turned down by the council, these people didn't give up, did they?

I told them they were right to be anxious. In the eyes of developers, no village is ever big enough – there is always one more field, one more paddock, one more outsize garden that could and should be built on. But to me it seemed obvious that Myddle had grown sufficiently, and that more large-scale building would threaten to overwhelm whatever character and identity it has managed to retain.

It has a primary school, which judging from the playground racket on a Tuesday seemed in good heart. What used to be the school is the village hall, where the youth club meet every week and there is bingo and table tennis, and the odd jumble sale and quiz night, and the Friendship Club. There is a handsome sandstone and brick pub, the Red Lion, which was closed for quite a while but was then taken over, done up and reopened by a development and building company which has its offices in Myddle (run, so I was told, by a family who used to be local farmers). There is no cricket or football club, but there is a village shop – although for how much longer may be in doubt, given its meagre and unappetising stock and the volume and flow of complaints from the bloke serving behind the counter about lack of village support.

The life of this place was once an open book, sufficiently so for it to be written down. It and its parish and its outlying settlements were engaged in a shared enterprise. Everyone had a part in it, whatever their station. But that shared enterprise ended a long time ago. The common stream has split into a multitude of separate, minute trickles. Some come together temporarily for particular purposes – the Friendship Club, the History Society, the school playground – but then go their own way again. Others stay apart for good.

In a way the story of Myddle now is that there is no single story any more.

12

MAKE-BELIEVE

Askrigg, North Yorkshire and *Rippingale, Lincolnshire*

After twelve years, seven series and eighty-seven episodes, the chairman of the parish council in Askrigg – the double for the fictional village of Darrowby in *All Creatures Great and Small* – said he was delighted it was all over. The myth-making power of the BBC had caused Askrigg an existential identity crisis. In one dimension it was as it had always been, a village of stone houses and cottages set in one of the loveliest of the Yorkshire Dales. In the other it was a fictitious construct given over to the antics of a trio of veterinary surgeons with posh accents dressed in tweed jackets and corduroys watched by a gallery of Yorkshire country folk, all mysteriously beamed in from a bygone age.

No wonder fans of the show were confused. They came on pilgrimage from all over the world and were perplexed to find that the Drovers' Arms was not the Drovers' Arms at all, but the King's Arms. The surgery where James Herriot treated Mrs Pumphrey's Pekingese Tricki Woo was not a

Looking towards Askrigg church in the 1960s

veterinary practice, but a care home for humans. They, and the residents of Askrigg, would sometimes wonder which world they were in.

All Creatures Great and Small was a TV phenomenon. It regularly pulled in 20 million viewers on Sunday evenings, that sacred slot in the nation's telly week. The opening sequence that accompanied the credits set the tone to perfection. A black car from an earlier time was shown bowling along a lane through misted fields, then through an antique village and over an antique stone bridge. At the wheel was Siegfried in battered tweed hat, with James at his side, the two of them hooting with laughter at some absurdity of life while a golden retriever of mature years stared inscrutably out the window. With Johnny Pearson's chirpy theme tune bouncing along in perfect harmony, it was an irresistible invitation to lean back on the sofa behind drawn curtains with the lights low and a mug of tea or cocoa to hand and slip back into an age of innocence.

The programme tapped into two wellsprings of notional Englishness: our love of animals and our intensive nostalgic reverence for life in the country. It belonged in that imprecisely dated golden age when the business of life was simple. People worked hard, knew their places, were not troubled by intractable social problems, stress, anxiety, depression or the threat of nuclear holocaust. They were grumpy because they were Yorkshire, not because they had anything to be grumpy about. Deep down they were happy because they were able to comprehend their world and where they belonged in it.

One of the many strengths of *All Creatures* was that it

was not, on the surface, overtly sentimental. Animals got ill, suffered and died. Largely because of the perfection of the casting of the main characters, it was able to sustain the illusion that it portrayed real professionals doing an authentic job. In almost every episode Siegfried, James or Tristan endured discomfort and were exposed to humiliation. These regular experiences were larded into the laughs and the joy. The vets were put upon, stretched, mocked and exploited; but deep down they were valued, even loved, because the community needed them.

The books were as remarkable a cultural phenomenon as the eighty-seven episodes. There was a touch of hyperbole, but no more, in the comment in Graham Lord's biography of their writer, Alf Wight, that he was famous 'even in the remote kampongs of south-east Asia and in the wilds of Africa'. It helped that he was Alf Wight and defiantly remained so, despite accumulated sales of around 50 million. Even after the publication of the sixth volume of Herriot adventures, *The Lord God Made Them All*, he continued to work in the practice in Thirsk which he had joined forty years before. When he finally retired in 1989 – six years before his death from prostate cancer – he was seventy-three.

The trick of *All Creatures* was to present and maintain a plausible version of real life while being nothing of the kind. It is revealing that Wight should have been deeply distressed when Christopher Timothy – who played James so wonderfully well – left his real-life wife and children for Carol Drinkwater, his on-screen wife. Adultery did not figure in the world Wight invented. Nor did vindictiveness, mean-spiritedness, depression, deception, abuse of wives and children, hatred between neighbours, alcoholism, cruelty to animals – all of which must have been happening somewhere close by as Alf Wight went on his rounds.

The brand created by the genial, good-looking, hard-nosed Glasgow-born vet was extraordinarily potent. The Dales ceased to be individual valleys and became Herriot Country. Visitors in their legions went on Herriot tours with Herriot guides who knew every twist and turn of every story. Walkers walked the Herriot trail, motorists used Herriot car-hire firms. Teashops and restaurants blazoned their Herriot credentials.

At the heart of it was this village, Askrigg/Darrowby, where the surgery looks across at the church with the Market Cross on the triangle in front, and the Drovers' a little way up the hill. The butcher's is A. Bainbridge and Sons, the cinema is the Plaza. The local bobby – variously named PC Blenkiron, PC Smith, PC Leach, PC Goole and PC Hicks – pedals the same beat on the same period bicycle in the same period helmet performing the same comic function: to be benign, literal-minded, slow on the uptake, solid, gullible, utterly reliable. Callers seeking an appointment at the surgery ask the operator for Darrowby 85 (later expanded, daringly, to Darrowby 385 to hint at a changing world). Visitors arriving by train alight at nearby Rainby Halt (actually filmed at Finghall on the Wensleydale Railway). News and trenchant opinion are to be found in the *Darrowby and Houlton Times.*

In Askrigg/Darrowby everyone knows everyone and everyone's business. The skies are generally grey and the streets are damp with drizzle. The people are dressed for the weather: women in hats and skirts and sturdy shoes, farmers in caps and mud-spattered rough trousers, vets in tweed jackets and sleeveless pullovers and corduroys or flannels, a shapeless hat or yellow waistcoat allowable. They all walk purposefully because they have purpose in their lives, but almost never so purposefully that they do not have the time to stop and gossip, because we all know that gossip is the lifeblood of village life. The shopkeepers know every customer's foibles; there is no urgency to be served or to get out of the shop. The barmaid at the Drovers' serves the regulars without being asked; she knows their tipples as well as she knows their names.

Askrigg/Darrowby is a proper village. It is self-contained and self-dependent, peaceful but not comatose, busy but never frenetic. Its people are warm and friendly at heart, but only once you get past the deep, instinctive suspicion of outsiders. They are generous despite the ingrained reluctance to part with 'brass'. They enjoy an unthinking oneness with the settlement and the fields and fells that enclose it.

What period is this? Alf Wight joined the practice (in Thirsk) in 1940, left to join the RAF, returned after the war and worked until 1989. He wrote the books between 1970 and 1981 (*Every Living Thing*, published in 1992, was a rather meagre sweeping up of leftovers). His gaze is backward but the period on which it rests is imprecisely defined. Siegfried's Hillman is an early 1930s model, but could easily be ten or twenty years old. James Herriot's arrival in Darrowby is dated 1937. There is no obvious division between pre- and post-war phases; the saga just goes on, although Wight's original stories were all used up by the end of the third series and the BBC had to persuade him to allow them to devise more.

All Creatures is timeless. Its existence (or non-existence) depends on it being entirely sealed off from the rest of the world, both spiritually and in time. The conditions in that outside world – threatening, troubling, rapidly changing – cannot be allowed to break the seal.

By a pleasing chance there is a history of the real Askrigg, precisely dated and rooted in its landscape setting. It is presented in a book called *Yorkshire Village*, a shining example of scholarly and elegantly written local history by two adoptive Askriggians, Marie Hartley and Joan Ingilby, which was published in 1952.

Yorkshire Village is a conventional narrative of the story of the settlement from its pre-Norman origins to the immediate post-1945 period: its gradual ascent to the status of thriving township in the eighteenth century and subsequent gentle decline back to being a farming village. Its most vivid chapter is one in which the two lady historians give a kind of real-time close-focus succession of snapshots of the surface of village life observed by them on an ordinary working-day morning from the village hub, the Market Cross.

It begins with the church clock sounding eight o'clock. The district nurse goes to her car, the caretaker of the Conservative Club crosses to the door to open up. Men turn up Pudding Lane on their way to work at the mill. The roadman and his wife get into a taxi in their best clothes ('a wedding, we surmise'). The dairy manager enters the yard, one of the workers behind him clacking in clogs. 'A soft-footed slouching figure, labourer, stone-waller, rabbit-catcher, handyman skilled at many jobs, passes along with a bag of mushrooms in his hand.'

The departure time of the first train of the day approaches, and a woman on her way to work in Hawes walks off to catch it, followed by a girl running. The postmen are off with the mail – two to the outlying districts, one with the letters and parcels for the village. The newspapers arrive from Northallerton and the newsagent is soon off on his rounds.

The tempo picks up. The milkman, dustman, builder, a farmer, the decorator are seen about their business. It's nearly nine by now: housewives with baskets over their arms make their way to the shops, and visitors staying in Askrigg buy their newspapers before going back for a leisurely breakfast. The blacksmith, the gamekeeper, the village bobby and the stationmaster's wife are among those making for the butcher's. At nine the bus draws up outside the grocer's and takes on five passengers. 'It is the signal for the orderly and less frenzied routine of the day to begin.'

Marie Hartley devoted her working life to studying and recording the traditional Dales life. Joan Ingilby was the second of her long-term collaborators, after the death of her friend Ella Pontefract. As well as writing, the three women assembled a great hoard of agricultural tools and accessories, cooking implements, domestic utensils and furniture which became the basis of the Dales Countryside Museum in Hawes. Marie Hartley and Joan Ingilby remained productive into old age – Joan dying in 2000 at the age of eighty-nine, and Marie in 2006 at the age of 100. They had lived long enough to see their village reclaim its own identity from the mythical incarnation represented in *All Creatures Great and Small*.

Although they respected and celebrated the old ways, they were commendably unsentimental about their passing. In *Yorkshire Village* Hartley and Ingilby recorded the huge changes in living conditions in their time: piped water, flushing lavatories, electric cookers in place of the kitchen range, stone floors replacing wooden ones. The shops now stocked tinned foods, factory-produced cakes, sliced bread – 'at most six housewives bake their own bread and no one regularly makes oatcakes,' they observed. A laundry van came to take linen away; a fish-and-chip van called on Fridays; there was no longer a village dressmaker. 'In the old days,' they wrote, 'the women rose at four o'clock to finish the washing of the blackleading before breakfast; if it was "all work i' them days" it is no longer so today.'

That was the early 1950s. In its eighteenth-century heyday Askrigg and its market – granted under Elizabeth I – flourished. There were dyers, hosiers, knitters, weavers, lead-miners, blacksmiths, masons, glaziers, plasterers, shoemakers, a cooper, a glove-maker, a slater, gardeners, grocers, butchers, bakers, tailors, haberdashers, drapers, a barber, an apothecary and more besides. In 1801 its population peaked at more than 750. Decline set in as neighbouring Hawes went from strength to strength, but it was gentle and relative.

By the time Hartley and Ingilby were writing *Yorkshire Village* change was accelerating rapidly. Sixty years later the shops they noted have all gone, as have the trades and crafts. There is a village shop, a delicatessen-baker-post office-gift shop and two tea rooms. There are several B&Bs, and – hearteningly – three pubs (the King's Arms, the Crown and the White Rose). I could find no evidence of club cricket or football, but there is a village hall and a busy church, a primary school and a splendid outdoor centre run by a local charity.

Two significant additions to Askrigg's commercial life were signs of the times. Building on the excitement generated by Yorkshire having hosted Stage 1 and 2 in the 2014 Tour de France, there was a cycle business on Main Street offering new bikes, repairs, hire bikes and guided tours of the Dales (now relocated to Hawes). Close by, in what used to be a milking parlour, was the Yorkshire Dales Brewing Company, the cherished child of Rob (I didn't catch his other name but I gathered he was in IT before the beer-making mania possessed him). His regular ales include Askrigg ('crisp golden ale with strong hoppy finish'), Butter Tubs ('dry bitterness of a good session ale') and Muker Silver, named after a brass band from the Swaledale village of Muker ('bittered with Hallertau Northern Brewer hops bursting with Styrian Goldings').

At the brewery I bumped into a large man called Miles, who was ordering supplies for his vinyl record shop-cum-bar in Skipton. We repaired to the King's Arms for a pint or two of the bitter bearing the pub's name (Rob told me he had produced 480 different beers in the ten years since he started the business). The bar is much as it was in its incarnation as the Drover's, the main room dominated by a massive stone fireplace. The passage is an *All Creatures* memory lane, lined with photographs of James and Tristan at the bar counter, Siegfried in tweed jacket and tie, James and wholesome Helen, her hand on his sleeve – all poignantly youthful.

But Askrigg has moved on. The pub is now owned by a superior timeshare company called Holiday Property Bond, which has spent a fortune converting the former stables and outbuildings behind into a complex of twenty-nine highly dinky holiday apartments. A steady flow of the company's bond holders helps keep the pub and the village shops in business. There are still Herriot pilgrims – mainly German, Dutch and American – but the flow has thinned to a trickle. It is another sign of the times that neither the barmaid at the King's Arms nor the girl who sold me my pork pie at the deli had ever watched an episode.

*

Almost twenty years before the publication of Alf Wight's first volume of Herriot stories the BBC's Home Service broadcast the first episode of a serial about rural life called *The Archers*. Today, twenty-five years after the last episode of *All Creatures Great and Small* was shown, *The Archers* is still going strong, and it's a fair bet that the everyday story of country folk will last as long as BBC Radio itself.

It has embedded itself in the national consciousness and helped shape our awareness of what village life and agriculture are. Its longevity is a testament to the vision and talent of all those who have helped make it, but more so to the power of the medium itself. Television can never match the pervasive influence exercised by radio. It requires a conscious act of engagement to sit down and watch, but the radio very easily becomes part of the flux of life itself, a companion through the waking hours.

Even so, for a daily serial to span two generations and nearly 18,000 episodes without ever facing a serious threat of being taken off air is astounding. It has managed it by evolving with society itself. It is middle class and middle-aged, of course it is; but even that broad sector of society has changed and changed again, shedding its skins. The trick of *The Archers* has been to keep step with that change, and to avoid becoming a vehicle for nostalgia and sentimental pastoralism.

All Creatures had, first and foremost, to comply with the strict requirements set down for Sunday-evening viewing. It had to be comfortable, cosy, gently escapist. It succeeded superbly by excluding the difficult aspects of community life. *The Archers* has done the opposite, embracing the darker side. Unfaithfulness in marriage, sexual abuse, hatred between neighbours and family members, crime, cheating, feuding, alcoholism, depression, class antagonism, mental decay, disease, death, sudden terminal accidents – these are the staples of *The Archers* menu, along with the shop and the panto and the cricket and the other froth. Collisions between countryside forces – conservation versus agribusiness, organic versus intensive, nimby versus developer, old village versus incomer – are readily and expertly worked into the storylines.

Unlike Askrigg/Darrowby, Ambridge is entirely fictional yet feels rooted in a recognisable version of reality. Over the years the makers of *The Archers* have cunningly engineered spurious connections with the real world – for instance, by persuading public figures from Princess Margaret to Sir Bradley Wiggins to make guest appearances. Another insidious ploy has been to provide a back story for the village itself. This achieved a high point of absurdity with the publication in 1982 of *Ambridge: An English Village Through the Ages* purportedly written by two of the characters – Jennifer

Aldridge and John Tregorran. Published in the name of the Borchester Press (proprietor Jack Woolley) it contained sections about prehistoric Ambridge, Roman Ambridge, Domesday Ambridge and even the deserted village of Ambridge. There were Ambridge recipes supplied by Shula Archer and Caroline Bone – who also did the sketches – and a collection of artfully aged photographs said to have come originally from Doris Archer, one of them of her mother, Lisa Forrest, captioned 'A Borsetshire Beauty'.

This farrago was actually cobbled together by the programme's editor at the time, William Smethurst. But its true origin was too mundane to be advertised, so instead it became a storyline in the soap opera. The research undertaken by the two authors – each married to someone else – became a bond between them. As surely as night follows day in Ambridge, shared interest in Roman pot shards begets troubling intimacy. Before long, tongues were wagging and marital relations were under strain. In this case it took the abrupt departure of the Tregorrans to begin a new life in Bristol for peace to be restored.

*

The makers of *The Archers* have never sought to deny that fictional Ambridge has a real-life twin in the Worcestershire village of Inkberrow, and that the focal point of Ambridge life, the Bull, bears more than a passing resemblance to Inkberrow's pub, the Old Bull. How much business has come the Old Bull's way as a result of the connection is anyone's guess, but it has long been a place of pilgrimage for *Archers* fans.

It could all, however, have been very different. The seed of the idea that would be realised in *The Archers* was sown, not in Worcestershire but on the other side of the country, in the flat, fertile land of Lincolnshire. In 1946 Godfrey Baseley, a BBC producer based in Birmingham and specialising in farming programmes, attended an agricultural show in Nottingham where he met a Lincolnshire farmer, Henry Burtt. Burtt lived at Dowsby Hall, a fine Georgian house near the village of Rippingale, just off the A15. He farmed the land around Rippingale, specialising in growing seed crops, particularly seed potatoes. He was one of very few producers of mustard and cress, and supplied the blackcurrants that went into Ribena.

Burtt was a good contact for Baseley, who had been charged with getting more farmers and country people listening to the radio and presenting agriculture in a sympathetic light. He invited the producer for an extended stay at Dowsby Hall, and he and his son Stephen were interviewed for a programme called *Farm Visit* which was broadcast in 1946. Two years later the BBC organised a conference in the Council Chamber in Birmingham to discuss farming and radio. Baseley and Burtt were both there, and at the end of a session of routine exchanges the Lincolnshire farmer stood up and said: 'I've listened very carefully to all that has been said and discussed but it seems to me that what is really wanted is a farming Dick Barton.'

Dick Barton was the radio hit of the time, a daily dose of suspense and derring-do in which the end of each episode was contrived to leave listeners on the edge of their seats gasping for the next improbable denouement. Burtt's suggestion was greeted with laughter in Birmingham, but when Baseley returned to Dowsby Hall to explore it further, the possibilities began to dawn on him. He was conducted around the farm, listening intently as Burtt and his son explained the complexity and cost of the operation and how fine were the margins between success and failure. At some point they lunched at the local pub – the Bull at Rippingale.

Baseley went away to chew on the idea. Eventually he commissioned the writers of *Dick Barton*, Ted Mason and Geoffrey Webb, to produce some trial scripts on the theme of working life in the country. In 1951 the BBC bosses, never at ease with the breathless sensationalism of *Dick Barton*, decided that it should be replaced as the daily serial by Godfrey Baseley's creation. *The Archers* rapidly built up a huge following, and Baseley served as its editor for the next twenty-two years.

Owing to its convenient proximity to the BBC's studios in Birmingham and even more convenient proximity to Baseley's home, Inkberrow – then still an old-fashioned farming village – became Ambridge by proxy. Coaches would bring parties out from Birmingham hoping to meet Dan and Doris and Phil and Grace (before her tragic incineration); and the BBC's publicity department would arrange photo opportunities at the Old Bull in which members of the cast – who never looked in the least like farming people – brandished their pints of Shires.

No one spared a second thought for poor old Rippingale's crucial part in inspiring the nation's best-loved radio soap opera until a retired journalist living in the village, Jim Latham, dug up the story. He did his best to promote the

Archers link for the benefit of the village. In November 2013 the Bull (the Rippingale Bull) put on an Archers Day, with a talk from Mr Latham and a themed lunch. The menu included the Lincolnshire bangers, mash and peas that Godfrey Baseley allegedly had when he lunched with Henry Burtt, Clarrie Grundy's Harvester Rabbit, Freda Fry's Rhubarb and Ginger Crumble, and – as a starter – Stilton, Celery and Pear Soup 'as served in Nelson's Wine Bar'.

Alas, Rippingale's attempt to supplant Inkberrow as the true home of the Archers, Grundys, Woolleys, Aldridges and the rest of them came to nothing. When I visited the village in September 2015 the Bull was closed and had evidently been that way for some time. It was dark and silent and the sign outside had lost its 'u'. But there is evidently more to Rippingale than its *Archers* connection, and I'm delighted to say that by Christmas the pub had reopened under new management.

13

LARK RISING

Juniper Hill, Oxfordshire

As self-appointed keeper of the nation's apprehension of itself, the BBC has played a major part in shaping perceptions – or misconceptions – of rural life. *All Creatures Great and Small* presented one version, *The Archers* an alternative. And there have been others.

A prime specimen, a generation ago, was *Miss Marple*, in which the bird-like Joan Hickson poked her genteel beak into assorted improbable crimes in the village of St Mary Mead, a confection of thatch, beam, mellow brick and flower-filled cottage gardens located in an entirely mythical, time-detached rural England (it was actually filmed in Nether Wallop, Hampshire). A little earlier came the vastly popular *To The Manor Born*, the manor in question being on the edge of another picture-book village, the fictional Grantleigh (both *To The Manor* and ITV's recent snob soap opera, *Downton Abbey*, observed a similar dramatic distancing of the grand house from the supporting, indistinctly realised village community).

A more recent BBC foray into an imagined rural setting was *The Vicar of Dibley*, a gentle farce or medley of farcical incidents revolving around the new woman priest and members of her congregation in an Oxfordshire parish. Filmed in Turville in Buckinghamshire – which has done long service as 'the quintessential English village' in the absurdist Chilterns crime caper *Midsomer Murders* and innumerable period fictions – *Dibley* owed its enormous popularity to the casting of Britain's best-loved *farceuse*, Dawn French, as the eponymous cleric. Although not even the BBC's publicity department would have dared to claim it as an authentic portrait of village life, the spinning out of its central comic premise – a big, jolly woman with a big smile and a big voice being in charge of a village's spiritual welfare – did depend on exploring her relationship with the villagers. That *Dibley* should have lasted thirteen years and been regularly voted among the nation's favourite sitcoms is testament to the ingenuity of its writers and the appeal of its irrepressibly mirthful protagonist.

Before *Dibley*'s run was over, the BBC commissioned a period drama based on Flora Thompson's classic account of rural life in north Oxfordshire at the end of the nineteenth century, *Lark Rise to Candleford*. The decision was taken early on that the title should be used as a flag of convenience, and that the contents of what had been a trilogy of books were to be regarded as a self-service store of characters and incidents from which the writers were to help themselves as and when they pleased. Faithfulness to the original was not a prime concern.

Thus, even though the stretch of countryside depicted in

the books was comparatively unchanged since the late nine-teenth century, the location was shifted to Wiltshire, which could be relied upon to provide the sort of conventional rustic setting expected by audiences brought up on endless Jane Austen adaptations. The appearance of the original village was evidently not quaint or picturesque enough to satisfy expectations, so the necessary mellow old brick and thatch dwellings were knocked up out of fibreglass and tacked on to the ends of some existing farm buildings. Small liberties were taken with some of the original names – for example Timms, the surname of the main character, Laura, was for some reason upgraded to Timmins.

The decision to import Dawn French from *Dibley* into *Lark Rise* sealed its fate. She exchanged clerical habit and pudding-basin haircut for tumbling locks, rustic hat, long skirts and a selection of blouses cut to display generous expanses of chest and cleavage. In the book her character, Caroline Arless, makes only one significant, albeit memorable appearance – 'a tall, fine, upstanding woman with flashing dark eyes, hair like crinkled black wire, and cheeks the colour of a ripe apricot.' She is attended by a multitude of her children – 'she was so charged with sex vitality', Thompson wrote, 'that with her, all subjects of conversation led to it.' On TV her output of offspring is reduced to four, her husband becomes an (absent) fisherman, her role is expanded to exploit Dawn French's star quality (and availability) to the full, and the original character vanishes from sight.

It is significant that in the original, Laura's move from Lark Rise to work in the post office at Candleford Green occurs at the start of the third volume, whereas in the television version it is placed at the start of the first of what would become forty episodes. The events used by the script-writers come mostly from the second and third volumes of the trilogy. Invented extra characters and all manner of addi-tional storylines – many in the form of love interests for all and sundry – are thrown in. Flora Thompson's first volume, *Lark Rise*, figures little. Yet it was this, with its unsparing, unsentimental, loving and lyrical depiction of a place and the hard lives it sustained, that won the status of classic for the trilogy. Thompson herself was well aware that it stood above the other two, which she referred to disparagingly as the 'light little gossipy books around it'.

In spirit the BBC 'adaptation' has almost nothing in common with Flora Thompson's masterpiece. It is a period soap opera, one more in a long line of good-looking con-tributions to what Richard Mabey, in his marvellously sympathetic and perceptive study of Flora Thompson's life and work (*Dreams of the Good Life*), referred to as 'the amor-phous comforting mythology of Old England'. The TV show, Mabey observed, had 'floated free from its physical moorings and its mortal creator'.

But that distortion of her work had begun long before BBC scriptwriters got their hands on it. The three volumes – *Lark Rise*, *Over to Candleford* and *Candleford Green* – were published separately in 1939, 1941 and 1943 respectively. They were well received individually (Sir Humphrey Milford, head of Oxford University Press, who acted as midwife to the first volume, said he regarded it and Arnold Toynbee's *A Study of History* as the two most important books he pub-lished in his thirty-two years in charge). But it was not until

Flora Thompson

they were brought together under the inspired collective title *Lark Rise to Candleford* that they were hailed as a modern classic. An important factor was the introduction commissioned by the OUP from the high priest of rustic fundamentalism, H. J. Massingham.

Massingham observed no scruple in claiming Thompson's work for his own back-to-the-earth agenda. Instead of seeing it for what it was – a closely observed, clear-sighted account of the lives of very different individuals bound by their situation in a particular place at a particular time –Massingham presented it as a generalised account of 'the irreparable calamity of the English fields ... the utter ruin of a close-knit organic society with a richly interwoven and traditional culture.' He asserted, without any foundation at all, that Thompson had described this 'at the very moment when the rich, glowing life and glowing culture of an immemorial design for living was passing from them'.

Massingham's introduction continued to feature in the Penguin Modern Classics edition of *Lark Rise* for more than sixty years, until it was replaced by a very much more accurate and sensible one by Richard Mabey. By then, however, the appropriation of Flora Thompson's masterpiece to the myth of the pre-Fall rural England of peace and innocence had been cemented by the publication in the 1980s of *The Illustrated Lark Rise to Candleford*, which sold not far short of a million copies. The text in this lavish production was severely pruned to make way for the illustrations, several of which were of paintings by the popular Victorian watercolourist, Helen Allingham.

Allingham was something of a phenomenon in her

heyday, famed for her innumerable depictions of English country cottages characterised by an intensely sugary *fin-de-siècle* sentimentality. Her cottages were old, low and crooked, with fat chimneys and small windows; often thatched, sometimes tiled, usually beamed, some of mellow brick, some of stone, some of rough cob; almost always enclosed in bloom-bursting gardens and shaded by spreading oaks or elms, often with blossoming or fruit-laden apple and pear trees close by and geese and chickens pecking outside the white wicket gate. The scene would be bathed in a misty, golden haze bestowed by a hidden but fruitful sun. The inhabitants of this Arcadia are outside: happy children at play, maids in bonnets and long skirts, matrons with baskets containing home-made cheese and honey over their arms. There are no interiors for Mrs Allingham, no studies of old men broken by toil sitting by meagre fires, no drunks, no paupers, no hint of disease or want or unkindness; above all, no hint of individuality.

*

Flora Thompson's triumph was to capture in words everything that Mrs Allingham with her brushes left out. She has been criticised by earnest academics for averting her eyes from the ugly side of working-class rural life: death, disease, cruelty, intolerance and so on. But as Richard Mabey pointed out, this is to misread her intent. She was not interested in writing a social history of rural conditions in north Oxfordshire in the 1890s. Her purpose was to produce literature: an imaginative realisation of a place and its people to achieve a deeper, more powerful truth.

She succeeded because she could write, and because she

had the true creative impulse. She is much more novelist than historian or memoirist; hence her inspired use of the literary device of casting an imagined version of her eleven-year-old self as observer and chief player in the action. She calls this girl Laura; as Flora Thompson she is left free to comment and elucidate, to be the authorial presence. The result is a wonderfully rich and multilayered texture of storytelling.

It is interesting to compare her with Miss Read: both female, both bookish girls, both evidently reserved emo-tionally, neither displaying much sign of strong attachment to their parents, both making conscious decisions at an early age to leave the place of their childhood behind, both infre-quent visitors in later life, both mining the experiences of childhood much later to create partially imagined worlds.

The big difference – apart from in terms of talent – was social class. Miss Read, from a modest but unmistakably middle-class background, wrapped the past in the soft tissue paper of nostalgia, distilling the elements that suited her ideal of rural life and discarding the rest. Flora Thompson belonged fully in the life she observed so minutely – as her first biographer, Margaret Lane, wrote, 'she was able to write the annals of the poor because she was one of them.' It is true that there was a small but significant social distinction between her and others in that her father, as a stonemason, was the only able-bodied man in the village who did not work on the land. But in the day-to-day existence, the lives of the Timms family were intertwined with those of their neighbours. For better or for worse, they were all in it together.

'The hamlet was in a state of siege,' Thompson wrote, 'and its chief assailant was Want.' But although they were all poor, they were not paupers. There was work for all the men on the farm, and for the boys who would join them as soon as they passed school age. At that same age the girls went away into domestic service, so as not to be burdens on the family. All the men earned the same, and all the wives were engaged in the same struggle to make ends meet. 'Their favourite virtue,' Thompson recorded, 'was endurance. Not to flinch from pain or hardship was their ideal.'

But this uniformity of circumstance did not make them all the same. 'In themselves they differed,' she wrote, 'as other men of their day differed in country and town. Some were intelligent, some were slow on the uptake; some were kind and helpful, others selfish; some vivacious, some taciturn. If a stranger had gone there looking for the conventional Hodge he would not have found him.'

She was equally insistent on the particularity of the place – Lark Rise as she called it, Juniper Hill in reality. It was unusual in having no extended history; indeed had not existed at all until the middle of the eighteenth century when the Poor Law overseers in neighbouring Cottisford raised a rate to build two cottages for the poor one-and-a-half miles away on what was open heathland. Two more cottages appeared soon after, and those four acted as a magnet for others, so that over the next hundred years Juniper Hill grew into a haphazard but coherent settlement of about thirty dwellings.

The defining event in the recent history before the arrival of Flora Thompson's family in the 1870s had been the enclosure of the common land on which the village stood. By then the historic open fields had long since been hedged and taken into the ownership of a handful of made-good local farmers. But Juniper Hill itself and the heath around it had remained as common. This meant that as and when it was enclosed, the people would lose their rights to graze animals and take wood, and – much more alarming – would risk losing their homes, to which they had no legal title. The arrival of constables armed with pickaxes to eject the villagers and take possession of the cottages provoked a two-day standoff. Eventually a compromise was agreed with the would-be enclosers, Eton College, under which nominal rents for the cottages were agreed and Juniper Hill was allocated eight acres of allotments, a quarter of an acre per household.

By standing together the village had seen off the threat to its very existence, which must have done much to pull the little community together. It was also extremely isolated, geographically, economically and culturally. Apart from its pub, the Fox, it had no amenities or facilities: no church, no shop, not even a smithy; there was therefore very little reason for anyone from outside to visit. Thompson described it thus: 'A huddle of grey stone walls and pale slated roofs with only the bushiness of a fruit tree or the dark line of a yew hedge to relieve its colourlessness. To a passer-by it must have appeared a lone and desolate place; but it had a warmth of its own, and a closer observer would have found it as seething with interest and activity as a molehill.'

Did she romanticise it? It's worth recalling her purpose – as Richard Mabey observed astutely, she became a writer 'by a gradual process of detachment from her roots and insinuation into a literary culture'. By leaving Juniper Hill to become an assistant to the postmistress at Fringford, a full three miles away, Thompson broke away from the norm, which was to become a domestic servant. Subsequently she moved much further away to work in other post offices, and eventually married a career postmaster and ended up living in Devon. When she revisited her childhood to write about it, she did so imaginatively only, and did not think twice about manipulating her material to serve that end. One example among many is the treatment of the postmistress in Fringford with whom Laura goes to live and work. In real life her name was Kezia Whitton and she was an enormous widow of nearly sixty. But in the book she is recast as Miss Dorcas Lane, 'a little birdlike woman in her kingfisher silk dress with snapping black eyes, a longish nose and black hair plaited into a crown on the top of her head.'

Overall Richard Mabey is surely right that what he calls her 'celebratory realism ... neither romanticises poverty nor underplays it.' Thompson herself wrote of Juniper Hill: 'The people were poorer and had not the comforts, amusements and knowledge we have today, but they were happier ... they knew the lost secret of being happy on a little.' Who is to say she was wrong?

*

'The hamlet stood on a gentle rise in the flat, wheat-growing north-east corner of Oxfordshire.'

It still does, although there is rape as well as wheat, and even sheep, which there were not in Flora Thompson's time.

Having cycled in and out and around, I can bear witness to the gentleness of the rise. Imperceptible would be nearer the mark; the hill of Juniper Hill is no more than wishful thinking.

The situation is not much changed, nor is the shape and appearance of the settlement itself despite a few twentieth-century additions. A significant number of the original cottages survive in an altered form, including End House where the Timms family lived, now Lark Rise Cottage. It doesn't look much like it did in Flora's day, but it is still 'a little apart, and turning its back on its neighbours as though about to run away into the fields.' There are no listed buildings in Juniper Hill; in fact no buildings of any distinction at all, with the possible exception of the pub – the Waggon and Horses in the book – which is now a private house. Even so – presumably because of the Lark Rise connection – the village has had Conservation Area status conferred on it, which means that it will not be allowed to expand significantly into the foreseeable future.

It is compact and discreetly blended into its landscape, as if it would rather you didn't know it was there. The countryside is flat, not pretty or picturesque, with no big views or surprises – just fields and copses and hedges (though not as many hedges as there used to be), quiet lanes, pale stone houses. When I came by in early summer the wheat was green but thickening, the yellow flowers of the rape pale and quite sparse. There was not a farm worker or a machine in motion to be seen, but that is to be expected these days. It is a pleasing, unexciting part of the country, far enough from London and Oxford and suburban sprawl to be genuinely rural.

It is arranged in a cluster off a very minor road that leads from Cottisford and Fringford north to meet the A43 trunk road. I spent a little while wandering around getting my bearings. With the closure of its pub in the 1990s, Juniper Hill lost its one remaining attraction for visitors – apart from the Lark Rise connection. There was a phone box, a post box, a green box containing salt to be spread in freezing weather and a noticeboard displaying the timetable for the nearest bus service – which does not serve the village – and something about roadworks on the M40. The long-established allotments are still on the edge of the village and were decently tended. Next to the allotments was a recreation ground but no sign of recent use. There had evidently been a football club once, but not for several seasons. The goalposts had been left beside a rusted metal shed in which, I assumed, the netting and line-marker had been stored.

Juniper Hill is too small to have a parish council and even when partnered by neighbouring Cottisford – Fordlow in the book – only warrants a lesser administrative body classified as a Parish Meeting. I met its chairman, who lives in one of the newish bungalows at the south-eastern edge of the village with his wife, who is Juniper Hill born and bred. They confirmed what I had already managed to work out for myself: that the life of the place, in the community sense, had steadily leaked away to the point at which it could hardly be said to exist at all. The closure of the pub had been a mortal blow; apparently the landlord had simply got tired of running it and decided to stop.

The one social event of the year was now the village party still held on the recreation ground. There was the odd coffee morning. That was it. There used to be a harvest supper and a fete at Cottisford down the road, but not for several years. Otherwise people just lived their lives in their homes and gardens, said good morning, discussed the weather and the prospects for a decent season on the allotments. The common cause that had once bound Juniper Hill together had disappeared so long ago that no one could properly recall what it was. Denied any opportunity to grow and become something different by its conservation status, it seems fated to remain little more than a kind of shrine to its one claim to fame.

Cottisford – the 'mother' village in *Lark Rise* – is much older and prettier than Juniper Hill, but no livelier. The school Flora and her beloved brother Edwin went to is on the crossroads at the eastern end of the straggle of dwellings that comprises the settlement. It shut down half a century ago, the supply of children having dried up, and in its much altered and smartened state no longer even looks like a school. The lane passes the Parish Clerk's House (there is no parish clerk), Manor Farm – where the Juniper Hill men came on Friday evenings to collect their wages – the Rectory, and the gates to Cottisford House. Here, in Thompson's day, the squire – Mr Bracewell in the book, Edwards Rousby in real life – lived with his family and considerable retinue of servants. Next to Cottisford House is the church where Flora and Edwin worshipped – 'a tiny place about the size of a barn with nave and chancel really, no side aisles.' Every Sunday morning the bells – 'cracked, flat-toned' – were heard across the fields, and the Juniper Hill churchgoers would start their familiar tramp along the lane. Once they had joined the squire and his contingent, the rector's household, the farmers and their families – all in the places determined by their social status, Juniper Hill people at the back – there were about thirty all told, filling the space.

The Church of St Mary the Virgin has not changed significantly. There are memorials to the Timms children and the rector of the time, the Reverend Charles Sawkins Harrison, who came to school each morning to teach Scripture and remind the children of the poor why God had ordered the world in the way he had. These days Holy Communion is celebrated there twice a month; the current owner of Cottisford House, who is one of the churchwardens, told me the average turnout was around twelve, 'not bad, considering'. Cottisford, like Juniper Hill, has been designated a Conservation Area; since 1945 its housing stock has increased by a grand total of six semi-detached council homes.

I finished my cycling tour of Flora Thompson country in Fringford, where as a fourteen-year-old girl she had begun her working life in the post office run by Kezia Whitton. Fringford was the basis for the Candleford Green of the third volume of *Lark Rise to Candleford*, although it is much more a composite than Lark Rise or Fordlow, with elements taken from several other sources. Unlike them it has been spared the restraining hand of Cherwell District Council's conservation officers, and has been allowed to grow and adapt to changing times. It has a population of about 600, a good-looking pub and an even better-looking cricket ground, a good solid red-brick village hall, a handsome church and a selection of pleasing old houses and cottages around The Green and along Main Street – of which Mrs Whitton's post office and forge, with its steep, low thatched roof and honey-coloured rough stone walls, is one of the most pleasing.

It is inevitable, given the standard of modern housing design, that Fringford's expansion should have cost it some of its old charm. As so often, the rot started in the 1960s – in Fringford's case with the lamentable string of bungalows along Church Close, and an equally dispiriting collection of houses in horrible pale brick around St Michael's Close. Subsequently the gaps which once gave the village its open, rustic look have been progressively filled. Some of the developments – Farriers Close, for instance, a cluster of big brick double-garage 'executive-style homes' – are more inept than others. But nothing I saw rose above the level of dull and derivative.

This is the deal that Fringford – in common with countless other villages – has made. It has surrendered a good deal of its historic distinctiveness, but – as its historian, Martin Greenwood, says in his splendid *Fringford Through the Ages* – 'it is smarter and more prosperous than it has ever been.' The primary school, built in 1973, is ugly but thriving. The village hall offers a rich programme of film shows, karate, Pilates, whist drives, dance teaching, bingo and more besides. The cricket club may not be setting the Oxfordshire Cricket Association League alight with its results, but when it was offered the opportunity to buy the ground a few years ago, it rose gallantly and successfully to the challenge. Fringford could certainly do with a village shop and post office, but apart from that it is evidently in reasonable health.

If Flora Thompson could see it now she would doubtless recoil at the way it has grown. She would be astonished and dismayed by the disappearance of the shops and trades, and would mourn the life and social intercourse they generated. She would be equally astonished by the complete erasing of the agricultural society in which she grew up, and by the emptiness of the fields. But she would be pleased, one feels, that the grinding poverty and constriction of mental horizons that went with that life are endured no more. And she would probably rejoice that the rigid social hierarchy whose God-given rightness had been drummed daily into her young head by the rector had been dismantled.

'Other days, other ways', she wrote somewhere, wisely.

14

POET'S EYE

Slad, Gloucestershire

Without Laurie Lee and *Cider with Rosie*, no one would have paid Slad – the Gloucestershire village where the book is set – any close attention at all. Of itself it is just a small, straggling settlement of ordinary cottages and houses distributed haphazardly along a steep valley side with woods above and fields around. Its situation is very beautiful, but so is that of other villages in this beautiful part of the county. Without its famous chronicler, it would be no more notable than any of them.

That one slim book – read by millions, never not in print in the sixty years since its first publication, twice filmed, a staple of the school syllabus – extracted Slad from the run-of-the-mill forever. It bestowed special status on it. It could never again be just one more village that came into existence in a particular place for a particular purpose, which was to give the people who worked there somewhere to live, and was then left to its own quiet devices once the

Slad Valley in 1910

work no longer existed. It became the village of *Cider with Rosie*, immortalised and almost sanctified by a writer who had actually left it behind when he was hardly even a young man – but who, in his imagination, could never leave it, and eventually became defined and bound by it.

There is a luminously lovely window commemorating the local hero in Slad Church, where he was notably disinclined to worship. The quotation engraved on the glass – '. . . bees blew like cake-crumbs through the golden air, white butter-flies like sugared wafers . . .' – is highly characteristic: a poet's words, distilled, jewelled, intensely and self-consciously literary. Through *Cider with Rosie*, Laurie Lee became Slad's spiritual curator. It was a post for life, from which he was unable to escape. Even twenty years after his death he holds it still.

In 2014 Slad celebrated the centenary of Lee's birth with a week-long festival. There was a Grand Opening at the church, followed by a fancy-dress parade and 'Village Fun Day'. There were readings and music in the Woolpack, the pub where he held court. There were exhibitions and dramatic realisations of scenes from *Cider with Rosie*, a programme of guided walks around the Slad Valley, a creative workshop for aspiring writ-ers. And so on, the events spilling out of the village into its mother town, Stroud, at the bottom of the valley.

The following year the BBC screened its second drama-tisation of the book. It was as one would expect: loving and lyrical, because the BBC is never more sure-footed than when breathing life into rustic dramas from bygone times. Unlike *Lark Rise to Candleford*, it was also faithful to its original. As in the previous adaptation, filming took place in the Slad Valley, as if it had not changed in a hundred years. The illusion of timelessness is supported from other quarters – Lee's widow still lives in their house behind the Woolpack, and the pub is much as it was when he was sipping from his tankard.

By returning to live there in early middle age, and remaining there the rest of a longish life, Lee conspired with his readers to keep Slad locked up in the past he had created for it. Wittingly or unwittingly, he was reluctant to allow the village to move on. In an essay called 'Harvest Festival' – recently published for the first time in a collection made by his daughter Jessy – Lee recalled going back after a long interval. 'The sloping fields and crested beechwoods were bathed in a rich sunlight more radiant than the airs of Greece ... apples and pears dropped like gifts into my hands ... the dear stone cottages shone like temples upon their hills and hollows ...'

He had left as a young man, moved to London, fought in the Spanish Civil War (although how much fighting there was remains a matter of dispute), lived the metropolitan literary life, conducted numerous love affairs, had a decent career as a factual film scriptwriter, endeavoured without much success to be recognised as a significant poet. In his mid-forties Lee wrote *Cider with Rosie*, returning to Slad in his imagination and reinhabiting it. Then, for complex and mysterious reasons not fully explained even by his sympathetic biographer, Valerie Grove, he came back in the flesh to live out the rest of his life a stone's throw from the cottage where he had grown up.

The immediate success of *Cider with Rosie* had made the move from London back to Gloucestershire possible. But, as

Valerie Grove makes clear, the book's irrepressible popular appeal turned it into a kind of spiritual ball and chain for its creator. The two sequels – *As I Walked Out One Midsummer Morning* and *A Moment of War* – came out at very long intervals over the subsequent thirty years, and although critically acclaimed and big sellers in their own right, they suffered in comparison with *Cider*. Lee himself had always longed to be known as a poet, but the three volumes of verse he published between 1944 and 1955 failed to secure the esteem he craved, and after the move back to Slad he hardly wrote poetry again. Late in life he said that his poems 'were written by someone I once was and who is now so distant to me that I scarcely recognise him any more.' Has there been a more poignant valedictory to a lost creative impulse?

The critic Robert McCrum wrote in his review of Valerie Grove's biography: 'In his prime he was known as a poet who had written a book, but in the end he was known as a prose writer who had formerly written poems.' During the extended coda of his life, Lee flitted back and forth between London and Gloucestershire as if never quite able to work out where he belonged. He was certainly not a countryman in the conventional sense. He observed the beauty of landscape and nature through his poet's eye, but he did not participate in it. He had no interest in shooting or fishing, or indeed in sport of any kind. He was no naturalist, nor even a great walker. His habitual haunt was inside or outside the Woolpack, and the pictures show him nattily turned out in shirt and tie with scarf and double-breasted cashmere or mohair overcoat, soft silvered hair flopping modishly over his ears, his half of light ale held in his violinist's long fingers.

Most accounts suggest that there was a gulf between the persona on display at the Woolpack or the Chelsea Arts Club – affable, chatty, humorously bibulous, gallant and flirtatious to women – and the private man. He was evidently difficult to live with, or be related to. His jealousy of his elder brother Jack – with whom he shared a bed in boyhood – is evident in *Cider with Rosie*. Jack became a successful film director and eventually went to live in Australia. In 1973, after many years apart, Laurie visited him there; but there was a falling-out, and thereafter Laurie cut his elder brother out of the rest of his life. 'He was one for taking offence' was Jack's only recorded comment.

By a very curious coincidence, Laurie Lee's only child with his wife Kathy was born on the same day as his granddaughter – whose mother had been the result of a pre-war love affair. For many years Jessy Lee was led by her father to believe that this earlier daughter was no more than a cousin. Jessy portrays her father as having been both controlling and alarmingly volatile. She attributes these traits to his epilepsy, although it is surely likely that they were also related to what Robert McCrum described as 'the agony of having nothing more to say'.

*

'Summer, June summer, with the green back on earth and the whole world unlocked and seething . . . with cuckoos and pigeons hollowing the woods since daylight and the chipping of tits in the pear-blossom . . .'

Slad's setting is as beguiling as Laurie Lee's prose. It was June summer when I cycled over from Gloucester, cutting through the edge of Painswick up a steep, dark lane to meet the Slad road at Bull's Cross. I took a bridle path along the top of Frith Wood, which Lee called The Brith, a great swathe of beech sweeping down the north-west slope of the valley enclosing the little Slad Brook. I had pale beech trunks to my left, sunlit foliage above, ungrazed meadows thick with buttercups to my right. At the end of the wood a steep, rutted drovers' track took me down to Slad's war memorial, recording the names of the forty or so of the village's fallen – most of them from the Gloucestershires, but some from other regiments, the Devons, the Worcestershires, the Northumberland Fusiliers.

The village reveals itself bit by bit. It is squeezed against the east side of a ridge which has Painswick and Pitchcombe on its far side, both hidden well away. The lane into it from the war memorial ducks down, then twists capriciously, one arm going off to Steanbridge Farm and the pond where Miss Flynn drowned, the other turning back to the main part of the village. The dwellings are at all heights and angles, wherever a space and level ground permit. There is no scheme, no centre; randomness is the guiding principle. Walking along one or other of the crooked lanes, you find yourself looking into a bedroom on one side, or even on to a roof. Then, around the corner, walls of grey stone leap above you. The stone is handsome enough but the houses tend to be tall and thin, as if starved of nourishment at some point in their growth. The one substantial residence, Steanbridge House – where the squire dropped two coins into the carol singers' box – is so discreetly hidden away that a view of its roof and a glimpse of its ivy-clad front is all that can be obtained from the public highways.

Slad has no obvious beating heart. It once had a village hall, or village room, but that fell down and no one bothered with another. The school where Laurie and his chums larked around became a private house long ago. There was a shop once, but not for many years. The lie of the land was inimical to providing a cricket ground or football field, so Slad never had a sports club. It is too small to have its own parish council, so it comes under the wing of Painswick Parish Council, which has plenty of Painswick matters to attend to and gives it little attention. The village notice-board – a good barometer of vitality – was silent about Slad. The Painswick Arts and Crafts Market, the Painswick Youth Centre, the Painswick Midsummer Ball were all advertised, as was the Stroud Dog Walking Service. But mention of Slad was restricted to a faded card for 'Cathy's Cushions . . . made in Slad.'

So it has its church and its pub, looking at each other across the road to Stroud. The church jogs along as do other churches in other Gloucestershire villages. But the Woolpack is not as other pubs. It stands straight and narrow at the side of the main road, and from the lower road behind appears improbably tall. It has been a pub, and therefore a key component of village life, for a very long time. In the 1980s Whitbread, which owned it, tried to close it and turn it into a private house, but there was uproar locally and in the end they sold it as a going concern to David Tarrant, who extended it inside and ran it successfully until the late 1990s. His decision to retire brought back the cloud of uncertainty, until it was announced that it had been bought by one of its more exotic regulars, the artist Dan Chadwick – owner of

Lypiatt Park in neighbouring Bisley, a part-medieval, part-Tudor, part-Victorian Gothic mansion bought by his father, the sculptor Lynn Chadwick.

There is an amusing account of the Chadwick takeover in a book by another son of a more famous father, Adam Horovitz – whose parents, the poets Michael and Frances Horovitz, came to live in Slad in the 1970s. Eccentrically entitled *A Thousand Laurie Lees*, the book is a highly coloured and charged account of an only child's sometimes painful progress from boyhood through adolescence to young manhood in the valley where the presence of Laurie Lee could be felt at every turn. Dan Chadwick, Horovitz wrote, was perfect for the Woolpack. He instigated 'a velvet revolution … everything changed and nothing did … brand new ancient benches appeared … everything was smartened up and faded … all the new-look, old-style Woolpack lacked was a daily coat of sawdust on the floor and barrels in the bar.'

According to Horovitz's well-spiced account, the locals became concentrated in one bar while the rest of the pub was given over to food and Chadwick's mates. Trade boomed as 'Dan's arty London crowd came roaring into the village.' Prominent among them was Damien Hirst – 'not gentlemanly in his cups', Horovitz reports. The partying and frolicking of Hirst and other celebrities drew media attention, and Slad was dubbed 'Notting Hill in wellies'. The locals, feeling they were being elbowed out, became restive. Chadwick took heed and – again according to Horovitz – 'the Woolpack settled back into tranquillity and Slad breathed deeply.'

I own to having been to the Woolpack a few times over the years, always with pleasure. One of my brothers, a considerable foodie, lives at Uley which is the other side of Stroud, and when I am down that way we usually meet at the Woolpack. The food is always interesting and sometimes first-rate, the Uley bitter is reliably decent and the place has a good, warm, homely feel about it. Locals and visitors may not mix but they coexist amiably enough. And who are the locals now, anyway? The time when Slad was populated by Slad-born-and-bred is almost as remote as that of the Annual Choir Outing to Weston-super-Mare chronicled in *Cider with Rosie*. They are all incomers now; the only question is when they came.

However, I did meet one who was almost pure Slad in the churchyard. She was keeping some gravestones spick-and-span: her mother's, her father's, her husband's. She had lived for sixty-three years in the village, then moved away towards Stroud because her husband's health was poor and they needed to be closer to the hospital and the doctors. Of course she had known Laurie Lee; they had had a good few sessions in the old Imperial Hotel in Stroud, always with a sore head afterwards. She missed Slad terribly, she said. 'It was my home – still is, really.' I wondered why she didn't come back now her husband was dead and didn't need the hospital any more, but maybe she couldn't face the upheaval.

The opinion I consulted was divided on the question of whether Slad functioned as a community or not. The bloke married to the landlady at my B&B – both fairly recent migrants from Bisley – was sceptical. Steve the parish councillor said there were things going on – the village picnic, the panto every couple of years, a *ceilidh* at the Woolpack. Everyone agreed that without the pub whatever little there was would be nothing at all. It sounded precarious to me.

After supper at the Woolpack I had a magical walk as the light faded and the colours darkened. I followed the lane down to the pond where Miss Flynn met her end, which was clasped by trees and very still and sombre. I took the path over the brook, pausing on the footbridge to marvel at how this thin trickle could ever have flowed vigorously enough to power one mill wheel, let alone the ten said to have been turning at the height of the cloth trade. The path cuts across the top of the field where Rosie took young Laurie under the waggon and initiated him in the pleasures of cider and the flesh; it is almost impossible to walk anywhere in this landscape without straying into the pages of the book.

I came out on to the lane below Elcombe, a minute huddle of old cottages pressed into the side of a wooded slope. Looking down over the wall by the road I saw the top of a white head below me. The body attached to the head was working on a richly filled fruit-and-vegetable garden, sturdily netted against the deer that maraud unimpeded in these parts. I complimented him on his brassicas and berries and we fell to talking about varieties of apple and gooseberry and the rapacious ways of pigeons towards purple-sprouting broccoli and some other of the burning issues that preoccupy and vex us fruit-and-veg types.

I walked along the bottom of the mound of Swift's Hill, bounded on one side by Laurie Lee Wood (one really cannot escape the man); then through The Vatch, which is the bottom end of Slad and is – if the truth be told – somewhat smarter and classier. The lights were burning bright in the Woolpack as I came back up the main road, but the deep, steep woods and the steep fields that shape the valley had merged into the darkness of the night sky. It felt like a place of enchantment on a June night. How else could it be?

*

'The last days of my childhood were also the last days of the village,' Lee wrote towards the end of *Cider with Rosie*. 'I belonged to that generation which saw, by chance, the end of a thousand years' of life.'

One of the odd things about the book – which I read for the first time while I was in Slad – is how little Lee reveals of that life, the real, hard, day-to-day working life. His father was absent, living in London with another woman and paying infrequent visits which his children dreaded and which evidently caused their mother infinite distress. Not surprisingly, Lee disdained his father. The household was overwhelmingly female in composition – Lee had three elder sisters as well as his mother, and as the younger son, and delicate in health, he tended to be petted and spoiled and indulged, and there was no working man to set an example.

Perhaps as a result, Lee had no interest in the world of men, which at that time meant labour. His depiction of the day in the fields which ended with him in Rosie's arms is lush and poetic and gives no idea at all of what else was going on – 'a motionless day of summer, creamy, hazy and amber-coloured ... it was the time of hay-making ... the whirr of the mower met us across the stubble, rabbits jumped like firecrackers . . . the farmer's men were all hard at work, raking, turning and loading . . .'

These farmer's men were, presumably, Slad men. But Lee has nothing to say about them as individuals, or the struggle they and their families would have been engaged in. He has no insights into the economy of the village, how it worked, nor any keen interest in its history beyond the shared store of old superstitions and folk tales. His focus is on himself – an essential in the best autobiography – and on his family. Although they were hard up, and he makes much of that condition, they were distinct from the rest of the village because their survival did not depend on anyone in the family working. They were kept by the absent, despised father, so the ever-present nagging need that shaped the lives of other families – to pay the rent, to feed the mouths – was unknown to the young Laurie Lee.

Hence his sense of the enchantment of the place was not darkened by exposure to its harsher side. He was not really curious about what went on in the village, except insofar as it affected him or his mother or his siblings. The other villagers – his school mates, girls, Miss Flynn, the squire – leap on to his stage, are vividly introduced, play their appointed part in the prank, adventure, tragedy or farce of the moment, then vanish. The portrait of the feud between Granny Trill and Granny Wallon – who lived one above the other in the same house as the Lees – is typical. They are presented, unforgettably, as an all-female Punch-and-Judy show, their antagonism no more than a comic turn. Their other dimensions – as human beings, which they must have had – are ignored. With Lee, the show is what matters.

In the final chapter he attempts a rapid impression of the changing world he was leaving – 'a world of hard work and necessary patience, of backs bent to the ground, hands massaging the crops, or waiting on weather and growth ... that is what we were born to.' But he was not born to it, and he cannot manufacture a close interest in it. Instead he leaps away: 'Yet right to the end ... the old life seemed as lusty as ever. The church, for instance, had never seemed more powerful ...' This cannot have been true, but it gives Lee a cue for sketches of the congregation – 'square-rumped farmers and ploughmen in chokers, old gardeners and poultry-keepers'; Miss Bagnall the Sunday School teacher polishing her nose.

It is the beauty of Lee's language that creates the magic of *Cider with Rosie*. His way with words, like the violinist he was improvising an air, plays on the beauty of the landscape, and on the place in it of an unusually self-absorbed boy reaching towards manhood. His trick was to convince almost everyone that he had left an incomparable picture of a village, a Gloucestershire village. But the picture is of himself.

*

Looking south-west from the top of Swift's Hill you can see the outskirts of Stroud thrusting like tongues into the green countryside. The Slad Brook runs along the top of a wedge of meadows between two of these tongues of newish housing. With that perspective, I – as an outsider, but aware of the intense pressure for more housing around Stroud – was surprised that the meadows had not been built over. But I was not reckoning on the enduring influence of *Cider with Rosie*.

A similar miscalculation was made by the development company Gladman – previously encountered at Foxton in Cambridgeshire – who identified the wedge of green, known as Baxter's Fields, as fruit ripe for the plucking. Gladman boast on their website that they are the most successful strategic land promoter in the UK, winning planning permission for more than 90 per cent of the sites taken on. With Stroud District Council they pursued their tested strategy of trying to bully the authority into submission. 'Gladman are passionate about winning', they proclaim. But with Baxter's Fields they lost. The council turned them down. They went to appeal as they invariably do, but the inspector – persuaded by a well-organised and passionate local campaign under the banner Save The Slad Valley – ruled against them on the grounds that, even though Baxter's Fields were well away from Slad, they still formed part of the context of the landscape celebrated by Laurie Lee, and that this made them worth more than the housing.

Gladman did not give up, not at once. They announced that they would seek to overturn the inspector's decision at the High Court. But almost on the eve of the hearing, they backed down. It would be pleasant to think that one of their barristers at last got down to reading *Cider with Rosie* and woke up to the realisation that the company slogan – We Promote | You Prosper – was no match for the power of the poet's pen, even a poet dead for almost twenty years.

15

Abandoned

Chopwell, Tyne and Wear

As a very small boy I and one of my elder brothers were taken by Sheila, our nanny, to stay with her parents in the mining village of Newbottle on the Durham coalfield. Her father was a miner and they lived in one of the back-to-back terraced cottages characteristic of the colliery settlements. It must have been around the time of the closure of Newbottle Colliery in 1956; a few years later, Sheila's mother and father and younger brother Ralph all came to live with us in Berkshire. Her father's health was by then shattered by bronchitis and smoking and he died a few years later, but her mother stayed with us for many years as our cook. That is how our very small part of the world was ordered then.

I remember nothing of the mine or the miners. But I do remember being astonished by the physical closeness of the life in the village. Everyone seemed to be living on top of each other, and there was no space and precious little privacy. The streets were full of noisy children playing football and

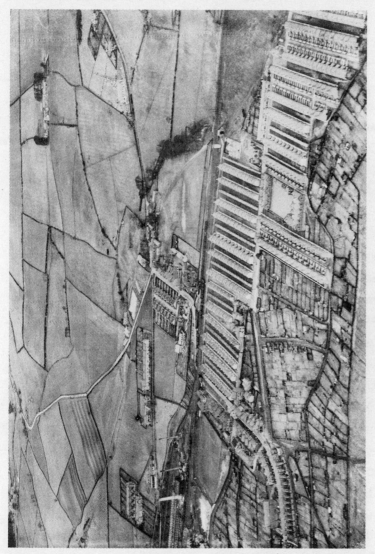

Chopwell mining village from the air, 1930

larking about. Washing hung from lines in every backyard, and women chatted over the walls between the yards. There were two highlights of my stay: the first when I choked on the yolk of a hard-boiled egg and Sheila swung me upside down and shook me until the obstruction shot out; the second having a bath in a tin tub in front of the fire, which I considered much more fun than the familiar and conventional washing experience I had to endure at home.

That remained the sum of my experience of a mining village until I visited Chopwell, on the western fringe of that same coalfield, in September 2015. By then tin tubs (actually zinc) and coal mining had both been relegated to the annals of history, along with a great deal else that had made this part of England so distinctive and important.

As I pedalled over the bridge across the River Derwent at the bottom of the valley below Chopwell, I was prepared for a display of coal-mining clichés: spoil heaps, sooty chimneys, rusting machinery, disused train track and the like. But apart from the upper section of a pit wheel placed across from Chopwell's Community Centre with a plaque commemorating the colliery, there was no obvious sign that there had ever been a mine here. The sites where the shafts were sunk are covered in woodland, and the paraphernalia of extraction – lifting gear, warehousing, drying ovens, chimneys and the rest – has been swept away as if it had never been.

The setting struck me as improbably rural. To the east is Chopwell Wood, ancient woodland now managed as a conifer plantation; to the west Milkwellburn Wood, mainly oak and ash with alder and willow along the stream. To the north the land rises to a great ridge as the once industrial landscape gives way to one of fields and copses dotted with isolated farmhouses. Further north still is the valley of the Tyne, one of whose main tributaries, the Derwent, runs along the wooded valley below Chopwell, a long necklace of pools and riffles alive with trout and grayling.

Exploitation of the deposits of coal in this area began centuries ago. But the scale of extraction, by means of shallow drift mines, was very modest, and Chopwell remained a tiny agricultural hamlet until late in the nineteenth century. It took the development of deep-shaft mining to unlock the potential of the vast blanket of carbon laid down millennia before to form the Durham coalfield. In the 1890s the Consett Iron Company acquired the mineral rights at Chopwell with a view to using the coal for its smelting works several miles to the south. Within a few years the first shafts were sunk, and the company set about providing its rapidly swelling workforce with somewhere to live.

The first cottages were built in accordance with the pattern familiar in mining areas everywhere, in terraces facing each other across an unmade street, with a narrower throughway behind where the earth or ash WCs were installed. The smallest cottages had one bedroom, a living room with fireplace and a minute kitchen. The largest boasted three bedrooms, two living rooms and a back kitchen. Each had a single cold-water tap. A few had gardens, but the usual practice was to provide allotments.

Tyne Street, Wear Street and Tees Street were ready for occupation in 1895. Six more streets were completed by 1901, and the first phase of building went on until 1911. By then there were more than 400 cottages arranged on a north–south axis in slender blocks, two terraces to a block. The streets were all named after British rivers – some (Thames, Severn, Tweed and Tay for instance) celebrated, others (Wansbeck) less so. The eastern expansion of the village was restricted by a steep dip in the terrain with Chopwell Wood on the other side. But there was plenty of room to the west and south, and Chopwell grew steadily. The main road through it, Derwent Street, was a dogleg that connected the eastern and western sections of the settlement. By 1901 there were several shops along it, as well as a hotel, a small block of flats and a branch of the Blaydon Co-operative Society. By the outbreak of war in 1914, Chopwell had grown in less than twenty years into a sooty, smoky, thriving settlement of more than 5000 people.

Post-1918 it continued to expand, mainly to the south and east. This housing was mostly undertaken by the council rather than the mining company. It left Chopwell in the shape of a lower-case 'r', with the stem running south. The classiest district was the north-west, where the houses of the colliery managers were built near their social centre, the Chopwell Officials' Club, from whose windows they could look down on the miners' cottages and keep an eye on the pit in case of signs of trouble.

In 1926, the year of the General Strike, Chopwell acquired a notorious, almost infamous reputation, in the national press. The colliery had by then been largely paralysed for the best part of a year after the 2000 miners refused to accept the demand of their employers that they should work longer hours for less pay. The union called it a lockout; the bosses called them strikers, malcontents and troublemakers. The right-wing newspapers damned the village as a hotbed of Communist subversion. The *Newcastle Chronicle* accused it of 'clutching at the hand of Communism'. 'Spectre of a miniature Russia' bellowed another.

For evidence they needed to look no further than Chopwell's recent past. In 1924 the local Miners' Lodge had proudly and noisily shown off its new banner for the first time – bearing the images of Lenin and Marx as well as that of the Labour Party's favourite working-class hero, Keir Hardie. Two newly built streets had been named Marx Terrace and Lenin Terrace – the latter in honour of a man publicly hailed by a member of Blaydon Urban District Council as 'the greatest and noblest of trade union officials that ever lived'.

In the year of the General Strike, Chopwell's best-known son, Will Lawther – later president of the National Union of Mineworkers and a long-serving Labour MP – was jailed for two months for fomenting unrest. A year later he led a trade union delegation to Moscow to join the celebrations of the Russian Revolution. Even more sinister in the eyes of the newspaper proprietors, editors and commentators was the way in which the infection of Marxist doctrine had reached the football field. The Chopwell Institute FC had won the Northern Football Alliance League in 1920, whereupon they applied to the Durham FA for permission to change their name to Chopwell Soviets. The Durham FA said no, so the club asked if they could be registered as Chopwell Reds. In the end they had to settle for being known as Chopwell White Star. Chopwell itself was regularly referred to as 'the

reddest village in England' and received the honorific –
shared with other centres of unrest – of Little Moscow.

Not for the first time or the last in the history of British
journalism, the name of a whole community was blackened
because of the activities of a small handful of individuals.
The village was indeed united in opposition to wage cuts
and longer working hours, and was led by trade union officials to whom the spouting of Socialist and even Marxist
slogans came easily. But there were never more than a few
card-carrying Communists among the rank-and-file miners.
'It was just a spirit of fighting the boss,' one union activist
explained, looking back. 'If you fought the boss, you were a
Communist, that's how they saw it.' Another remembered it
thus: 'We never knew anyone in the village that was Red . . .
no one preached Communism. It was because Chopwell
Lodge fought for every privilege they could get in the pits.
We had loyal pioneers who fought . . . it made a lot of people
jealous.'

The Chopwell miners and their womenfolk may not have
been closely concerned with the finer points of Marxist
dialectic, but they were acutely conscious of the common
cause that bound them together. 'Community spirit' is an
inadequate term for the bonds clamped around Chopwell
and other mining villages. At its heart was a proud shared
awareness of the dignity of the work. In his autobiography, *A
Man's Life*, the ex-miner and Labour politician Jack Lawson
wrote of the watershed in his life when, aged twelve, he went
to work: 'I was now a man, for a man is not really a man in
Durham until he goes to the coal-face.'

Underground, miners depended on each other to an

extent perhaps only paralleled between soldiers in war. That communality bred a unity of purpose and thinking that made dissent extremely difficult and unusual. From that grew the violent hostility bordering on hatred towards those who dared to break ranks: strike-breakers, blacklegs, scabs. The most detailed study of the social background to the strike is *The 1926 Miners' Lockout: Meanings of Community in the Durham Coalfield* by Hester Barron, an academic from Sussex University. She had the nerve to suggest that strike-breaking itself took a kind of courage, an idea greeted with predictable disdain by a former miner who posted an online review: 'A scab adopts an entirely alien persona. Gives up membership of a community, turns his back on everything of value and worth.' The isolation of a blackleg within the community was absolute, and the wives were as pitiless as their husbands. 'It was the women who went to the pithead with their rolling pins,' one Chopwell veteran of 1926 recalled. 'Wherever they [the blacklegs] lived, about fifty or sixty women would sing them home or we'd get them in the middle of us and be sticking them with our hatpins.'

*

In 1947 the coal industry was nationalised and Chopwell Colliery ceased to be the property of the Consett Iron Company and became part of the empire of the National Coal Board. Less than twenty years later it closed; its reserves of easily recoverable coal were exhausted and what was left was deemed unviable.

Soon afterwards the village was, unknowingly, included in one of the most infamous programmes of social planning – or destruction – ever devised by the bureaucratic mind. Faced with the challenge of deciding what should happen to scores of similar settlements that were economically dependent on their pits, Durham County Council compiled what became known as the Category D list. It comprised mining villages assessed as being beyond redemption or salvation once the coal ran out. Some were scheduled for demolition, others were simply to be starved of funding for new development and left to decay. The policy was discreetly drawn up and never publicised, and was eventually ditched in the late 1970s. But by then Chopwell was well advanced along its downhill path.

Without the colliery there was no work, and without investment there was no hope of work. One by one the threads that helped make up this rich community life withered and died. The colliery band packed up, followed by the St John Ambulance and the British Legion. The Colliery Institute closed. The Co-op Women's Guild, Mother's Union, the Male Voice Choir and the WI went the same way. The annual Chopwell Fair was discontinued. The Youth Club, Scouts and Guides all folded, as did the Ex-Servicemen's Club, the Men's Club, the Boxing Club and the Old Age Pensioners' Club. In November 2010 the football club that had once proudly topped the Northern Football Alliance League withdrew because of lack of players.

Chopwell has not ceased to exist, far from it. But the population is half what it was in its mining heyday, and its heart is palpably on life support. The primary school is running at two-thirds of capacity, and along Derwent Street the hotel is boarded up and rotting away. Bargain Zone and the betting shop have closed, and the windows of other empty shops are filled with old photographs of the colliery from the time when the coal trucks were running and the band was playing and the heart was beating strongly.

There is virtually no job opportunity in Chopwell. In addition the old housing stock is progressively deteriorating, most of it now in the hands of absentee landlords not in the least particular about who they put in their properties as long as someone picks up the bill. The week before my visit a noisy protest was staged outside a house in Forth Street after it became known that two women on remand charged with the murder of their two-year-old son (and subsequently convicted) had been placed there by the Probation Service. Police were called out in force to disperse around seventy local people, and the women were taken somewhere else.

The unfunny joke is that the original late Victorian cottages are actually neat and a pleasure to look at, with their front doors opening on to a rectangular green shaded by flowering cherry trees; and if they could somehow be airlifted to Berkshire or Hampshire or Surrey they would be prettified and gentrified and sold on at £300,000 each instead of being accumulated by shady property companies at fifty grand apiece and used to keep society's unwanted discards out of sight.

Blyth Street is one of the originals, but shorter than others, having been squeezed between Severn Street and an abbreviated Tees Street. I knocked on one of the doors. In times past no one in Chopwell ever locked their doors, but now it took some time for the bolts to be undone and the key turned. A lively old lady welcomed me in — I had been put in touch with her by the landlady of the pub in Shotley Bridge where I was staying and where she still worked a couple of shifts a week. Her husband had been a miner, as had her father and grandfather and all her uncles. 'That's how it was,' she said. 'And it were a lovely place to live.'

What had gone wrong? She told me that recently a lad just out of prison had been put in next door, and he'd come to ask her if she could lend him a bowl and a spoon. 'He'd nothing to eat with, poor bairn,' she said shaking her head. Before that she had had a prolonged run-in with 'a druggie from Portsmouth,' as she put it. 'They put her in four different houses in Chopwell, can you believe that? Because there were that many complaints against her. Gone back to Portsmouth now, hasn't she.'

I went to talk to an ex-miner now living in a bungalow towards the bottom of the village. He'd gone down the mine at fifteen, a couple of years before it closed, then worked at other pits until shortly before the 1984 miners' strike, but not since. He had multiple sclerosis and had been left with two boys to bring up after his wife went off with someone else. He blamed the council for ruining Chopwell by using it to dump what he referred to contemptuously as 'the rubbish'. A lifelong union militant, he remained intensely proud of the village's history. His sons, he said, both still had houses there, but had made their lives elsewhere. 'There's nothing here for them,' he said.

In 2009 Gateshead Council published a Draft Masterplan for Chopwell. Why a Masterplan rather than just a plan or a modest proposal is a matter for them, but the stated intention was to help bring the village back to life – or, as the preamble put it, 'to identify the problems within the village and build upon its inherent strengths and link this to spatially and thematically linked interventions.' Who in God's name writes this stuff?

The proposals were few in number and short on specifics: to support, retain and develop economic opportunities, to create a sustaining and balanced community through investment and regeneration, to protect and enhance the local environment, to tackle the problems of poor housing stock (and who could argue with any of that?). The one firm project was for a private housing development on a roughly triangular piece of land owned by the council to the east of Mill Road, and known as the Heartlands.

The Draft Masterplan spoke of a 'phased and prioritised approach to regeneration' which may explain why, six years later, I could find no evidence of any 'intervention' of any kind. The council did produce a Planning Brief for the Heartlands, but the area itself remains a wide open space of rough grass and scrub intersected by informal paths for exercising fierce-looking dogs. However, Chopwell's representative on Gateshead Council disputed the suggestion that they had given up on the village. Negotiations, he told me, were at an advanced stage for a big housing development – not on the Heartlands, although that would surely happen in the fullness of time – but on a site to the west which was favoured 'because of the view'.

One major but invisible sign of progress, he said, had been a licensing scheme for landlords, requiring them to maintain properties in a decent condition and vet their occupants. Most of Chopwell's absentee property owners were said to have signed up for this voluntary agreement, and pressure on the rest would be maintained. The councillor insisted that community spirit was good and antisocial behaviour was 'under control'. I pointed out that there was no work available, no business park, no small units for start-up businesses, nothing to stimulate economic revival. He said he had hopes that the deficiency would be addressed by Gateshead Council's Rural Growth Network Initiative. I was glad someone had hopes.

There was one business in Chopwell that caught my eye, possibly because of the life-sized blue swordfish over the door. It is a brick warehouse of modest size on the north side of Derwent Street and is the premises of a company called Ultimate Fishing Supplies. Confident of a warm welcome, I went inside. It was stuffed to the ceiling with boxes of flies, fly-tying gear, feathers, fur, rods, reels, spinners, spools of line – all the wonderful variety of stuff that supports the angler's happy pastime. The chap running it was away, but his dad was there, sitting in the office chair watching his wife and daughter-in-law scurrying about dealing with mail orders and very happy to hold forth about what was wrong with Chopwell.

He, like the ex-miner, blamed the council. 'Killed it, haven't they?' was his verdict. 'Used to be full of shops, Chopwell did,' he said. One was his own fruit-and-veg business. 'What did they do? Laid on a free bus to take Chopwell folk to the Tesco at Consett. Everything's gone now.' He told me he'd expressed an interest in buying the old hotel and moving the fishing-tackle business there. 'They wanted £80,000 for it, with the roof half gone. I ask you. It's had it, Chopwell has.'

But it hasn't had it, nor should it have had it. The mining and the way of life that went with it have gone, and will not come back. But that should not mean the end of the place. People still live there and some of them retain a deep fondness for it. There is a school, a pub, a busy community centre and a spanking sports centre with floodlit outdoor courts and an indoor hall. There is decent housing which has not been engulfed in cloned, characterless estates. There is glorious countryside all around, a walk away. There is plenty to build on.

There is also the small matter of a trout stream at the bottom of the hill. Across much of industrial Britain one of the unsung dividends of the end of coal mining and the factories it powered has been the rebirth of rivers. For a hundred years the main function of the Tyne was as a conduit for the filth spewed out by the factories along its banks. But over the last thirty years or so it has been not so much cleaned up as resurrected, and has been able to resume its position as England's premier river for salmon.

The Derwent is but one of the Tyne's many tributaries, but it is an important one and has a long and proud angling history. Up to the 1980s much of that history concerned pollution incidents, fish kills caused by discharges from the factories and plants along its course and battles to obtain compensation from polluters. It is an irony not lost on the loyal and committed members of the clubs that control the fishing on the Derwent that the dramatic improvement in the river's condition and their sport is an accidental dividend from the end of the coal-mining and associated industry across the North-East in which their forefathers worked.

For £55 a year you can join the Derwent Angling Association and fish the fifteen miles of water between Derwent Reservoir, out to the west, and Lintzford, a mile or two upstream from Chopwell. It is full of wild trout and grayling, as well as some bigger trout that the club put in. In early summer, so I learned from the club's website, the hawthorn fly with its dangling hind legs gets the fish up and feeding. There is a good mayfly hatch to follow, and olives and sedges later on.

I had a good long look at it from the bridge at Blackhall Mill that carries the road into Chopwell over the Derwent. I had not heard of the river before, and I thought how fishy it looked. But being where I was, I did not have trout in mind, so I asked the old bloke who was also watching the flow if they used worms and maggots. He looked at me with disgust and spat eloquently on the ground. 'It's fly-fishing, lad,' he said. We chatted for a while, and he told me that not many fished this stretch but it was good on its day. He recommended a Grey Duster as a dry fly, and a Pheasant Tail Nymph for below the surface.

So, if the stream can be brought back to life, why not Chopwell itself?

16

VILLAGE OBSERVED

Luccombe, Somerset

My bicycle chain snapped on the first hill out of Porlock, so I had little choice but to proceed on foot. It was a nice, soft summer's day with no rain threatening, so I didn't mind. I walked down through the ancient oaks of Horner, over the stream and on to the lane which led me to the signpost for Luccombe.

You would have to have a heart of stone not to be stirred by the situation and appearance of Luccombe. Whichever way you approach, it is the realisation of the dream of the classic English country village. It rests at the bottom of a vale below the bare, brown hump of Dunkery Hill, fitting into it in the same comfortable way that an old dog sleeps in its familiar bed. Bands of woodland stretch across the lower slopes beneath Dunkery Beacon, giving way close to the village to irregular meadows defined by thick, old hedges where sheep graze amid drifts of buttercups and clover.

It consists of two streets of houses and cottages roughly

Times past in Luccombe

at right angles to each other, meeting in the centre in a quavery T. The stem, Stoney Street, leads south-west in the direction of Dunkery but shrinks to a bridle path as it reaches the woods. The cross of the T heads north-west then west towards Horner and Porlock, and east towards Wootton Courtenay. But such is Luccombe's seclusion that all these destinations – not to mention Minehead, which is only four or five miles away to the north as the crow flies – seem remote to the point of being almost theoretical.

The forty or so dwellings of Luccombe are arranged in no systematic way. The majority are seventeenth or eighteenth century in origin, cottages with thick walls of stone rubble and low thatched roofs, although some of the thatch has made way for tiles over time. The only significant nineteenth-century buildings are the school – now doing duty as the village hall – the Rectory, spuriously renamed the Manor House, and a pair of delightful red sandstone cottages at the road junction, which were built in 1897. There are three dull but unobtrusive modern houses on what used to be the Rectory gardens, and other gaps have also been filled. The most noteworthy recent additions to Luccombe were three small Housing Association cottages in Stoney Street, built in the early 1990s in appropriate vernacular style let down – in the stern judgment of the Luccombe Conservation Area Appraisal drawn up by officers of the Exmoor National Park – by their PVC windows.

But we can forgive the PVC windows and other uninteresting twentieth-century elements, because as a composition Luccombe is well-nigh perfect. Any minor blemishes are more than compensated for just by the glory of its Grade I listed church with its square, embattled towers, its 700-year-old chancel, its 600-year-old nave, its 500-year-old aisle, its ancient stone glowing with a slightly pink flush in summer sunshine, standing majestically in its grassy graveyard in the company of Luccombe's departed. The Church of St Mary the Virgin stands tall and dominant, as it was meant to, but the rest of the village is modestly and comfortably embedded in its setting among big, sheltering trees – oak, ash, copper beech, sweet chestnut; the dwellings looking modestly out from behind grassy banks, low walls, hedges and shrubs.

The composition is enhanced by a tiny brook that runs down beside Stoney Street and then turns left along the road to Horner. The brook is contained within steep, stony embankments thick with ferns, and is crossed at intervals by miniature stone bridges. An iron railing keeps it company, set at a convenient height for leaning on and worn smooth by generations of Luccombites lingering to contemplate the cheerful progress of their watercourse.

There is very little that is regular or repetitive in Luccombe. The dwellings stand where someone chose to put them long ago, at angles to each other and the road. The roof line goes up and down and up and down, thatch then tile then thatch again. There are square chimneys, rectangular chimneys and some round chimneys. The walls are rough, bulging and crooked. No vision of how a village should be arranged has been applied here, perhaps because Luccombe has no big house and never had a resident squire. It is a medley of expressions in brick and stone of different tastes, different means and different needs, which over time has grown together to fit pretty exactly the conventional notion of what a West Country village should look like.

It looks perfect. But it is worth considering what it does and does not have. It has its church and its village hall. It has no pub and never had one. It once had a school, but not for a long time. It once had a village shop, but not for a long time. It was once lived in by people who also worked there, and they all knew each other, but no more.

*

Towards the end of the Second World War Luccombe came under the microscope in a way no village before or since has experienced. It was chosen for treatment by Mass Observation, the organisation set up in the late 1930s to document everyday life among ordinary working-class people. The ambition of MO was high-minded. Its founders – the anthropologist and ornithologist Tom Harrisson, the Communist poet Charles Madge and the film-maker Humphrey Jennings – believed that one of the chief reasons for conflict and rivalry between nations was that the voice of the people had been drowned out by governments and power groups and newspapers pursuing their own agendas. Their mission was to counterbalance the propaganda and misinformation by raising awareness of how working families lived, what mattered to them, what their opinions were. They called it 'the science of ourselves', 'an anthropology of our own people'.

A small army of volunteers was recruited to do the observing. They were not trained – several were poets like Charles Madge, including William Empson, Stephen Spender and

Madge's wife, Kathleen Raine. Others – Tom Driberg, Woodrow Wyatt and Richard Crossman – later became Labour MPs. The method was to send one or two observers to a specific location for an extended period with instructions to watch people as discreetly as possible and eavesdrop on their conversations, and then to inquire about their views.

The main effort was concentrated on industrial towns and cities, and Luccombe was the only village to receive the MO treatment. It was to have been the first in a projected series under the generic title British Ways of Life, intended to have a wider public appeal than the earlier compilations of data. The idea was to gather material in the usual MO way, but then to have it edited and written up by an established author and published with attractive illustrations with a view to making money. *Exmoor Village* was published in 1947; probably because it failed commercially it was not followed up and the series did not materialise.

The established author originally commissioned to produce the text was Compton Mackenzie, who had achieved critical success with his novel *Sinister Street* and would hit the jackpot with *Whisky Galore*. But for some reason the task was switched to an Australian poet and music critic, W. J. Turner. Turner – remembered now, if at all, for his mystical poem 'Romance' with its refrain of 'Chimborazo, Cotopaxi' – was an established figure in London interwar literary life, much admired by Yeats and Sassoon among others. But he was a strange choice for a book about rural life in Somerset – as James Hinton says in his history of MO, *The Mass Observers*, it is 'an odd mixture of pedestrian detail and nostalgia'.

Turner had no part in collecting the material, and

is believed to have visited Luccombe only once, which may explain the hit-and-miss nature of his judgments on it. Most of the groundwork was undertaken by a young woman called Desiree Ivey, who had not previously been involved in MO and seems, from her communications with her handler in London, to have had a very sketchy idea of what was expected of her. She spent the best part of two months in the village, but naturally enough everyone knew from the start who she was and what she was doing, and considered it most peculiar. 'Some of the detail you ask for is very personal,' she protested to London at one point, 'and the people resent it.'

Towards the end of her stay in Luccombe she was joined by an experienced MO volunteer, Nina Masel (later Nina Hibbin), who helped knock the material Desiree Ivey had gathered into shape. Nina Masel was a dedicated Communist who had previously worked on an MO project in the East End of London during the Blitz. But there is no obvious sign of the story of Luccombe being overtly touched or coloured by a Marxist perspective – although the absence of the rector or any gentry from the action could perhaps be seen as a subtler form of manipulation.

But overall the picture presented of the village belongs to an earlier school of thinking about country life, in which it is invested with a noble innocence, as if it represented some kind of eternal truth about Man's relationship with the land. One of the several oddities is the almost complete absence of any awareness of the war, which at the time the material for *Exmoor Village* was being drawn up was approaching its final crisis. It is as if there was no war, or not one that had an impact on village life. None of the men are mentioned as being away on war duty, yet there must have been some, even though the great majority of farm labourers were designated as 'reserved occupation' and continued to work on the land.

'In this Exmoor village,' the preamble to the book states, 'we may see country life very much as it was hundreds of years ago.' It is a life dictated by the demands of the land. Apart from the agricultural workforce of four farmers and four farm labourers, Luccombe has three carters, a carpenter, a mason, a house-painter, a haulier, a timber-cutter, two gardeners and two men employed by the council to mend the roads. There is a total of thirty-one cottages housing a population of ninety-four. The equine element is almost as important as the human – every man and boy (no mention of women and girls in this context) can handle a horse.

Mrs Baker, aged seventy-eight, runs the village shop, opening and closing it when she feels like it. There is a post box but no post office. There are five homes with private telephone lines; all but three have a wireless set, but very few a flushing lavatory and almost none a bath.

And so the detail is piled up, relentlessly and impersonally. All but four households take a daily newspaper, but none has the *Times, Telegraph* or *Daily Graphic*. Few people go regularly to church. The parish hall – described as a cold ex-Army hut – is rarely used. Social life, such as it is, takes place in the street or on the doorstep. The teacher at the school, Miss Sims, keeps out of village life. A policeman comes once a week. No one discusses politics. The principal entertainment is the local stag hunt, which the villagers follow on foot.

The overall impression is close to unreal – of a place magically detached and isolated from its neighbours, its region, from the country as a whole, and from the world outside. That impression is enhanced by the photographs used to break up the spare, sober text. These were taken by John Hinde, a painter as well as a well-known photographer (and, for several years, a circus performer) and are far from being casual, spontaneous snaps. They are carefully composed studies of village scenes or villagers engaged in mundane tasks or activities – children dancing, a mother tending to an infant by the fire, the interior of the village shop – but reproduced in rich, almost gorgeous, colour, as if intended as backdrops for a theatrical, cinematic or operatic production. The front cover displays a vista of Luccombe set in its rolling landscape of woods and fields, with a glimpse of the sea in the far distance. It is like the vision of a promised land; you would not guess that this was a country at war, emerging from a struggle for its very existence, soon to have a Labour government, on the verge of social and technological transformation.

Instead we are invited to accept the implausible proposition that Luccombe is representative of the working country village all over England; and that this life exists as a kind of eternal, timeless counterweight to the frenzy of change going on elsewhere. 'In a world where so much changes so rapidly as almost to obliterate memory,' the concluding valediction goes, 'it is good to think that Time has a foothold in Luccombe; where the continuity of the life of individual men and their families imparts a sense of permanence and duration to all things.'

This amazing piece of make-believe could surely have been written only by someone who was drunk, or who had no care about what they wrote, or – most likely – knew nothing at first-hand about Luccombe in particular, and next to nothing in general about agriculture and rural conditions in England. In fact, of course, it was not 'typical' of anywhere else. Its location and its history – in which W. J. Turner took no more than a cursory interest – had determined both its physical reality and, to a great extent, the way it functioned.

In Domesday the Manor of Luccombe is recorded as having a population of '18 villeins, 6 bordiers, 2 serfs, 1 horse, 6 swine, 100 sheep, 50 goats.' It passed through the hands of various owners over the next few centuries until it came into the possession of Sir Thomas Acland in the middle of the eighteenth century. He was the 7th baronet and was already the owner of estates at Killerton near Exeter and Petherton Park, on the edge of the Quantocks, when he married Elizabeth Dyke, who had inherited the 12,000-acre Holnicote Estate, including Luccombe. But Luccombe was well away from the heart of the estate, Holnicote House; and anyway Sir Thomas Acland's principal residence continued to be Killerton (with its modest 6000 acres). His use of, and affection for, Holnicote arose from the exceptional opportunities it afforded for indulging his passion, which was hunting the red deer of Exmoor. He maintained packs of hounds at Holnicote itself, and at two of his wife's other properties on Exmoor, making use of one or other of them according to where that day's chase would take place. It was said of the 7th baronet that he 'hunted the country in almost princely style ... : respected and beloved by all the countryside'.

The passion for pursuing and killing stags burned with almost equal brightness in the breasts of the next two Sir Thomas Aclands, but died down somewhat with succeeding generations. They retained the estates, though, and encouraged others to keep up the old hunting tradition, and the semi-feudal life went on much as before. In politics, in contrast, the Aclands inclined increasingly to the radical. The 11th baronet, also Sir Thomas, succeeded his father in 1871 and served initially as a Tory MP and later – for twenty years – as a Liberal MP, in which capacity he campaigned energetically for agricultural and educational reform. He was succeeded in 1898 by his eldest son, another Thomas, who also became a Liberal MP.

In 1917, two years before his death, this Sir Thomas Acland took the momentous step of handing over the Holnicote Estate on a 500-year lease to the National Trust. According to the chairman of the Trust's executive committee at the time, the Earl of Plymouth, he did so 'to safeguard this beautiful country from such dangers as might arise in future from disfigurements or injury through building development or otherwise.' His decision was taken in conjunction with his brother Arthur – who succeeded him to become the 13th baronet – and his nephew Francis, who became the 14th baronet. But it was Sir Francis's eldest son, Richard – who succeeded to the baronetcy in 1939 – who proved to be the most radical Acland of them all.

Richard Acland was elected as Liberal MP for Barnstaple in 1935. But he drifted left, and in 1942 left the Liberals to form a new party, known as Common Wealth, with J. B. Priestley. Common Wealth was an overtly Socialist grouping, which proclaimed its core principles as Common Ownership, Morality in Politics, and Vital Democracy. In keeping with the first of these Acland – by now Sir Richard – transferred complete ownership of both Holnicote and Killerton to the National Trust in 1943.

His subsequent career was varied, to put it mildly. He stood as a Common Wealth candidate in the 1945 election at Putney and was defeated; defected to Labour for whom he fought and won a by-election at Gravesend in 1947; defected from Labour in 1955 in protest at the decision to support nuclear defence; fought Gravesend as an independent and lost. He subsequently became a teacher of mathematics at Wandsworth Grammar School, was a founder member of the Campaign for Nuclear Disarmament, and spent fifteen years as a lecturer at St Luke's College of Education in Exeter, which his great-grandfather had helped establish.

As no Acland had ever lived in or near Luccombe or had anything much to do with it, the fortunes and activities of the various baronets were regarded with indifference there, and the transfer of ownership made no difference to their daily lives. The National Trust ran the village in much the same way as the Acland bureaucracy: dutifully with regard to the maintenance of the buildings and the land, but with no lively concern as to how it might adapt to a fast-changing world.

Horner, the hamlet just to the west, developed a commercial dimension in the form of teashops, a caravan site and an open farm where visitors could pat the sheep and watch cows being milked. Luccombe, by contrast, remained stuck in its time warp. The school closed in 1946 having taught a grand total of 303 pupils in its 54-year history. It became the village hall in succession to the previous parish hall which had rotted away and eventually blew down. The Acland ban on a village pub was upheld by the National Trust, so that thirsty villagers had to tramp two miles to Wootton Courtenay for a pint.

Some visitors did come to Luccombe because it was so quaint and pretty; but they did not linger because there was nowhere to linger, and they did not spend money because there was nowhere to spend money apart from at a couple of B&Bs and the sparsely stocked village shop. Meanwhile the agricultural revolution so conspicuously ignored in *Exmoor Village* spread its reach even to this distant corner of Somerset.

*

Forty years after being exposed to the attentions of Mass Observation, Luccombe found itself in the public eye again – this time through the wrong end of a TV camera. The publication of *Exmoor Village* had been a bruising experience for some of those featured in the book, who felt that they had been tricked into cooperating and objected strongly to what they saw as the violation of their privacy ('all the other people in the other villages got to know about our private affairs and that's not right,' one complained). They even consulted a solicitor about taking legal action against the publishers, although this came to nothing.

So it is perhaps slightly surprising that the village should have agreed to be invaded over the summer of 1987 by a film crew from the independent network HTV. It may well be that the impetus to welcome the TV people came from the National Trust in return for a promise of favourable publicity for its humane and far-sighted stewardship of the Holnicote Estate. It was also the case that quite a number of those involved in the book had died or moved away by then, and that certain financial inducements – to support the church and the village hall, for instance – were on offer. Whatever the factors, the result was four half-hour programmes with the same title as the 1947 book, which were shown on HTV in 1988 and later on Channel 4.

They were fronted by a well-known presenter and journalist, Dan Farson (less well known as an alcoholic and predatory homosexual). At the start of each programme he is seen leaving the Groucho Club in London in a well-filled lightweight suit and heading by taxi, train and bus for the infinitely remote Somerset location, rather in the manner of an explorer of old setting off for darkest Africa. Much of the first episode is taken up by a curious dramatisation of the original Mass Observation material staged in Luccombe village hall and performed by two professional actors with a ruddy-faced Farson providing the narration. The atmosphere in the hall is one of somewhat forced hilarity, with gales of raucous laughter greeting such absurdities as 'What do people listen to on the radio in Luccombe?' and 'Is anyone courting?' and 'Where is Lovers Lane?' Other events – including the stealing of a knife and the unmasking of the culprit – are recounted to the perceptible discomfort of the white-haired old folk involved.

Nina Masel, the MO observer who was latterly involved in the Luccombe project, was also in the audience, a small, curly haired, twinkly eyed woman then in her late sixties. In an interview with Farson she dismissed his suggestion that the book had idealised the village. She said that for her – recovering from the experience of recording the impact of the Blitz on east London – her stay in rural Somerset had indeed been idyllic. She had been aware, she said, of deep divisions in the village society, and she agreed that these were not explored in the book. She was also clearly troubled by the question of whether the intrusion she had participated in had been justified, and had no clear answer.

Many of the other interviews were stilted and unrevealing, others overextended. Some Luccombites clearly did not really wish to talk, others had too much to say for themselves, and overall the programmes come over as an awkward mixture of social documentary and rustic sentimentality. Members of the Gande family – originally wartime evacuees from London – received a disproportionate amount of airtime; interestingly in the case of the mother, Louise; tediously in the case of her son Terry, playing up to his self-appointed role as long-haired, bearded, singlet-wearing village rebel.

Dominant themes were the absence of anything happening in Luccombe and the loosening of the ties that had bound the village together. Apart from a tiny handful still working on the land, everyone went to work elsewhere. The school had gone, the weekly village dance had gone, the drama group had gone (though its surviving members were persuaded to reconvene in wigs and rouge for the benefit of the

HTV cameras). Hardly anyone went to church any more and judging from the gloomy assessment of the couple running the village shop, it too was heading for the scrapheap.

The final programme attempted rather half-heartedly to look ahead over the next forty years. Some Luccombites, including the rector, expressed the fear that it was doomed to be turned into a holiday centre. Shots of overflowing car parks and flourishing commercial enterprises in Horner were contrasted with Luccombe's somnolence and lack of amenities. The best sense was talked by an elderly, bespectacled farmer, Bill Partridge. He pointed out that as long as the National Trust maintained its policy of not making cottages in Luccombe available for holiday lets, discouraging the opening of a pub and making it as difficult as possible to start up anything resembling a teashop or other money-making enterprise, it would be difficult for it to become a holiday village. But people would still want to live there. 'They'll be absorbed as they always have been,' Mr Partridge observed sagely.

*

Thirty years after the HTV series Luccombe is as lovely and unspoiled as ever. There is still no pub, and the shop is but a memory. There is no rector either; services at St Mary the Virgin are conducted by the vicar from Porlock. The village hall is decently maintained but the noticeboard outside gave no indication that a lively programme of events was in the offing. The church fete, prominently featured on television, has fallen by the wayside, as has the flower show.

Most contentious has been the forced erasing from the

Exmoor scene of stag-hunting. In 1990 the National Trust banned it on the Holnicote Estate (and all its other properties) in direct contravention of Sir Richard Acland's stated wishes and intentions. The hunt was Luccombe's great day out, bringing together all classes from the toffs on horseback to the ordinary folk in cars or on foot. It had been gleefully seized upon in the TV series and depicted as a comical relic of the feudal past amid a welter of clichés about red coats and red faces and frequent emptyings of the stirrup cup. But the outlawing of a sport that had been woven into the fabric of Exmoor life for centuries was bitterly opposed by most local people and remains considerably resented to this day.

My first encounter was with a woman living in one of the new Housing Association cottages in Stoney Street. She told me Luccombe was the most unfriendly place she'd ever lived in. Nothing ever happened, no one ever talked to her and after being a regular churchgoer for a while, she had lost her faith and was about to lose the cottage because she couldn't afford the modest rent.

There was something about her testimony that made me slightly dubious about her reliability as a witness. I went and introduced myself to a couple who had moved into the village from High Wycombe for no other reason than its beauty. They gave me tea and home-made cake and told me it was paradise, which I suppose it might well appear to be after High Wycombe.

For a broader view I dropped in on Eric Rowlands, the historian of Luccombe. I had already obtained and closely studied his admirable guide to the village's history and buildings. One of the most characteristic of these is his own cottage along the road to Wootton Courtenay, where he was born and still lives. I found him gently saddened by the way the life of the community he had known had slowly drained away. It was still very much a working village when he was a lad. The men had work in and around the village, there were young families, everyone knew each other and got together to do things. But now everyone had aged or moved away, and the young families had not been replaced by new young families. It was never a paradise, Mr Rowlands said, but it had something and that something was gone.

What has not gone is the farming – in the sense that the farms that were in operation when *Exmoor Village* was published are still farms today. East Luccombe Farm, on the edge of the village towards Porlock, was at that time let to a Fred Partridge, who had taken it over from his father-in-law. It then passed to the Bill Partridge featured several times in the HTV programmes; he continued to live there until his death in 2013 at the age of ninety-six, by which time one of his daughters had assumed the tenancy. I found her at home at the farmhouse, which sits back from the yard and its glorious set of thatched outbuildings. She was hard-pressed by calls on her time. She said she could spare me ten minutes, and ten minutes is what I got.

I wanted to know if the National Trust were good land-lords. She didn't say that they were and she didn't say that they weren't, but I had the firm impression that dealing with them was one of the more taxing trials in her life. The viability of the farm depended to a significant degree on an animal feed business that her father had established many years before in one of the barns; but the Trust, I was told, had persisted in restricting the terms of the lease so that it could not be defined as a retail enterprise and therefore could not sell directly to the public. In the old days there was a local Trust agent whose ear could be bent with local gripes, but now she had to deal with the central bureaucracy which liked to remind her that the Trust had to operate as a business and not a charity. 'That's not why the Aclands handed it over,' she said bluntly.

I asked her if this was the life she would have chosen. She had left home early and spent years away, and then come back to help her father after her mother was overtaken by dementia. She looked thoughtful. Maybe I would anyway, she said. Her son, who had trained as a vet, had already committed to taking the farm over from her. So at least it'll stay in the family, she said. Then she said: your ten minutes is up.

I called on another Luccombite, born and bred like Eric Rowlands. She was in her early eighties and had featured in both exposures of village life. In the book she appeared twice in John Hinde's photographic compositions – in the village shop, a little girl with neat flaxen hair accompanied by a boy, and with her grandfather holding up a flower from his garden. There was also a reference to her going outside the cottage where she lived with her grandparents at night, in her nightdress. Even now, seventy years later, she was indignant: 'That was not true, they would never have allowed it. That book should not have been written.'

Her indignation over the intrusion probably explains her reaction in one of the TV programmes to being accosted by Dan Farson and asked what she thought of the book. She ducks away, saying in a palpably uncomfortable way that she doesn't want to talk to him (it does not explain, however, why the makers of the series saw fit to include the brief encounter).

But she seemed happy enough to chat to me in the little sitting room in her snug, thick-walled cottage. It was true that there were no more than a handful of the old village people left that she knew. But she had wonderful neighbours who did so much for her, and her son and daughter-in-law and grandchildren were just down the road, and she had more family over in Minehead and Taunton. What about her landlords, the Trust? I asked. 'Oh they're very good,' she said. 'They put in a new wood burner and fixed the Rayburn for me. I just have to ask and they come round.'

I asked her if she had been happy in Luccombe. Oh yes, she said, smiling brightly. It wasn't any good being sad about the way things used to be. 'It's the way things are now that matters,' she said. 'This is my home, the only one I've ever known. Why would I ever have wanted a different one?'

Then her face darkened. 'But I did not like that book.'

17

HIGH IDEALS

New Earswick, North Yorkshire and *Bar Hill, Cambridgeshire*

Luccombe is a perfect specimen of a village that was not planned nor needed to be. It just came into existence in response to its setting and landscape, as if it had grown from the Somerset soil and rock. That way of growing – little by little over a long period, adding something here, losing it there, replacing, rebuilding, a multitude of small decisions and actions taken by a host of individuals – is how the great majority of English villages achieved the form they have now, although not often with such happy results as at Luccombe.

There is another type, the planned village – purpose-built to fulfil a specific function and usually built in a comparatively short period to achieve a near-finished form. The earliest of these were commissioned by a handful of outstandingly rich members of a new breed of landowner that emerged in the period after the Glorious Revolution of 1688.

These plutocrats — some of them aristocratic, some made-good merchants — accumulated vast estates to go with their vast wealth, and naturally enough wanted to let the world know how well they had done. One obvious way was to have an enormous mansion built and to surround it with many acres of rolling parkland. What these men did not want was a squalid huddle of hovels and tumbledown cottages visible from the drawing-room window.

At Chippenham in Cambridgeshire half the village was removed to make way for the park and lake that Edward Russell, Lord Orford, required to complement his very splendid residence, Chippenham Park. Fifty new cottages were built in pairs along the approach to the gates; very neat and pretty they looked, and still look today. Other magnates followed suit. Sir Robert Walpole had the village at Houghton in Norfolk demolished and rebuilt outside the gates to his Palladian pile, Houghton Hall. In Nuneham Courtenay, near Oxford, the existing village was razed to enhance the view from Lord Harcourt's mansion across the park created for him by Capability Brown. It was replaced by the two rows of regular-as-clockwork little cottages still facing each other across the main road today.

The most notorious of these acts of relocation was the erasing from the landscape of the village of Milton near Dorchester on the orders of the vainglorious and pathologically touchy Earl of Dorchester, Joseph Damer. He had a lake dug in its place and had most of its people rehoused in two rows of thatched whitewashed cottages arranged at intervals along a sloping street some distance away in what became known as Milton Abbas.

Even at the time, these exercises aroused unease and were seen by some as nothing more than displays of arrogance. Goldsmith based his poem *The Deserted Village* on the fate of Nuneham Courtenay, and Fanny Burney was one of several who complained about the artificiality of Milton Abbas. But there were few audible complaints from those who were housed in this first generation of model villages. The new cottages were in every way better built, more comfortable, more spacious and more salubrious than their old ones, and they were not bothered by a change in the view.

As the Industrial Revolution gathered pace and force, a different kind of purpose-built village appeared, combining utility with elements of paternalistic philanthropy. There was a clear and obvious need to provide the workforce in the great factories with somewhere to live. In the cities that generally meant putting up rows of basic cottages as fast and as cheaply as possible wherever there was space for them – the first slum settlements. But in some cases the location of the manufacturing centre opened another possibility – one that appealed to that characteristic Victorian impulse felt more strongly by some of the new breed of industrialists than others: to combine the pursuit of profit with doing good and being seen to be doing good.

Well-known examples included New Lanark on the Clyde, Elsecar near Barnsley and Sir Titus Salt's Saltaire near Bradford. All these went much further than merely providing somewhere for the worker to eat, rest and be with his family in the brief periods between shifts. Their owners saw improving the lot of the lower orders as part of their civic duty: to nurture their minds, to tend to their welfare and even to provide them with amusements (as long as these did not involve alcohol or gambling). These model villages boasted a range of amenities – reading room, library, allotments, sports room and so forth – as well as living accommodation vastly superior to the city slums. Such villages were, of course, the exception. Settlements like Chopwell in County Durham – regimented rows of tiny, basic dwellings put up as fast and as cheaply as possible, offering the barest minimum of comfort – remained the norm.

The nature of the synergy between the making of sweets and chocolate and the Quaker conscience may not be immediately obvious. But it is a fact that the three great sweet-making dynasties – Fry of Bristol, Cadbury of Birmingham and Rowntree of York – were all closely involved in the Society of Friends, and all took the duty of promoting a better life for their workers and for humanity at large as seriously as they took the business of making and selling tooth-rotting temptation.

In 1902 Joseph Rowntree – following the example of George Cadbury at Bournville – acquired 150 acres of land a couple of miles north of his factory in York with a view to building a decent place for working people to live. To achieve his vision he secured the services of two brothers-in-law, Raymond Unwin and Barry Parker, who would later mastermind the first Garden City, Letchworth. The site was flat and without notable features except for a stretch of the River Foss down the eastern side. Unwin's plan for what became known as New Earswick shows a sort of perimeter road following the bends in the river, then running across the northern edge to intersect with the existing through route, the Haxby Road, and feeding into the western section and curving around the southern perimeter.

Thus enclosed, the estate was divided into sectors by traversing streets. Each sector covered five or six acres, and they were built on successively over the years. The approach to the layout of homes was original and dictated by Parker and Unwin's determination to get away from the regimented terraces typical of the industrial slums. They placed small terraces and groupings at all kinds of angles to each other: some fronting the street, some sideways to it, some accessible by footpath only. The cul-de-sac became the favoured method to fill in the gaps; the guiding principle was liberation from the street pattern.

The inspiration for the early house designs came from the Arts and Crafts movement. The first homes were built along Western Terrace, in the south-east sector, country cottage in style with low eaves and thick, whitewashed pebble-dashed walls. Others were built of the distinctive wine-dark bricks fired at the local brickworks. A prime concern was light – living rooms were placed to be open to the sunlight even if that meant facing the street rather than the garden. Each dwelling had an internal WC and bathroom – distinct novelties at that time – as well as a coal store. Each had a garden with fruit trees and space to grow vegetables. Open green spaces were provided on a liberal scale and planted with English broad-leaved trees.

Although Joseph Rowntree and his sons were impelled by their sense of obligation to better the lives of working people, New Earswick was not intended as an act of charity. The rents were fixed at a level calculated as affordable, but sufficient to

Station Avenue, New Earswick – built 1905

fund the provision of amenities and services. Between 1902 and 1918 a total of 250 houses were built without any subsidy from the Joseph Rowntree Trust. Subsequently the need to fit the homes with improved facilities combined with higher building costs meant that the 259 houses built between 1919 and 1936 were subsidised by the Trust. This was despite significant modifications in Barry Parker's designs (he and Raymond Unwin had gone their separate ways in 1914 after Unwin accepted a post with the Local Government Board and devoted himself to public-sector housing).

Post-1945 New Earswick has continued to grow, albeit much more slowly. Inevitably – given the waning influence of the founding fathers – the style of building has become less interesting as time has gone on. The grim, concrete-clad flats in Garth Way, off White Rose Avenue, the chimneyless boxes in Oak Tree Grove, the black-clad flats in Maple Court, the 1990s development between White Rose Avenue and Alder Way – these could all have appeared anywhere.

But overall New Earswick remains a magnificent and inspiring illustration of what can be done with mass housing for ordinary working-class people, when those responsible have vision, boldness and imagination, care passionately about what they are doing, and – most important – have the time and resources to see their vision through to fulfilment. With its splendid Folk Hall doing duty as a very superior village hall, its primary and secondary schools, playing fields and leisure facilities, allotments, library, nurseries, churches and health centre, New Earswick is remarkably well provided for. True, it has no pub – the Rowntrees would not countenance making the demon drink available. But it has almost everything else that a village needs to sustain itself and thrive. It remains under the overall control of the Joseph Rowntree Trust, and although some of the houses are privately owned, most are still 'social housing' at affordable rents.

It is not surprising that people like living there and want to live there. Demand for the houses remains intense. It is green, leafy, spacious – a pleasure to cycle around. It is full of small delights: fine, mansard gables, overhanging eaves, neat picket fences, sweet little gardens, fine, upstanding mature trees. It even has its own nature reserve tucked into the south-west corner, with a lake and a fishing club.

*

Rowntree expressed the hope that the model he helped create at New Earswick, with its emphasis on high-standard housing and village amenities, would be adopted elsewhere. And for a time the impact of the Garden City movement did continue to make itself felt – for example in the housing schemes drawn up in the 1920s by Raymond Unwin when he was in effect the government's chief town-planning officer.

But over time the balance shifted from high-minded philanthropic individuals towards government departments and local councils. Rowntree at New Earswick, Cadbury at Bournville, Lever at Port Sunlight – and, indeed, Ebenezer Howard at Letchworth and Welwyn Garden City – were able to do much as they wished. They and the architects and planners they recruited shared a vision of what modern living could be and how it could be achieved. They were not significantly constrained by regulation or the need to negotiate with and satisfy a local or national bureaucracy.

The 1914–18 War and the pressing requirement to provide mass housing afterwards gradually took the power away from the visionaries. The scale of what was needed was too great; only the state could provide it. And with state control came the inevitable accompaniments: bureaucracy, the imposition of general standards, the stifling of flair and distinctiveness. The Town and Country Planning Act of 1947 completed that process. Thereafter the duty to provide housing rested with a new generation of trained planners employed by local authorities and necessarily obedient to orders from central government.

Scroll on from the beginnings of New Earswick to Cambridgeshire in the 1960s. The county was faced by an acute shortage of housing. The obvious solution – to let Cambridge itself expand across the surrounding countryside – was deemed unacceptable; the planners took the reasonable view that to do so would be to destroy the character and value of the ancient university city. A policy was drawn up to restrict the city limits, and to concentrate new housing on the villages around. But it soon became clear that the villages could take only so much before their facilities were overwhelmed and their residents rose up in revolt against the swamping of their communities.

The answer, clearly, had to be entirely new settlements. The man put in charge of implementing it was Cambridgeshire's chief planning officer, W. Leathley Waide. He set about finding a location for what was intended to be the first in a necklace of new villages that would loop around the north of Cambridge. He identified it on a tract of treeless and featureless farmland just off the A14 road to Huntingdon. This was to be the village of Bar Hill.

The rationale for building 'new villages' had been laid down by the then director of the Town and Country Planning Association, Wyndham Thomas (the prime mover in designing and building Peterborough). He wrote optimistically of smaller settlements providing 'much superior conditions for family life and an increased degree of civic and community consciousness and participation in community life.' In his evidence to the Bar Hill planning inquiry, W. Leathley Waide specified four criteria for all future developments in Cambridgeshire: that they be able to use existing public services; that costs to the public should be minimised; that the pattern should be best suited to the long-term needs of the county; that there should be 'major improvements' in the standard of layout and design (presumably over what had been the norm in the 1950s).

With hindsight it is evident that the only one of Waide's principles to have any significant practical application was the minimising of costs to the public. It meant that the building – and in effect the designs and layout – would be undertaken by private companies in pursuit of profit. High ideals were not involved. Several big construction firms were sounded out before one – Holland, Hannen and Cubitts – signed up for the project. They appointed a Scottish firm of architects, Covell Matthews, to design the village.

The decision was taken to adopt the Radburn Principle in determining how Bar Hill should be configured. Named in honour of a new town in the American state of New Jersey, the Radburn Principle attempted to resolve the dilemma posed by society's increasing reliance on the motor car as the primary means of transport. Its essence was that a settlement should be encircled by a perimeter road that fed the connecting roads between the sectors; but, crucially, car and pedestrian circulation were kept separate. Access to the front doors of the dwellings was generally by footpath only and the car was exiled to the back. The original plan for Bar Hill envisaged groups or 'nests' of around a hundred houses facing inwards on to a shared green open space. The total population would be about 2500.

Outline planning consent was given in December 1964 and detailed consent for the first phase six months later. Cambridgeshire County Council had pressed for this consent to be conditional on the provision of facilities, but in the event this was watered down to a soothing assurance from the developers that this would happen. It did not. Building work began in November 1965. The architects' plan envisaged the first 300 homes being ready for occupation within eighteen months, and another 500 by the end of 1970. By then the village centre – shops, village hall, school and so on – would also be ready.

The plan and reality soon parted company. The construction of houses proceeded at a snail's pace, that of the accompanying facilities not at all. HHC, the development company, needed to sell homes quickly to raise the cash for more building. But the selling was put in the hands of London agents with no experience or knowledge of the housing market in Cambridgeshire, where demand was concentrated to the south of the city. A drip-feed of bad publicity about Bar Hill – everything from the absence of

Bar Hill from the air

shops to problems with drainage to windswept situation – conspired with marketing incompetence to hold back sales.

In 1968 HHC sold Bar Hill to the Ideal Building Corporation, which set up a new company, Bar Hill Developments, and entrusted the construction work to a local subsidiary, J. Nunn and Sons of Ipswich. By that time fewer than 100 houses had been completed, and with the sale of the whole project, the undertakings made by HHC for the village became null and void. The new owners sacked the original architects, ditched their layout designs and imported standardised house designs from their existing range. Complaints about the standard of the workmanship multiplied, as did the concerns of planning officers about breaches of the consent. In 1975 J. Nunn and Sons went bust.

The original concept for Bar Hill had been to 'create a community'. Whether such an ideal is achievable at all in the public sector is arguable. Certainly the manner in which the Bar Hill project was pursued made it wholly impossible, at least in the short term. One by one the aspirational elements, or social aspects, of the concept were jettisoned or trampled underfoot by the developers. Instead of being concerned to create a community, they were compelled by market forces to regard Bar Hill as a composite of more or less lucrative financial opportunities. The building proceeded piecemeal rather than incrementally, on sectors often far apart from each other, while the accompanying facilities lagged far behind. A parade of shops was completed but several of the units proved impossible to fill. Bar Hill Developments then proposed a large supermarket next to existing shops, which – in 1977 – became a Tesco.

In December 1975 an influential Cambridge academic, poet and cultural commentator, David Holbrook, had a letter published in the *Cambridge Evening News* in which he described Bar Hill as 'an environmental death ... ill-sited, bleak, muddled, hideous and anarchic' with a 'a horrible little windswept centre which lacks all human touch'. In retrospect the mid-1970s can be seen as the low point in the Bar Hill story. By then – in defiance of the chaos and cynicism evident all round – the people actually living there were building their own community spirit from within. It was most evident in the work and increasing outspokenness of the parish council, the church and the residents' association. In particular the residents' association newsletter gave a voice to those who felt themselves – and they generally were – powerless to influence developers and the remote policy-makers of the county council.

The opening of the village hall and social club at the end of 1979 represented a crucial step forward for the village's social dimension. With the arrival of Tesco and the building of a flyover junction with the A14 to replace the previous, highly hazardous T-junction, Bar Hill was maturing into a coherent, independent settlement. By now the building of the houses was progressing more smoothly, so that by the end of the 1980s Bar Hill was finished. By then it had a population of 5000, twice as many as projected in W. Leathley Waide's original plan.

One more convulsion lay in store. In the early 1990s Tesco proposed to replace its existing large supermarket with a truly enormous superstore, with an appropriately expanded car park. The negotiations – sweetened by Tesco's offer to pay the parish council more than a million pounds for the various parcels of land it needed – lasted for several years. In the end the objections of the villagers of Bar Hill counted for very little against the muscle of the giant retailer and the reluctance of the local authority to submit to a trial of strength. Tesco, which was then nearing the zenith of its ambition to control every facet of retailing in the country, won the day. Its gigantic glass and steel box with its curved front awning and acres of black tarmac opened in time for Christmas in the year 2000, sealing Bar Hill's primary status – in the eyes of the planners anyway – as shopping destination rather than village.

There it stands today: the store and its associated delivery ports and car park like a huge right-angled wedge driven into the heart of what was once intended as a contemporary version of a peaceful, rural settlement. The south-eastern flank of the car park is a matter of yards from Bar Hill's primary school, library and church, with its playing fields just beyond. To a first-time visitor the dominance of this slab of *Imperium Tescorium* is brutal, its closeness to the heart of the supposed village shocking.

But Bar Hill has learned to live with it.

*

I talked to a little group of mums who had just dropped children off at the school. They all said they were living in Bar Hill because nowhere else around could offer comparable facilities and amenities at a comparable price – around £250,000 for a three-bedroom semi. They all spoke warmly about the school, the library, the village hall, the fact that you could walk or cycle everywhere; about the friends they had made and the social activities; about the openness of the place and its safeness. What about Tesco? I asked. Isn't it rather overbearing? But handy, they said. We don't even have to park.

They liked Bar Hill and liked living there. But they clearly regarded it primarily as a convenience, a staging post on a progression that would lead somewhere else. I got no sense from them of loyalty to it, or a strong feeling of belonging. One said she had grown up in a 'proper village' in Warwickshire and would love to live somewhere like that again.

The elderly people I met were just as contented, and had no intention of going anywhere else. It was safe, which was the most important thing. Good health centre, welcoming church, sound paths for mobility scooters, friendly people. Tesco? They all liked Tesco.

It being mid-morning on a working day, there were no blokes of working age for me to ask, but I'm sure they would have had much the same view. Nor were there any teenagers around, who would undoubtedly have told me that Bar Hill was deadly dull and there was nothing to do. (Interestingly, both Bar Hill and New Earswick installed skate parks at great expense to give the young people something to do; in both cases the amenity came under sustained attack from vandals and graffitists from the word go, to the point that they became hazardous and had to be demolished.)

Bar Hill's range and quality of amenities would be the envy of any village. It has all the essentials – schools, pub, church, library, village hall, sports ground, shop (if Tesco can be called a shop) – and pretty much all the desirables: health centre, dentist, garden centre, allotments. Overall, despite all the setbacks and compromises, it is recognisably derived from its original concept. It has its village green and village centre. It is largely contained within its perimeter road. It is possible to walk from any part of it to the centre without having to cross anything more threatening than one of the feeder roads. It is leafy, grassy, quiet and self-contained. I spent some time walking a few of the many miles of paths that thread their way around the maze of closes, glades, rises, spinneys, drives, avenues and ways; I became lost, and I defy any stranger not to lose their bearings, but it was all perfectly pleasant.

But let's not get carried away. Aesthetically there is nothing in Bar Hill that rises above the mediocre – not one building that can match the charm and character of one of Parker and Unwin's cottage clusters in New Earswick. Every dreary cliché of Sixties and Seventies housebuilding – coloured panelling, tile or timber cladding, pop-up garage doors, windows flat to the exterior and the rest – are on display in row after row of terraced or semi-detached dwellings. The homes are packed in tight. Rooflines are monotonously unvaried. The big builders involved – Bovis, Wimpey, Ideal and others – imported their standard designs of the time; pallid brick, PVC windows and concrete tiles rule. The blocks of garages with their corrugated roofs and metal doors – for instance along Gladeside, which is the vehicular approach to the village centre – were clearly jerry-built and have fallen into a dismal state of decay. There is no spark of imagination or inventiveness or originality on show in Bar Hill; the best you could say is that it is not bad.

My final encounter was with an elderly lady who was getting into her car outside her home in Acorn Avenue. This was the first row of houses to be completed, and hers was the first to be occupied – back in 1967, by Rob and Stella Burry and their daughter Elizabeth. The current owner had bought it ten years later, for £11,750; the fact that she was still there – her children having long gone and her husband having died – was, I thought, a considerable testament to the good things about Bar Hill.

I asked her if she regarded it as a village. She shook her head decisively. 'It's not a village. It's a settlement.'

*

Bar Hill was to have been the first of a new generation of Cambridgeshire villages, but it remains the first and the last. In the final analysis too much went wrong for the model to be more widely adopted. For a long time it was tainted, and the fact that it has come good in the end says more about the resilience of people and their capacity for making the best of things than for the value of the concept.

The pressures that brought Bar Hill into existence have not diminished, but intensified. The demand for housing outside Cambridge has grown and grown, to the point at which any village within reach of the city is threatened as speculative developers scrabble for potential sites. The latest 'solution' is taking shape a couple of miles away from Bar Hill, on the other side of the A14, on what used to be an RAF airfield. Called Northstowe, it is projected to become a 'new town' of up to 10,000 homes – possibly even an 'eco-town'.

Will the lessons available from Bar Hill be studied and learned by the planners of Northstowe? It would be nice to think so. But the experience of housebuilding in this country does not encourage optimism.

18

CHANGING FACE

Pitton, Wiltshire

The village was hidden in a streamless valley between two folds in the rolling sea of green that is the south-eastern edge of Salisbury Plain. I came upon it suddenly, freewheeling down an old road called the Whiteway which cuts away from the A30 Winchester to Salisbury highway. There was a solid, handsome Victorian school on the right, a church steeple visible over to the left, a scattering of old cob and thatch houses. The road climbed up the other side of the village, the Whiteway becoming White Hill. This is chalk country, and there is a good deal of white around.

The place is called Pitton. It is at the northern end of a crescent of similar sized settlements east of Salisbury, with Adderbury at its southern tip. It is not at all remarkable and never was: a village on the boundary between the downland and the great expanse of ancient woodland known as Clarendon Forest, owing its existence and character to both. People settled there in Anglo-Saxon times and for more than a thousand years went about the business of taking a living from the woods and fields. Within my lifetime that way of life came abruptly to an end, and now Pitton is something else entirely.

But even fifty years ago the arrangement of the village had not changed that much. The old farmhouses – Parsonage Farm, Taylors Farm, Coldharbour Farm, Webbs Farm, Whitehill Farm and some others – were spread out along the Whiteway and the lanes off it with barns and yards and paddocks between. Then a resourceful local with ambitions to be a builder rather than a farmer got down to filling some of those gaps with new housing, and discreetly edging the village outwards. The new dwellings – for instance the bungalows along Beeches Close on the west side – were of their time, uniformly uninspiring in design and owing nothing to local building traditions or materials. They did nothing to enhance the charm of Pitton, nor did they make their developer a popular man, although he was doubtless consoled by the profits.

However, the village did at least retain its nucleated form and the integrity of its setting in the landscape. To the north and east the downs – chalk with a thin covering of soil – rise and roll away. To the south and west extend the remnants of the great forest of Clarendon, much reduced but still considerable, also rising and falling with the undulating landscape. A couple of miles south-west of Pitton are the ruins of Clarendon Palace, which began as a mere royal hunting lodge but grew in the twelfth and thirteenth centuries to be a very splendid complex of apartments and halls and kitchens and ancillary buildings, surrounded by terraced gardens; all

Pitton and its fields in the mid-1960s

of it left to crumble and be reclaimed by the forest as the tastes of kings and queens changed with the times.

To the villagers of Pitton the forest was an opportunity for poaching when the backs of the gamekeepers were turned. But they also enjoyed legitimate, time-honoured rights in the less-favoured expanses of woodland. They took their faggots of firewood, and cut hazel rods to make their wattle fencing and hurdles. They took the spars for pegging the thatch roofs of their cottages, and larger poles to make the frames of the cob walls. They shaped the handles of their scythes and other tools and made gates and ladders and whatever else they needed.

So some Pitton men worked in the woods, and their sons and grandsons after them. And others took their living from the open land, which for centuries meant sheep above anything else.

Sheep meant wool and wool meant shearing. The downland shearers were a special breed. They worked in gangs, moving from farm to farm in customary sequence around an area in a twenty-mile radius from the village. They were away from home from Monday to Friday, sleeping in barns, up at first light to fit in four hours of clipping before breakfast. Often the barns were far from any farmhouse, so there was no access to a kitchen. Someone would light the fire and put the kettle on, and when it was singing they broke off from their work and squatted down in front of the heat and held out rashers of fat bacon on wooden skewers until the grease dropped and sizzled. They ate and drank strong sweet tea among the bleating sheep. Then they went back to the work through the day, until the flock was done, when they would wash from a barrel of water filled by the farmer. Then they would eat again: bread and cheese and sliced onions, maybe boiled eggs if they were offered, or spoonfuls of cocoa powder mixed with condensed milk. With the light now gone, they rolled over in the straw and slept.

One of the Pitton shearers remembered the scene at breakfast thus: 'The bearded men with ragged coats held by binder-twine at the waist, squatting close together on the dewy grass, the dancing flames casting glows and shadows on their gaunt faces ... in the east the climbing sun is just beginning to shed a little warmth, and all the myriad dew-drops sparkle in a final blaze of glory before evaporating into oblivion. Freer than the villagers, freer than the Gypsies, we shearers were more to be compared with the downland curlews and larks as we feasted.'

If the language sounds improbably, even suspiciously, flow-ery for a humble sheep-shearer, there is an explanation. The speaker, in old age, was Edwin Whitlock, a Pitton farmer born in 1874, one in a line of Whitlocks going back to 1655 – when the first page of the first parish register has one recorded – and beyond. The writer of the words was Edwin's son, Ralph Whitlock, who was born to be a farmer like his father, but had a gift rare among those of that calling. Ralph Whitlock found that writing came as naturally to him as song to the curlews nesting in the meadows. While still in his teens he began contributing a column about country matters to the *Western Gazette*, and continued with it for more than fifty years. For many years he wrote a similar column for the *Guardian*, an arrangement ended only by his death in 1995. He was farming correspondent for *The Field* for the best part of thirty years, wrote and presented *Cowleaze Farm*, which ran weekly as part of Children's Hour on the BBC's Home Service, and produced an astonishing number of books – more than 100 of them – on every conceivable aspect of natural history and rural life, from water dowsing to the life cycle of the pig.

Whitlock was a phenomenon of productivity. The problem with such a vast output of words is the separation of wheat from chaff. All his flood of journalism has gone the way of such work, into oblivion, and almost all of his books are out of print. It is not easy to envisage much of a demand for a reissue of his volumes about penguins or ducks or even eels. But the three books he wrote about Pitton and the Whitlock connection with it – *A Family and a Village*, *The Lost Village* and *A Victorian Village* – together constitute a uniquely informed and authentic picture of agricultural life in the last age before the revolution that changed the face of the countryside for good. It is focussed entirely on one small settlement, but that is its strength. Ralph Whitlock knew the place and the life of that place from the inside, and he made it his business to make a record of it, to give it its due after it was gone.

His father and mother had Whitehill Farm, on a track called Coldharbour which led south-west from the village towards Clarendon Palace. Pitton had ten farms altogether and ten farming families – some related to others, none of them conspicuously better off than any other. They lived in houses with thick cob walls – there was no natural stone available in the vicinity – and thatched roofs. In addition to the farmhouses there were fifty or so cottages, giving the village a total population of around 300. Since 1850 Pitton had had a school; the agricultural labourers paid a penny a week for each child, the smallholders two pence, the better class of farmer three.

The farms were of fifty to a hundred acres each, with two or three labourers to a farm. The other able-bodied villagers worked in the woods, or travelled elsewhere. The dairy fields were mostly along Bottom Way, north-west of the village. In the afternoon the herds of cows would be led along the flinty track to the milking parlours at a leisurely pace, allowing time for them to munch at the grass along the fringes. Sheep were grazed on the downs, and some of the land was suitable for wheat which was cut by gangs of mowers with scythes, after which the sheep and pigs would be turned out to graze the stubble.

There had been two great events in Pitton's recent history. The first was a fire in 1861 which gutted a number of houses and cottages on the north-west side of the village; they were replaced by new dwellings near the lime kilns under White Hill. The second, in 1912, was known simply as The Sale, when the Earl of Ilchester, the ancestral owner of Pitton and the neighbouring village of Farley, decided to get rid of both. As he lived in distant Dorset and had nothing to do with them, the people of Pitton did not miss him. But those who were able to scrape together the means were able to buy their farms, which at the time was – or seemed – an extraordinary opportunity for betterment. Almost overnight Pitton's farmers became men of property.

After the 1914–18 War the village acquired a reading room in the shape of an ex-Army wooden hut with a galvanised iron roof. There was a stage at one end for theatrical and musical performances, a piano, a dartboard, table tennis, a collection of books and old magazines. The village had its church, St Peter's, which was next to the pond, but many Pittonians, including the Whitlocks, were Methodist. According to Ralph Whitlock, the books commonly found in people's homes were the Bible, Bunyan's *Pilgrim's Progress*, a volume of Wesley's *Sermons* and perhaps Foxe's *Book of Martyrs*. Unusually there was no pub and had never been one, until the Silver Plough opened its doors in the 1930s.

The main diversion, which grew out of the field and forest work, was killing birds and animals. Whitlock recalled that when he and his father took on 230 acres of downland for sheep in 1934, they shot more than 2000 rabbits in the first year and paid the rent with them. As a boy he and his chums had delighted in shooting blackbirds with their air rifles and netting the hedges for sparrows. There was no stream through the village so no fishing, but otherwise every living creature that could be sold or eaten was fair game.

Reviewing the Pitton of his boyhood in *A Family and a Village*, Ralph Whitlock listed the comforts and amenities they did without: no radio, no newspapers, no running water, no electricity, no car, no indoor lavatory, no bath, no telephone, no gas, no fridge, no doctor or nurse, no shop apart from the basic village store; and very little money. But they provided for themselves: chickens, eggs, pig meat, lamb and mutton, fruit and veg, home-baked bread. Everyone helped everyone else and labour was cheap. On Saturdays they went to shoot rabbits, on Sundays they went to church. They organised concerts, fetes, dances – everything dictated by and revolving around the farming calendar. 'Would I go back to it?' Whitlock asked himself. 'That is hard to answer. But we were vastly content.'

That, of course, is him speaking for himself, the view filtered through hindsight. His father, also looking back as an old man, identified his golden age as his carefree days as a sheep-shearer. Their perspectives on the past bring to mind Raymond Williams' metaphor of the backward escalator, offering the memory the opportunity to jump off at its time of perfect contentment. Did Ralph Whitlock mean his 'vast contentment' to include the whole village? Or just himself and his carefree schoolfellows? His own father was fifty years of age when Ralph was ten, and must – given the economic climate of agriculture – have had a multitude of worries about how to make the farm pay. Would he have thought himself vastly content? Or would he have thought himself overworked and weighed down by burdens of anxiety?

Certainly the 1930s brought acute difficulties for the Whitlocks in common with other small-scale farmers in Wiltshire. Sheep-farming could not be made to pay and was in headlong retreat. Edwin and Ralph Whitlock got rid of the flock, diversified into vegetables and flowers, sold butter and chickens. All the money Ralph earned from his writing went into the farm, but the overdraft grew. They went into dairy and expanded the acreage, but the struggle was unending. Whitlock recorded bleakly that when his father died in 1963 at the age of eighty-nine, he left nothing.

By his own account and that of others, Ralph Whitlock was a far from successful farmer. But it was in his blood and he kept at it a long time, combining it with his prodigious output of words. In 1967 he was accused of bad husbandry on land rented to him by the county council; he contested the charge, but after a bitter court battle he lost the fields, which were divided up between neighbouring farms. A little later he finally gave up, and spent the next five years travelling on behalf of the Methodist Missionary Society in India, Africa and the West Indies, giving advice on farming methods. On his return to England Whitlock devoted himself wholly to writing, including the second and third volumes about Pitton.

In *The Lost Village* – published in 1988 – he seems less sure than before about the balance between profit and loss: 'Is the village better or worse than it used to be? Immeasurably better, from the standard of life ... Each generation adapts to its environment and local atmosphere and develops its character accordingly. What can be said is that the village of 1919 to 1939 has been irretrievably lost in the mists creeping up from the horizon.'

*

At first glance the landscape and the place of the village in it do not seem so different. The fields that Edwin and Ralph Whitlock and their forbears and fellow Pitton farmers worked are still worked today. It's mainly arable now – wheat, barley, rape – although there are some cattle and even a speckling of sheep on a few meadows. A great swathe of woodland still sweeps up and over the ridge where the ruins of Clarendon Palace are hidden. The woods to the east – Hound Wood and beyond that Bentley Wood – survive intact. On a hot June day, with the rise and fall of the downland pale green with ripening wheat and splashed with the brilliant yellow of rape against the richer green of the pastures and the deeper green of the woods, it would be quite easy to conclude that nothing had changed too drastically.

Then look a little closer, and scratch at the surface. Blocks of conifer dominate Clarendon Forest. The fields are empty of men and machines. The conversion of the downland landscape from sheep-grazing to arable – made possible by the ever-more sophisticated application of herbicides, insecticides and chemical fertilisers – has brought about an extraordinary ecological degradation. Hardly more than half a century ago Ralph Whitlock and his aged father were noting the disappearance of wheatears, stonechats, stone curlews and corncrakes. Twenty years later the son was lamenting the vanishing of the wildflowers – tormentil, viper's bugloss, eyebright, sheep's bit scabious and the rest – and the precipitous decline in the abundance and variety of butterflies and moths: Adonis blues, fritillaries, skippers, green hairstreaks and burnet moths.

Two generations ago a drive across Salisbury Plain at dusk or during the night in summertime would have left the margins of the car windscreen thick with the corpses of insects. The air was filled with them and the birds thrived on eating them. But today anyone who fishes for trout on the famous Wiltshire chalk streams – the Avon, the Wylye, the Nadder and others – will testify that the hatches of standard insect invertebrates are a shadow of what they once were. The silence along the riverbanks is matched by the silence of the downs, which were once alive with the songs of the birds.

Pitton itself has clearly secured a new and viable function for itself. There are twice as many houses as there were in Whitlock's youth, and if it is a tenth as picturesque as it was then, does that matter so much if it works as a place to live? The agricultural labourer has gone the same way as the stone curlew; Pitton is now populated by an overwhelmingly middle class and prosperous mix of retirees and families in which the breadwinner drives off to Salisbury or further afield to work.

The school is apparently thriving, even if a significant majority of the pupils are from outside the village. The church is well supported. The number of weekend cottages is very small, so Pitton is not afflicted by the seasonal flux that devitalises so many prettier villages. As a result it is able to support a decent, basic village shop which – crucially – retains its Post Office counter. The pub, the Silver Plough, is distinctly gastro rather than village boozer, but none the worse for that. The old wood and iron reading room was replaced by a proper village hall in the 1970s, which is well used. The whole village turns out every July for the Pitton Carnival. Although there is no cricket or football club, there is a slightly eccentric enthusiasm for pétanque, and part of the little recreation field behind the village hall has been levelled for a 'terrain' on which league matches are played.

On the face of it, Pitton is a quiet, decent, friendly place to live – if you can afford it. The absence of low-cost 'social housing' at one end of the scale, and of substantial gentri-fied mansions at the other, has given it a social cohesiveness which fosters a distinctly contemporary brand of community spirit – one based not on the need to work together to sur-vive but on a shared economic (and, one suspects, political) outlook. The flavour of this spirit is aptly displayed in the

Parish Plan, which also covers the next village, Farley, and was produced in 2007.

This document concentrates largely on a familiar cocktail of middle-class concerns: excessive road traffic and speeding, the risk of flooding, noxious weeds, street lighting, inappropriately timed cutting of hedges, litter, the maintenance of play areas and so forth. The sections on the economy and housing are revealing, bearing in mind that for almost all its long history Pitton was a working, working-class village. Current economic activity is minimal and the villagers clearly want it to stay that way; the Plan states that any new business should be small-scale, inconspicuous and silent, which rules out most options.

On housing the Plan virtuously declares theoretical support for 'planning applications that provide lower-priced housing for locals and families on appropriate sites whilst protecting open village spaces.' A cursory look at the way Pitton is laid out reveals that – apart from the recreation field – there is only one sizeable area within its present form that has not been built on. Known as Coldharbour Field, this is an area roughly square in shape between the gardens along The Green and The Street, the two side roads off White Hill. Some years ago it was placed on a list of notional sites for housing across the Salisbury District Council area, thereby setting off a considerable village rumpus. The owners of the land found themselves under fierce attack spilling over into personal abuse, which ended only when the field was excluded as a potential housing site under the Salisbury District Plan.

*

Just one of the old farming families listed by Ralph Whitlock still has a presence in Pitton: two brothers whose father followed his father on the farm, but who themselves plumped for careers in teaching in preference to lives of toil in the fields. But the impulse is not that easily shaken off. The brother I met has held on to sixty acres on the western downslope of White Hill; having spent a small fortune fencing it off, he is farming some sheep there – not for the profit, he hastened to assure me, because there isn't any profit, but because it's in the blood.

Otherwise the rupture between Pitton's past and its present is almost complete. Despite occupying the same position in the streamless valley, and retaining a significant proportion of its old buildings, it has become a wholly different place, observing a set of values, priorities and objectives that would have been literally unimaginable when Ralph Whitlock was a boy. He wrote: 'I knew every hedge, every tree, every gutter, every dog and cat, every holiday visitor as well as every village resident.' And that was but a small part of what he knew. No one will have that kind of knowledge again.

19

LAKELAND STATESMEN

Troutbeck, Cumbria

On a raw, rainy day early in November 1799 two of England's greatest poets walked over the Garburn Pass from Kentmere, through the straggling village of Troutbeck, down to the shores of Windermere and across by the ferry to Hawkshead. The landscape through which Wordsworth and Coleridge strode at their customary forced-march pace – accompanied by Wordsworth's brother, John – was as grand and rugged then as it had ever been, and is still today. But even then, two centuries and a little more ago, the old Lakeland life and ways were changing fast.

Writing to his sister Dorothy, Wordsworth pronounced himself 'disgusted with the new erections and objects around Windermere' – the erections being vulgar villas paid for by plutocrats from the proceeds of commerce. After a night in Hawkshead, the party went on to Rydal and then Grasmere. Crossing in front of Rydal Hall they were rebuked by a serv-ant for straying on to private land – an impudence likened by

Town End barn, Troutbeck

Troutbeck in the 1880s

Coleridge to the 'trespass on the eye' caused by the 'damned whitewashing' of the house, a form of tarting-up regarded by both poets as an outrage to the senses.

They did not linger in Troutbeck. Had they done so, they may not have been offended by any whitewashed houses – not yet. They would have found a place apparently rooted in its past and traditional patterns of life, but actually on the verge of great and irreversible change.

It is called a village and functioned as a village. But it is made up of a string of minute hamlets, clusters of housing each separated from the next by a field or two, stretched along a mile of hillside from Town Head in the north to Town End in the south. Troutbeck's church and school were both built at a distance from the village, on the valley floor next to the main road from Windermere up towards the Kirkstone Pass, where the eponymous beck flows and where they could serve the outlying farms on the eastern side.

The founding fathers chose carefully, to suit their needs rather than any notion of what a village should look like. There was rich grazing along the stream, so they built their homes and barns to look down on their best land. Higher up rose the fells, where their sheep could be turned out to fend for themselves for most of the year. They took stone from the quarry beside the old Garburn track for their building: thick slabs for the walls, split stones for the roofs. Houses and barns stood together as one, right by their land.

The earliest written records, from the sixteenth century, reveal Troutbeck to have been a loosely grouped community of yeoman farmers – the Lakeland 'statesmen' so revered by Wordsworth. They held their land by customary tenure, which meant that they owned it except for any minerals that might be found underground. Wordsworth, in his romantic way, chose to portray this society as a kind of democracy or republic of shepherds. In fact, of course, the age-old determining principle – that there should be haves as well as have-nots – applied just as firmly in Lakeland as anywhere else. By the end of the sixteenth century fifty or so families of statesmen had established themselves in Troutbeck. But the scale of their land holdings varied considerably, and by no means could they be regarded as a community of equals.

Nevertheless, in the way they lived and worked, in their situations and in the challenges they faced, they were as one – 'a race of men singularly sturdy, independent and tenacious of their rights', as they were described by Samuel Haslam Scott in his history of Troutbeck, *A Westmorland Village*, which was published in 1904. They raised and tended the Herdwick sheep of the fells, each attentive to his own but ever ready to lend a hand to help another, and all expected to join together in the necessarily cooperative enterprise of rounding up the animals at shearing-time.

They lived in exactly the same way: they grew some oats and ate bread cooked on the griddle, with salted beef, mutton or bacon (but rarely a green vegetable and never any fruit). They wore grey coats, knee breeches, shirts of hemp and flax, leather clogs with wooden soles. They were solitary in their work, their only regular companions being their staffs and their dogs. Their duty was to provide for themselves and their dependants, and to pass on what they held to the next generation, increasing the inheritance if the chance came.

They built their chapel where the Jesus Church still stands.

Early on it had an earthen floor, considered 'more convenient when there were frequent burials', but in 1707 it was decided that it should be flagged. Twenty-two of the Troutbeck statesmen are recorded as having sent a man and a horse and 'trayled flags' from Applethwaite Quarry. Fourteen of the villagers gave a day to 'mossing the church', which meant clambering on to the roof to plug the gaps between the flat stones with moss to stop the rain and snow getting in. The school was built across the road from the church in 1657; George Longmire and Stephen and George Birkett were responsible for the walls, while Myles Sewart, Troutbeck's carpenter, took charge of the roof.

Life was hard, but it was not all toil and travail. They had their amusements, which they cherished and took seriously. The village was the home of the Troutbeck Players, who toured Lakeland performing their 'Play Jiggs', characterised by Samuel Scott as 'short dramas in verse, the interest arising from the incidents of low rustic intrigue and sometimes terminating in the most extraordinary moral application.' The village celebrity in the late seventeenth century was Thomas Hoggart, known as 'Auld' Hoggart, who was originally from Bampton and combined sheep farming with writing plays likened in style to those of the Spanish master Lope de Vega. One of his hits, *The Siege of Troy*, began with a procession through the village of 'the minstrels of five parishes ... followed by a yeoman on bull-back.'

Wrestling in the Cumberland and Westmorland style was a big draw in Troutbeck as elsewhere. So too was hunting, which spread deep and strong roots in the statesmen communities. This was very different from the gentlemanly and aristocratic version adopted further south. The Lakeland huntsmen came from all levels of society and walks of life. An account of hunting around Loweswater in the late eighteenth century speaks of a hound being kept at almost every cottage – 'two or three qualified inhabitants take licences to kill game and command the pack . . . as soon as the harvest is in, an honest cobbler shifts his garb and becomes huntsman.'

Less than half a century after Wordsworth's and Coleridge's walk Troutbeck listed around sixty owners of land. The biggest was George Browne of Town End with 735 acres. Four farmers had between 100 and 400 acres each. The rest made do on what were little more than smallholdings. Most of the villagers were still Troutbeck born and bred.

Over the next half-century, up to the death of Queen Victoria, there was a social revolution. The development of the Applethwaite slate quarry brought an influx of workers and required the building of new cottages. A number of the old dwellings that had fallen into disrepair as the families that owned them died out or moved elsewhere were replaced by smart new residences. Others were extended and modernised. The old track through the village was widened and macadamised. The Mortal Man, the village inn of great antiquity, was entirely rebuilt. Most significant was the provision in 1869 of the Village Institute, a sturdy stone expression of Victorian self-belief built opposite the lane going down past Low Fold Farm to the main road.

By then many of the old statesmen families had moved out or disappeared altogether, although the most prominent – the Brownes – held on at Town End, the magnificent old farmhouse at the southern tip of the village. Five years after the opening of the Village Institute, the village's long-serving parson, the Reverend William Sewell, died at the age of eighty-eight. He had been in charge of Troutbeck's spiritual welfare for more than forty years, combining his duties at Jesus Church with farming his own land, hunting and teaching at the grammar school in Ambleside. On one occasion the bishop visited, and came across Sewell helping his neighbours with the sheep. When the bishop dared to suggest that this was unworthy of him, Parson Sewell retorted 'when you find me better remuneration, I can probably afford to lay aside assisting my neighbours and I shall be very glad to give up tending my sheep.'

The opening of the railway to Windermere and the consequent influx of outsiders had done much to erode the self-contained isolation of Troutbeck. But it remained a working, farming, hunting village. Samuel Scott's book summed up the life at the dawn of the twentieth century thus: 'The people are better educated, better clothed, better housed; travelling is no longer beset by hardships, and sanitary conditions are vastly improved. But in the main the Westmorland farmer lives the same life as his forefathers did . . . The methods of farming have changed very little.'

Local priorities were clearly indicated in the school log-book: 'An hour lost through scholars being permitted to go hunting . . . punished three boys for running sheep . . . many children absent through sheep-shearing . . . cautioned boys against grappling fish in the stream.' The schoolmaster was a man called George Joyce, who was also the organist and church choirmaster and treasurer of the Village Institute. He organised concerts as well as magic lantern entertainments, using the money raised to equip the library with books and the playground with swings.

In 1914 the last of the many George Brownes of Town End died, and the flag over Troutbeck School was flown at half-mast. The Brownes had been a dominant presence for more than four centuries and over that period their social status had risen from that of yeoman farmer to considerable landowner and gentleman. The last of the line was a noted scholar and antiquary, a great collector of old books and manuscripts, and an occasional contributor on historical matters to the *Transactions of the Cumberland and Westmorland Antiquarian and Archaeological Society*. His chief skill was in carving wood, and many examples of his craftwork can still be seen at Town End, which remained in the ownership of his family until the 1940s when it was handed over to the National Trust.

That same fateful year, 1914, saw the election of Richard Clapham as Troutbeck's Hunting Mayor. The Mayor's Hunt originated back in the eighteenth century. Initially it was a purely local affair in which harriers chased hares, but over time the tradition evolved of inviting the famous Coniston Foxhounds over from beyond Windermere. In some ways Clapham illustrated the changing nature of the times – he was a Yorkshireman who had lived in Canada and New Zealand before returning to England on the death of his father. It was the opportunities for sport that lured him to Troutbeck, and in his forty years living there he identified closely and passionately with the Lakeland sporting herit-age. He hunted three times a week, with the Coniston and Ullswater, Blencathra, and Eskdale and Ennerdale packs. He acted as whipper-in for the Kendal Otterhounds, shot grouse and blackcock across Wansfell and deer in the Troutbeck Park estate (owned by Beatrix Potter), and fished for trout and salmon wherever and whenever the opportunity presented itself.

Clapham wrote voluminously about his sporting life in the field sports press, and produced several books, including the definitive *Foxhunting on the Lakeland Fells*. Anyone wishing to know what a Lakeland hound should be need only consult Clapham: 'Light in frame and particularly well let-down and developed in hindquarters . . . good neck and shoulders and loin . . . long in pattern and ribs carried well back . . . a good nose, plenty of tongue, and, last but by no means least, pace.'

The Mayor's Hunt, held each November, was one of the great events in the Troutbeck calendar. The other, linked with it and held at about the same time, was the Shepherds' Meet, at which the stray sheep gathered off the fells before the onset of winter were identified by the marks on their ears, horns or fleece and claimed by their owners. The location for this time-honoured get-together was always the yard behind the Queen's Head Hotel at Town Head, the northern outpost of the village where it comes down to the main road. In times past the reclaiming of the animals was followed by a great gathering of shepherds and hunters in the hotel over steaming plates of a local delicacy known as 'tattie pot', washed down by much ale and enlivened by the singing of old hunting songs, 'D'Ye Ken John Peel' among them.

The Queen's Head Hotel was gutted by fire in June 2014, and was still a blackened ruin when I was there in September 2015 – despite a large sign on the road promising that it would reopen 'early in 2015'. The Shepherds' Meet and the Mayor's Hunt do still survive in a somewhat reduced form, but in almost every other way the Troutbeck that Richard Clapham finally left in 1947 to return to Yorkshire has had most of the life taken out of it. It is now three-quarters given over to second and holiday homes, which makes for a muted atmosphere over the winter months. The property prices are startling – £300,000 for a decrepit semi-detached cottage requiring another £200,000 to make it habitable. The Village Institute is kept solvent by the weekly meetings of the Penrith Christadelphians (although why they cannot discuss God's intentions for the Earth in Penrith itself is not immediately obvious). The village shop and café had recently shut down when I was there because of some trouble with the tenants, although they have subsequently reopened.

The night I spent in the village was that of the Annual Parish Meeting in the Institute, although I managed not to hear about it until the morning after, which was rather irritating. A grand total of eleven residents turned out, I was told: the burning issues were the reluctance of South Lakeland District Council to put up any signs on the A592 to indicate the existence of Troutbeck; and the reluctance of anyone to do anything to restrain 4x4s from roaring up and down the track past the old quarry.

Economically it is the walkers – devotees of the cult of Alfred Wainwright – who keep Troutbeck from relapsing into the status of seasonal holiday settlement. At the Mortal Man they deal with a steady stream of them in any half-decent weather all the year round. They also make a speciality of welcoming dog-owners; the evening I was there I watched a couple with their two Labradors who had hardly a word to say to each other but chatted to their pets as if they were fully sentient human beings. The landlord of the hotel was extremely friendly and helpful to me, but he looked profoundly exhausted by the demands of tending to dog-lovers and fell-trampers fourteen hours a day seven days a week.

After my excellent supper I cycled the whole length of the village very slowly, from north to south, and then again from south to north. I stopped at each of the little huddles of old houses to marvel at their construction: the massive walls, low porches, strange cylindrical chimneys, thick-slated roofs, mullioned windows and mighty exposed beams; and at the way they speak so honestly and directly of the lives of those who made them. They lie at rest in the grassy churchyard below the village: Birketts, Longmires, Forrests, Brownes and others.

But the race of Troutbeck statesmen is not quite extinct, not yet. The next morning, after breakfast at the Mortal Man, I was introduced to a vigorous, elderly chap in mud-caked wellingtons who said he could spare me half an hour before he had to get 120 Cheviots (sheep, if you please) ready for collection. He was actually an outsider, from Windermere, but had married a Troutbeck girl in the 1960s and had taken the tenancy of one of the few farms not controlled by the National Trust. When the owner died he had managed to scrape together enough to buy it, and had subsequently built his holding up to 600 acres, doing sheep and beef cattle. 'I thought it were paradise when I came here,' he told me. 'And it were.' But everything changed in the 1970s: house prices rocketing, locals selling up and moving out to Windermere and Bowness, no building allowed because of the village's conservation status, therefore nowhere for young families to live. It was a familiar story, with a familiar coda: the shutting of the school in 1976.

'In winter it's just dead,' Mike said, shaking his head. 'Except for us farmers, the ones that's left.' He handed over his tenancy to his son a while back, but he still keeps working. He said he had no hobbies, no interest in holidays, no thoughts of retiring – 'it would put me in the ground,' he said. I asked if they had any trouble with the walkers who stream over from Ambleside by Wansfell Pike and down the old track known as Nanny Lane into the village. He grimaced. 'Bloody Wainwright,' he growled. 'You know he advised taking wire-cutters in case you had to get through a fence. Fancy that!' But he acknowledged that without the Wainwright devotees, Troutbeck would be hard-pressed to retain the life it has.

But would anyone go back to the way it was? Samuel Scott posed the question more than a century ago, when the old structure was already crumbling. He pointed out very wisely that those who groaned and sighed thinking of the times departed were liable to forget what had also departed – the toil, the discomfort, the squalor, the actual and spiritual darkness. 'They are unmindful,' Scott observed, 'that when people are unlearned and credulous, they are rude and cruel too.' How futile it is to moan about the 'destruction of village life' as if somehow the best of it – the closeness of community, the friendships and bonds that went with it, the sense of worth and shared identity – could have been salvaged to complement underfloor heating, Wi-Fi and the multichannel TV experience.

Of course there has been loss. Of course a heavy price has been paid for our material comforts. Troutbeck is a little like Robin Hood's Bay, pretty much detached from its past and from the impulse that brought it into existence in the first place. Superbly preserved in terms of its fabric, cherished and nursed as it never was before, watched over by the local council's conservation officers who come down like avenging angels on anyone who dares interfere with an old barn door or even contemplates a PVC window or a satellite dish, Troutbeck has become an installation rather than a village, a facility, an amenity.

What cannot be taken away from it is the glory of its situation. To the south-west the valley is open, showing the gleam off the waters of Windermere with the blue outline of the Langdale Pikes beyond. To the east rises Applethwaite Common, where the Garburn track cuts over to Kentmere. Wansfell and Idle Hill, dark and rugged, block the way to the west, while northwards the road climbs steadily and steeply to the Kirkstone Pass, where Parson Sewell had the famous inn rebuilt in the 1840s. Along the side of the valley is the village itself, sombre grey stone mixed with bright white-wash, the low cottages overshadowed by the sycamores and oaks beside the lane. Higher still the crooked little fields with their wandering stone walls give way to bracken and heather and stone outcrops.

When the sun shines, the meadows dropping down below Troutbeck to its stream glow a brilliant green. The beck is thickly treed along its banks, but where the sunlight breaks through, it strikes the stony bed and turns it gold.

In 1615 an early George Browne, well known for his quarrelsome and litigious character, challenged the King's right to take fish from the Troutbeck. He installed a weir and helped himself to 'kipp trowtes and salmonds . . . in great abundance about 400 in number.' The 'kipp trowtes' were the big lake trout of Windermere which migrated late in the year to spawn in the stream. They are not seen these days, but trout there certainly are. I saw them darting between the sunbeams, their flanks flickering, and I was heartened that the beck still deserved its name.

20

SWALLOWED UP

Three Mile Cross, Berkshire

'Go on, 'ave a go.' The one urging me on was Snowy, one of a quartet of white-haired stalwarts of the Three Mile Cross Bowling Club gathered on a soft June morning for a spot of chat and gentle ribbing and the rolling of a few bowls. I stepped cautiously on to turf as smooth as satin. Snowy pointed at the jack, pressed the bowl upon me and gave me a few tips as to how I should proceed. I crouched and sent the shiny black missile on its way. To my amazed delight it came to rest about six inches from the jack. 'Not bad,' one of the other old bowlers said. Snowy bowled and finished further away than me. Old timers' abuse rained down on him.

I asked Snowy about the village. 'Ain't a village no more, is it?' he growled. He'd come in 1959. There were seven pubs then, he said. I think this must have been an exaggeration – an inflated abundance of licensed premises is a common feature of the village viewed in a golden haze of nostalgia – but there were certainly three, of which one, the Swan, survives today.

Three Mile Cross, pre-1914

A decade after Snowy's arrival in Three Mile Cross a different Golden Age was reaching its zenith, that of British road construction. The M4 motorway was nearing completion, having thrust its noisome way around the village's northern flank and severed it from Reading. Another decade on and the M4 was joined by the A33 Swallowfield bypass, a spanking-new dual carriageway immediately to the west of Three Mile Cross connecting booming Reading with booming Basingstoke.

The old Reading–Basingstoke turnpike road had gone straight through Three Mile Cross, and had been the source of whatever prosperity and importance it had ever possessed. The road connected a string of villages south of Reading and by the time of Snowy's migration to Three Mile Cross, it was doing duty as a major trunk route, a role for which it was wholly unsuited. The traffic jams were appalling and the residents of all the villages along it hated it, so the construction of the M4–A33 axis brought relief. But Three Mile Cross got the worst of the deal. Caught between the two new roads, it had its life and identity squeezed from it.

*

I left the haven of the bowling club to investigate further. The old village is strung out along the turnpike road, with offshoots along the lanes leading east towards Shinfield and west towards Grazeley. There are no fine buildings, but there are a few nice eighteenth-century cottages left, keeping company with Victorian villas and twentieth-century additions, and the Swan looks not that different from the way it did a couple of centuries ago.

The land between the original village and what is now the A33 used to be fields, but over the past twenty years or so has been progressively gobbled up by housing. The south side of the road to Grazeley was built over first. Now the triangle on the north side has been similarly transformed into an estate called Mitford Fields, the name in honour of Miss Mary Mitford, the celebrated chronicler of life in Three Mile Cross almost two hundred years ago.

I cycled slowly around Mitford Fields at mid-morning on a working day in school termtime. Except for the odd straggler, it was deserted; it was as if it had been evacuated after a warning of imminent chemical or nuclear attack. Pedalling along the main thoroughfare, Tabby Drive, I passed Fawn Drive, Elk Path, Caribou Walk and Sika Gardens (but no Muntjac Meadow or Red Deer Rise, which was slightly disappointing). I quickly lost my bearings, a common experience in the modern housing estate, where straight lines and right angles are anathema. This was the conventional interlocking maze of curves and irregular ovals and cul-de-sacs with houses arranged in clusters interspersed with units of garages, rectangles of marked and unmarked car-parking spaces and 'green spaces' in the form of play areas, patches of turf and beds with thick coverings of bark around council-approved varieties of ornamental trees, shrubs and perennials.

Two of the major housebuilders – Bellway and Bovis – shared the spoils at Mitford Fields. The Bellway portion contains a selection of their standard homes, the names given a literary flavour: the Yeats and Wilde have two bedrooms, the Scott three, the Christie (presumably Agatha), the Cookson and the Carver (?Raymond) four, the Shelley, Wordsworth and Dickens five. Bovis favour names suggestive of harmony, comfort and middle-class respectability. At Mitford Fields may be found the two-bedroom Amberley and Camberley (but no Ramberley or Shamberley); the four-bed Canterbury, Albany, Beaumont and Thatcham ('stunning'); the five-bed Melville, Gaskell ('offers stylish family living') and Wallace.

On the Bovis site plan the different models are colour coded – green for the Wallace, apricot for the Amberley and so on. But the 'affordable housing' provision stipulated by the local authority in the conditions for planning permission do not have a designated colour or brand name. They are left an anonymous white, which suggests that they are there on sufferance.

One or two of the house-type names on Bovis's Mitford Fields estate crop up at other Bovis developments around the country – the Canterbury, for instance, and the Amberley. But the company's inventiveness in the matter of nomen-clature is considerable. Knights Mount in Hampshire, for example, boasts the three-bedroom Sheringham, Chilworth, Southwold and Beaulieu, the four-bed Montpellier, Salisbury, Hersley and Austin, and the five-bed Chester. At Windmill View, near Petersfield, the Chester, Sheringham and Salisbury mix it with the five-bed Arundel and Dorchester, the four-bed Andover and Selsey and the three-bed Durrell. Speed north to Bedfordshire and Saxon Grove, and you will find the familiar Canterbury and Sheringham alongside the Olney, the Lavendon, the Malmesbury, the Wimborne, the Chellington and more besides. Shoot across to Eden Park near Rugby and you may encounter the six-bed Baxterley together with the Rowington, the Bickenhill and the Alveston.

Too much choice? An excess of diversity? Rest assured. There is no choice. There is no diversity. All these houses are the same. The homes built by Bovis are the same as those built by Bellway which are the same as those built by Taylor Wimpey, Barratt, Persimmon and the rest of the volume builders.

Of course I do not mean that they are exactly the same. Some have slate roofs and some have tiled roofs. Most are red-brick, but some have rendered frontages. Some have some pebble-dashing or cladding or panelling. Some have brown window frames, some have white. Some have porches, some don't. Some have dormer windows, some don't. Different-coloured bricks in different patterns can be a feature, or not. Some are one storey, some two, some three.

But these are variations on a single, simple theme, embraced by housebuilders great and small across the land. Our estate dwellings are clones, bricks-and-mortar equivalents of the children produced by the Central London Hatchery and Conditioning Centre in Huxley's *Brave New World*. Spawned from a 3-D printer linked to a database located in some cultural and geographical non-place, they belong nowhere and everywhere. They spread a deadening uniformity that repudiates regional difference and denies any glimmer of individuality. Like our cloned town centres filled with the same chain outlets selling the same products from Wick to Penzance, our estates offer no clues as to where they are. The occupier of a Bovis or Bellway home in Somerset could be beamed across to one in Northumberland and notice no material difference.

The big companies have one defence to the charge that

the houses they build are banal, derivative and characterless, and that is that their customers like them and want to live in them. It is the same defence offered by the supermarkets to justify their efforts to hegemonise food retailing and strangle local food shops. Of course people want these houses – first and foremost because there are precious few alternatives, and secondly because they are warm and comfortable and convenient.

That is not the point at all. The strength of demand is irrelevant to any debate about whether or not this is the best model for mass housebuilding. So too are the opinions of the volume builders. They have devised this model because it suits them. It requires nothing from them in terms of decent design or sympathy for place or setting. They do not have to employ architects; all they need is a bank of design blueprints to dip into. The scale of operations makes huge savings possible through bulk buying of materials and labour. With profits for the ten biggest builders up by a third to £2.4 billion in 2015 they are not likely to look kindly upon any challenge to their way of doing business.

But a challenge there should certainly be, because these companies are peddling a grand deception. The Bellway Homes brochure for Mitford Fields states that 'Three Mile Cross is a story of thriving village life and a sought-after gem of a location.' This is highly fanciful, to put it charitably, and the implication that moving into a house on the estate will somehow provide a route into vibrant community life is a ridiculous misrepresentation. Snowy, stalwart of the bowling club, is spot on. This is not a village any more and Mitford Fields – with no shop, no pub, no church, no school, no sports club – is no more or less than an agglomeration of brick boxes bolted on to its side.

And the planners have much more in store for this 'gem of a location'. The local authority, Wokingham Borough Council, have given permission for an estate of 172 homes on the land immediately to the east of the bowling club green. The winners of these spoils are Taylor Wimpey, who are also set fair for several hundred more houses a little way to the south, at Spencers Wood. Croft Gardens, the brochure warbles, 'is modern village living in a growing community with its streets and pathways set in open space nestling in the village of Spencers Wood, where Berkshire village life is a tradition with some family businesses dating back 100 years . . .'

The council's officers refer to Croft Gardens as 'a sustainable urban extension to the existing settlement' which is PlanningSpeak for 'we are happy to see Spencers Wood swamped in new housing.' In all, Wokingham Borough Council is favourably disposed towards the construction of 2500 new houses over the next ten years around Three Mile Cross, Spencers Wood and Shinfield. It has in effect surrendered the entire area to an alliance of developers on the grounds that its location between the M4 and the A33 is not much use for anything else, and that by concentrating new housing there, it can relieve the pressure on other villages more worthy of being protected.

Which is bad luck for Three Mile Cross, not that anyone seems to care very much.

*

By a neat twist of fate the old cottage in which Mary Russell Mitford lived and wrote her bestsellers about village life now contains the offices of Woolf Bond Planning, a firm of planning consultants specialising in trying to cajole .or bully reluctant local authorities into granting planning permission for large housing developments on greenfield sites. The building, now called The Mitfords – why the plural? – is very smartly turned out in gleaming whitewash, which it certainly was not when the celebrated authoress arrived to live there in 1820. She described it to a friend as 'a messuage or tenement . . . it consists of a series of closets, the largest of which may be about eight feet square which they call parlours or kitchens or pantries . . . behind is a garden about the size of a good drawing-room . . . on one side a public-house, on the other a village shop and right opposite, a cobbler's stall.'

She was then thirty-three. Miss Mitford she was and Miss Mitford she remained: an only child, servant and slave to her parents, in particular her parasitic monster of a father. It was entirely due to his pathological selfishness, snobbishness, profligacy and addiction to high living and gambling that the three of them should have been reduced to finding refuge in Three Mile Cross at a rent of £20 a year. Their previous home had been very splendid: Grazeley Court, on the other side of what is now the A33. It had been rebuilt and renamed Bertram House by Dr Mitford in a characteristic burst of *folie de grandeur* which exhausted the residue of what had once been his wife's considerable fortune as well as the £20,000 (worth around £1.5 million today) which his daughter had won with a ticket on the Irish Lottery.

The family's finances were in a desperate state when they arrived in Three Mile Cross. Miss Mitford set about repairing them in one of the few ways open to a woman at the time, with her pen. Encouraged by a friend from Reading with literary connections, she began submitting articles to the London magazines. In 1822 the *Lady's Magazine* published a sketch entitled 'Lucy' about the Mitfords' maid. She followed this with two helpings of 'Boarding School Recollections' and then, in December 1822, with 'Our Village'. This, in a revised form, became the opening chapter in the first volume of *Our Village*, published in 1824. Four more volumes appeared between 1826 and 1832, and they were followed in 1835 by *Belford Regis* – a thin disguise for Reading, Berkshire – and *Country Stories* in 1837.

By then Miss Mitford had established herself as a kind of national treasure. By locating herself so precisely in a particular place and by describing events, scenes and characters that were recognisable to everyone, she was able to give her multitudes of readers the impression that she was talking to them about a world they all knew and shared; that she was their personal friend. She became a celebrity; visitors to that part of Berkshire would be driven out to see her humble residence, even – if they were in luck – to take tea with her. She earned well, but whatever she earned her father contrived to spend. After her mother's death in 1837, she became his nurse as well. He was as demanding an invalid as he was a devious and insatiable spender of her money. Poor woman, night after night she was required to read to him and sit playing cribbage into the small hours, and only when he was ready to sleep was she free to write.

By the time this egotistical leech breathed his last in 1842, Miss Mitford's own health had been broken by the years of toil and anxiety. She was wracked by rheumatism, a condition not helped by the decay of her famous cottage. 'The foundations seemed mouldering like an old cheese with damp and rottenness,' she wrote. 'The rain came dripping through the roof and streaming through the walls. The hailstones pattered upon my bed through the casements and the small panes rattled and fell to pieces every high wind . . . the poor cottage was crumbling about us.'

She clung on until 1851, when she was persuaded to move to a more comfortable cottage a mile or two away at Swallowfield, where she died in 1855. One of her visitors towards the end of her life was the energetic Rector of Eversley, Charles Kingsley. He found 'the little figure rolled up in two chairs . . . packed round with books up to the ceiling . . . with clothes on, of course, but of no recognised or recognisable pattern . . . and somewhere at the upper end of the heap, gleaming under a great deep globular brow, two such eyes as I never perhaps saw in any other English woman . . . and such a tongue, for the beautiful speech that came out of that ugly face. She was a triumph of mind over matter, of spirit over flesh.'

*

Admirers of Miss Mitford's stories assert that she was the first to reveal and do justice to the daily lives of ordinary country people. It is true that she was not at all like Jane Austen, who set her fictions in comparable places but had no interest whatever in how the agricultural working class lived. Miss

Mitford focussed on the labourers, servants, gardeners and traders who lived around her in Three Mile Cross. She certainly did her best to bring out their dignity and humanity by chronicling the small things of life: an act of kindness or eccentricity, a cricket match, the hunt, haymaking, a walk in the woods, gathering primroses or nuts, going to the races.

There have also been valiant attempts to recruit her into a 'rural realism' school of writing, as a gentler female ally of William Cobbett. In a valuable book called *The Rural Tradition*, Professor W. J. Keith claimed that close reading of her work revealed 'the darker side of her rural picture . . . there is shadow as well as sunshine in Three Mile Cross.' He instanced her references to the agricultural depression, absentee landlords, the savage game laws and – most tellingly – an extended passage about the Captain Swing riots and what she called 'the awful impression of that terrible time'. Professor Keith conceded that she may have 'overemphasised the idyllic circumstances of village life in her time' but insists that 'she is never misleading'.

Well, perhaps. My own view, for what it's worth, is that for a reader of today she is rather hard going. Whatever Professor Keith may say, she resolutely steers clear of the dark side of her own and other people's lives. She is, I'm sorry to say, trite, sentimental, long-winded, short-sighted, arch, chatty and twee. This paragraph, taken from the second volume of *Our Village*, is representative:

It is a pleasant lively scene this May morning with the sun shining so gaily on the irregular rustic dwellings intermixed with their pretty gardens; a cart and a waggon watering [it would be more correct, perhaps, to say *beering*] at the Rose; Dame Wheeler with her basket and her brown loaf just coming from the bakehouse; the nymph of the shoeshop feeding the goslings at the open door – they are very late this year, those worthy little geese; two or three women in high gossip dawdling up the street; Charles North the gardener with his blue apron and ladder on his shoulder walking rapidly by; a cow and a donkey browsing the grass by the wayside; my white greyhound, Mayflower, sitting majestically in front of her own stable, and ducks, chickens, pigs and children scattered all over ... A pretty scene!

If you care for that kind of thing, there is plenty more where that came from. W. H. Hudson, who stopped off on a walk from the 'hated biscuit metropolis' of Reading to talk to the sexton at Swallowfield about Miss Mitford, was very stern about her more ambitious works, which included several lengthy verse plays. 'Poor stuff' he called them, but he liked *Our Village*: 'There is no thought, no mind stuff in it,' he wrote, 'and it is a classic. It endures, outliving scores of better books, because her own delightful personality manifests itself and shines in all these little pictures.'

She certainly did provide a uniquely detailed layout of the village at that time. Starting at the bottom of the road, she described the 'tidy square red cottage' belonging to the retired publican on the right, the 'pretty dwelling of the shoemaker', the blacksmith's 'gloomy dwelling where the sun never seems to shine', a 'spruce little tenement, red, high and narrow', the village shop 'multifarious as a bazaar', her own cottage and the pub next door, 'the white house opposite the collar-maker's shop, with four lime trees before it', the carpenter next door 'famed ten miles round and worthy of all his fame'. The last building combined the curate's lodgings – with 'fine flowered window-blinds, the green door with the brass knocker' – and the wheelwright's shop. Ahead the lane climbed up 'between its broad green borders and hedgerows, so thickly timbered'. And that was Three Mile Cross in 1820.

But even then it was menaced. Miss Mitford was inclined to insist at frequent intervals on its unchanging nature – 'in outward appearance it hath, I suppose, undergone less alteration than any place of its inches in the kingdom.' But even she occasionally raised her gaze to the swelling urban growth to the north. 'This little hamlet of ours,' she exclaimed, 'is much nearer (to Reading) than it used to be. Our ancient neighbour, whose suburbs are sprouting in all directions, hath made a particularly strong shoot towards us.'

To W. H. Hudson, Reading was not so much a vigorous plant, but 'a stupendous octopus ... which threw out tentacles miles and miles long ... little rows and single and double cottages, all in red, red brick and its weary accompaniment, the everlasting hard slate roof.' By the time he walked through Three Mile Cross, Miss Mitford's cottage had become a Temperance Hotel established by William Palmer of the Huntley and Palmer biscuit empire, a prominent campaigner for abstinence from alcohol. Hudson said the building was in a 'degraded state' and considered the whole place 'no longer recognisable as the hamlet described in *Our Village.*'

The garden behind the cottage, where Miss Mitford had found much solace for her troubles, had by then been filled with a village institute built of iron and also paid for by William Palmer. An article in the *English Illustrated Magazine* in 1895 reported that the cottage itself had acquired a new front and 'modern windows'. The writer described the village as 'quite the most commonplace collection of country habitations that can well be imagined.' A little later Thackeray's daughter, Anne Thackeray Ritchie, visited while preparing a new edition of *Our Village*. 'I saw two or three commonplace houses skirting the dusty road,' she wrote. 'Except for one memory, Three Mile Cross would seem to be one of the dullest and most uninteresting of country places.'

*

Commonplace still seems an apt adjective for Three Mile Cross, only more so. I cycled there from Reading on a June morning, early enough to witness the daily mass exodus from the housing estates at Three Mile Cross, Spencers Wood, Shinfield and other settlements to the south of Reading: a solid line of cars waiting to get out on to the mighty road junction and disperse to all points of the compass. To reach the bottom of the village, where the old turnpike has been blocked off, I had to lug and push my bike up, over and down a network of footbridges high above the flowing, roaring rivers of traffic. The crescent of land between the M4 slip road and the bypass is disconcertingly rustic; rough meadows grazed by cattle and fringed by trees, with a footpath along one edge.

The retired publican's tidy square red cottage is long gone; the first dwellings are a cluster of generic 'executive-style' detached houses half-hidden behind electronic security gates. Further on some of the cottages featured in *Our Village* do survive in much-altered form, including the spruce little tenement, the village shop, the Mitfords and the curate's lodgings, now Wisteria Cottage.

Behind the Mitfords is a clutch of dark maisonettes where the village institute used to stand. Behind the maisonettes is the Church Centre run by the Pentecostal Christian Fellowship, and behind the Church Centre is an L-shaped development of modern semis protected by another set of gates. Beside the church car park is a garage, Montelle Motors ('Quality by Nature'), with the bowling green behind that. A petrol station occupies the site where Miss Mitford's collar-maker lived, with a tyre-fitting centre nearby. The carpenter's house, where three-year-old Lizzie, 'the plaything and queen of the village' held court, is a Londis store and post office. Opposite the curate's lodgings and the wheelwright's are the allotments, a tiny playground, a patch of grass and a seat, and a parish noticeboard with – at least on the day of my visit – no information at all about Three Mile Cross on it.

The swathe of land including Three Mile Cross and the other villages that has been ceded to the housebuilders by Wokingham Borough Council has been designated, in a prime example of the dead language of planning, a 'Strategic Development Location' – otherwise known as 'the South of M4 SDL'. The shared website set up by the developers to advertise their intentions is entitled Creating Communities. The lesson of the story of Three Mile Cross – which was told because a woman born to write with a father born to spend happened to end up there – is that communities cannot be created. They grow, of their own accord, in their own way. But they can be destroyed, very easily.

21

My Village

Sonning Common, Oxfordshire

The only remarkable thing about the village where I have lived for the past twenty years is how deeply unremarkable it is. If there is a village in England that is more lacking in distinction than Sonning Common, I would very much like to visit it.

The list of attributes it does not have is impressive in its way. There are no buildings in it with any reasonable claim to architectural merit or historic interest. There are no authentically ancient dwellings – one house of Tudor origin, much altered, is not really in the village at all. There is no village green. The church, 1960s functional, is tucked away next to a car-repair workshop. There is a pond, but it – like the Tudor manor – is on the edge of the settlement, and anyway there are many prettier village ponds elsewhere. There is no cricket ground, picturesque or otherwise.

In short, there is nothing in Sonning Common worth a detour to look at. Nor has anyone with any claim to public

Wood Lane, Sonning Common – my road between the wars

attention ever lived there or had anything to with the place. No event of any significance has even a tenuous connection with it. The county histories of Berkshire and Oxfordshire – it has been passed from one to the other – are silent about it. It is most unusual in having no past extending further back than a century or so; and even the history it has is so lacking in interest that it hardly qualifies as such. I have heard tell that there was once a Sonning Common History Society. If so, it expired because – having exhaustively picked over every trivial incident in a meagre store – there was nothing more for it to do.

Even a hundred years ago, which is roughly when the house I now live in was built, Sonning Common was not really a village in any meaningful sense. A hundred years before that it was no more than an expanse of rough grazing, scrubland, furze, gorse, bracken and woodland, designated as part of the common land assigned to the Thameside village of Sonning, three miles away to the south, but actually an unclaimed tract of wilderness where a handful of poor families had staked out smallholdings, built basic habitations and were eking out survival livings, not bothered by landowners and unnoticed by the outside world. The decent agricultural land in the area was allotted under an Enclosure Act of 1816 to the usual alliance of gentry and made-good farmers. But the part where Sonning Common now stands was not included.

By the end of the nineteenth century there were four significant farms on the periphery of the fledgling settlement: Bishopswood to the north, and Blounts Court, Reddish Manor and Blackmore to the east and south-east. These and the surviving smallholdings sustained a scattering of cottages along Hog Lane (now Woodlands Road) and Wood Lane (on which my house stands). There was a choice between four public houses in the area — all of which are still going today, although not always in quite the same place — but only one, the Hare and Hounds, was actually located in the village itself.

The building of new houses along the through roads got going in earnest from 1902 onwards. In 1907 Sonning Common was sufficiently noticeable to warrant an entry in Kelly's Directory. Six years later it acquired its school. By then it was spreading in all directions, but it was not until 1952 that it became significant enough to be detached from the parish of Eye and Dunsden and be designated a parish in its own right. By then there was a population of 1450 which rose steadily through the 1960s and 1970s before gradually flattening out. It is currently around 3800, making Sonning Common one of the biggest villages in south Oxfordshire.

Roughly speaking the settlement as currently constituted is in the shape of a wedge aligned north-west to south-east, with the narrow end towards Reading. It is framed between two roads that come together at the Reading end: Peppard Road, which heads north towards Peppard and Nettlebed; and Kennylands Road, which runs along the western flank before changing into Reade's Lane and eventually petering out in the hamlet of Gallowstree Common.

Sunk into a dip at the narrow end of the wedge is a small development of modern detached houses, with some older dwellings further north. There is then a large gap in the settlement made up of an open stretch of grassland known as the Millennium Green, which was given to the village by its most devoted benefactor, a great lady called Isabella Bonham-Carter (of the great and high-minded Liberal dynasty), who was determined that it should not fall into the hands of developers.

Most of Sonning Common is laid out over the broader section of the wedge, between the Millennium Green in the south and, to the north, an ancient wood, Old Copse, with the fields of Bishopswood Farm to the west. The most pleasant parts are the earliest, which followed the plotland model of development: detached and semi-detached houses fronting the roads but set back behind modest front gardens, with much bigger and generally well-wooded gardens at the back. There is nothing remotely distinguished about any of the architecture, but there is a diversity in the styles and materials which gives the street scene a certain charm. In contrast the estates that came later – from the 1960s onwards – are as bland and generic and uninteresting as they are everywhere else; perfectly pleasant to live in, for sure, but without any aspiration towards character or individuality.

But at least the accretions of modern housing have not – in my view anyway – been allowed to overwhelm Sonning Common. Not yet. They are boring to look at, but have not significantly affected the overall character of the place. 'Pleasant' is the adjective that comes most readily to mind, followed by 'handy'. These are not exciting terms but then my life is not very exciting either.

The village pleases me because it suits me. It takes me ten minutes to walk from my house into woodland or open fields; three minutes on my bike to be in a country lane. The countryside is not in the least spectacular – just an unfolding of fields and copses and bigger woods cut across by footpaths and bridle paths and windy, hedged lanes. Much of it is included in the Chilterns Area of Outstanding Natural Beauty, but ours is not the Chilterns of steep escarpments and hidden valleys and absurdly cute little villages of ancient brick-and-flint cottages. Our landscape rolls gently and unassumingly in all directions. What is important to us is that there is enough of it to give our village the feel of being genuinely rural – even though the tentacles of the urban octopus that is Reading are just visible over the furrows of the fields and around the edges of the woods.

For a village, Sonning Common is unusually blessed with amenities. It has a secondary school and a primary school, a flourishing health centre and dental surgery, and a village hall which – although too small – is in constant use with choir, Monday market, yoga, Zumba, Pilates, dance classes and the rest of it. There are pubs, an Indian restaurant, a Chinese takeaway, a fish-and-chip shop, a sandwich shop. There is an excellent small Co-op supermarket, a more than excellent butcher, an incomparable hardware store and several other useful shops. There are two car-repair workshops, a petrol station, a car showroom and a small, classy garden centre.

The village has its troublemakers, but the youth club helps contain the menace. It is full of do-gooders of the best kind. Some get together to plant up and weed the village flowerbeds, some to take the old folk shopping, some to run the Guides and Cubs and the library. I will not itemise everything that goes on because to do so would be extremely tedious, as well as invidious to those I failed to mention. Suffice to say that since I came to live here – quite by chance – I have never regretted it.

*

It was just good luck, at a low point in my life. After divorce and its attendant wretchedness and impoverishment, I inherited some money, just enough to put down the deposit on a house of my own. The first I looked at in my price bracket was a 1930s semi on a lane leading west out of Sonning Common to its neighbouring village, Kidmore End. I knew nothing about the place until I went to live there.

At that time I made no effort to involve myself in what was going on in the village. I was commuting into London from Reading railway station for work. Periodically I had three children on my hands and was struggling to discover how to try to tend to their needs. I had an elderly mother living a few miles away in Henley and requiring a certain amount of attention. In addition, my house was right on the edge of the village, so its life went on largely unnoticed by me.

I got married again and we moved to a house in the centre – insofar as Sonning Common can be said to have a centre – across from the village hall. We had children, two girls. We began to get to know some other parents through the normal channels: National Childbirth Trust classes (I didn't go), nursery, pre-school. By then I had stopped commuting to London and was at home much of the time, working on one book or another. I began to pay more attention to what was going on in front of me. I went to the newsagent next to the village hall every morning to get my newspaper. I bought meat at the butcher's and other stuff at Somerfield (later the Co-op). I banked at the NatWest next to the garage. I recognised people who recognised me and said good morning to them, even if I didn't know their names. The ease of familiarity began to settle on me, a feeling of home, which I had not experienced for a time.

School opened new pathways. My wife continued to work in London, leaving me to a good deal of hanging around in the playground. I was significantly older than most of the other parents there, who were mostly mums anyway, but I used to chat to one or two of the regular dads and in time to some of the mums as well. Our elder daughter had a particular friend who was often picked up by her grandmother, who is a few years my senior, and we naturally got to exchanging news and views. She was – still is – an essential cog in the running of village affairs: founder and organising genius of the Village Gardeners, fundraiser, member of this committee and that, proofreader for the village magazine, doughty campaigner against those who would let their dogs shit on the pavements and other social criminals, scourge of litter bugs – the list is endless.

At that time she had recently joined the parish council. She needed allies, she said. Would I . . .?

Ah, the parish council! That fusty, musty, cobwebby, infinitely middle-class, absurdly outdated village institution; that puffing, gasping generator of futile hot air; that laughable talking-shop refuge for bores and cranks and busybodies and ineffectual spinster do-gooders. As a young and appropriately jaundiced local newspaper reporter I had stretched, yawned, fiddled, doodled, dozed and stared at the ceiling through countless parish council meetings, marvelling at the tedium they engendered, marvelling that educated human beings should choose to waste their precious spare time on such mind-boggling trivia. Litter collection! Dog fouling! Street lighting! Repairing the village clock! Grass cutting! Yobboes trashing the playground! Potholes!

Of course I said yes. I am one of those who always says yes, always sticks his hand up when volunteers are sought for some dull, time-consuming chore. In this case I was already being pricked by my conscience into thinking that I needed to contribute in some way, to 'get involved'; plus my daughter's friend's grandmother is a difficult person to refuse. Almost before I realised it, I had been co-opted on to the council.

To my surprise I found that – far from being an arena of vacuous windbaggery – it was a quietly seething maelstrom of tensions and rivalries, fascinating to behold. The chairman at that time was in her late seventies, a woman of formidable energy and personality who had grown used to treating the council as her personal fiefdom and directing it to implementing her will. Her disposition was tyrannical and her demeanour towards anyone who dared challenge her – or even mildly question her wishes – was ferocious. The majority of the other members of the council were docile, and the clerk was no more than an instrument of the chairman's purpose.

She had so arranged matters that all decisions of any significance were taken by the General Purposes Committee, whose composition was carefully arranged by her and the clerk. These decisions were subsequently endorsed by the full council under standing orders that prohibited any discussion of the issues. In the context of democratic debate the monthly meetings of the council thus came to resemble those of the Politburo in Soviet Russia.

Any attempt to raise an issue or voice a doubt as to what useful purpose was served by these charades would be met with impatient scorn by our chairman. But the grandmother of my elder daughter's friend – let us call her Chrissie – was not one to be cowed by anyone. She raised questions and duly came to be hated by the chairman. A particular source of tension between them was Chrissie's efforts to get modest funds from the council for her pet project, which was to enhance the centre of the village by restoring three neglected raised flowerbeds and planting them with pleasing blooms and shrubs. Our chairman hated spending council money except on her own pet projects and therefore hated Chrissie all the more.

I was supposed to be Chrissie's ally, but I confess that – certainly in the early days – I was somewhat intimidated by our chairman's forceful personality and capacity for sudden outbursts of alarming rage. I once, rather timidly, raised the matter of the flowerbeds. 'Don't talk to me about those bloody beds,' our chairman snapped at me, and to my shame I complied. She was then engaged in a disgraceful, but ultimately successful, manoeuvre to divest the council of responsibility for the village's recreation ground, arguing that the cost of maintaining it and the clubhouse with it could not be afforded. She did not care about those who wanted to play football or cricket, and was obsessed with keeping down the precept – the minute proportion of the council tax that goes to parish councils – and increasing the financial reserves.

Exceptions were made for her particular enthusiasms, chiefly children's play areas and the welfare of the ducks on the pond. On one occasion it slipped out that a bill for £2500 had been nodded through the General Purpose Committee and the Finance Committee for a new structure on the pond for the ducks to sit on when they didn't want to get their feet wet. Meanwhile the sports fields were relinquished into private ownership; I still feel ashamed that I was one of those who allowed this to happen without significant protest.

Our chairman met her nemesis in the form of another, much more effective ally enlisted by Chrissie, a retired teacher abundantly equipped with the stomach for a fight. She tried to bully and silence him, but he would not be bullied or silenced. Unlike the rest of us, he took the trouble to study our standing orders and knew exactly where they were defective. Our meetings turned from rubber-stamping exercises into a succession of tense and enthralling battles for power. Time and again he disputed our chairman's rulings, and time and again she lost her temper and failed to quell him. Like two beasts of the savannah they fought it out. But his strength was greater than hers, and gradually she lost her dominance over the pack. Her allies – chosen for their submissiveness – proved inadequate as open warfare broke out. Eventually, like the king of the lions, she was toppled.

She resigned and a new chairman was chosen, ushering in a new era of comparative peace. For a while she circled around, roaring in an echo of her old majesty about our disgraceful profligacy. When election time came she attempted to stage a comeback. Contested parish council elections are not the norm (a more familiar problem being finding enough volunteers to fill the slots). But she persuaded enough of her supporters to stand to force a vote, then orchestrated a venomous leaflet campaign alleging every kind of malfeasance against the new council. But her day was done, and she finished at the bottom of the poll. She slunk off into the undergrowth and was hardly heard from again.

In time her nemesis became chairman (as he is now). All the old divisions and enmities were forgotten. We became a team, working together for the good of the village. We acquired a new clerk, a retired businessman of strong personality and abundant energy, with an apparently inexhaustible capacity for mastering the intricacies of council responsibilities and getting them properly discharged.

Instead of hoarding our reserves we began to spend them on village needs. We helped keep the library and the youth club open when they were threatened with closure by county council cuts. We had footpaths repaired and the allotments' car park resurfaced. We paid for a weatherproof noticeboard recording the salient details of the history of the pond (I wrote the text!). We gave funds to the Village Gardeners, to the Scouts, to various other worthy bodies (although we were never able to get our sports ground back). Our formidable clerk now has an equally effective deputy; and we spent and are spending money on a scale that the old chairman would have viewed in the same way that the Popes of the sixteenth century viewed the heresies of Martin Luther.

The personnel of the council has changed somewhat, but quite a few of the old faces remain. We are all friends now and our meetings are exercises in teamwork. I have no doubt that we are doing a better job for the village. But I confess that I sometimes look back to those epic tussles of old with something like nostalgia. I miss the drama. It's all quite boring now.

*

In 2011 a piece of government legislation called the Localism Act came into force. Among its provisions was one that offered – or appeared to offer – the opportunity for villages to decide where new houses should be built, and what sort of houses they should be. The right to draw up what were to be called Neighbourhood Development Plans was presented as a way to appease or accommodate the growing sense of helplessness felt in many parts of the country by communities confronted with a developers' land grab. People wanted to challenge, or at least to have their voice heard, as development companies pursued their ambition to exploit for their gain the unarguable need for more homes, and in doing so to take advantage of every conceivable fault line in the incoherent hotchpotch of regulations that constitutes our planning system.

Sonning Common was one such community. Its location and road and rail connections made it a juicy target for developers. It was all the more alluring because its extreme ordinariness meant that it was free from those pettifogging conservation restrictions that in more picturesque regions so easily impede the turning of paddocks and fields into useful housing estates. Property and building companies were beginning to circle us like hyenas scenting a new kill.

Applications were lodged to build on the east and west sides of the village; and although these were sturdily rejected by the local authority, South Oxfordshire District Council, it was obvious that these hungry predators were not going to be fobbed off indefinitely, or persuaded to go and hunt elsewhere.

Knowing next to nothing about what would be involved, the parish council decided to venture boldly down the path of a Neighbourhood Development Plan for Sonning Common. Volunteers were sought, both from the council and the village as a whole, to form a working party. And, yes, I put up my hand.

We went to work, full of noble aspiration but notably short of awareness as to what we were letting ourselves in for. Once the scale of the enterprise became slightly clearer several of the early enthusiasts dropped out. To guide us we hired a firm of consultants, experts in the field. They advised us, suggested pathways, drew up documents and came to a few of our meetings. Because of other commitments – that was my excuse – I was less engaged than others, and rarely had a clear idea of what the consultants were on about. Even now I am unclear how much use they were.

As time went on, the quantity of documentation produced from within our group, from the consultants, from those we recruited to survey potential development sites, from the district and county councils and various other more or less interested outside bodies grew to unmanageable proportions. Each new document was like a bale of hay added to a haystack that grew so vast it threatened to blot out the sun altogether.

To give some idea of what I am talking about, before set-
tling down to write this account of what turned out to be a
four-year marathon I asked the member of our group who
gallantly undertook most of the detailed number-crunching
how much, in volume terms, it had all added up to. He said
that in his NDP file he had stored 5.5 gigabytes of documents. These included maps, charts and photographs, but
still amounted to a veritable mountain of words. He had
5000 NDP emails on file, and he calculated that he had
given 4000 hours of his life to the project, *excluding* those
spent at meetings.

We did surveys, organised public meetings and exhibitions, put leaflets through hundreds of letterboxes, surveyed
traffic, surveyed businesses, surveyed our heritage assets (the
pond and Old Copse, so that was not too onerous). We held
meetings for the residents affected by the sites chosen for
housing, so that they could tell us that they accepted the need
for new homes but please could they go somewhere else. We
commissioned a report on wildlife that ran to many pages.
We commissioned an expert on traffic management to tell
us how the traffic might be better managed. We produced
reports on recreation needs, housing needs, retail needs,
health and education needs, power lines, environmental
impacts, drainage, flooding, how to safeguard the Area of
Outstanding Natural Beauty, demographics, landscape, sustainability and a host of other matters.

In addition to the public meetings and the meetings with
consultants, landowners, developers, the district council's
planning officers and even, occasionally, with our MP, we had
a working party meeting most weeks at the home of one of

our members. It is these I remember most vividly – not what happened, because I rarely had a firm mental grip on what was under discussion, but my own sensations. I felt like a man sinking into a swamp of verbiage, being sucked down into a bottomless pit by exchanges of opinion which – because of my ignorance and inattention – seemed to have had no beginning, to have no middle and to offer no hope of ever reaching an end.

The proceedings reminded me vividly of attendance at church when I was at school. As the vicar inched his way through the Nicene Creed or busied himself interminably with the intricate preparations for the Communion, I would experience an intensity of boredom so acute that I would wonder how it could be that time could slow in such a way as to seem at risk of stopping altogether. Our NDP meetings began at 6.30 p.m. and at around 8 p.m. I would plead the pressing need to feed my daughters or help them with their homework or see my wife – anything to escape before I went under. And I would depart, shame yielding to relief; and I would hear later that the meeting had gone on for another ninety minutes or two hours.

As month succeeded month and year succeeded year, we gradually discarded the high ideals with which we had started out. We had talked of remodelling the village centre, providing a new library, upgrading the village hall, promoting business opportunities, solving the parking problems. We had even indulged in dreams of social engineering, arresting the ageing of the demographics, opening arms to young families.

But increasingly the focus narrowed to the issues involved in housing: how to divide the allocation imposed on us by the district council – originally 138 homes – between the sites we had approved, what kind of houses they should be, how they should be arranged and screened and landscaped. The one noble aspiration we clung to was that of securing land to provide the village with its own recreation ground and – one fine day – its own sports centre.

It was necessary for us to have extensive dealings with various versions of that proverbially slippery customer, the developer. The role of the developer – who may or may not be the same as the company that actually builds the houses – is to find a way in which that unkempt, unnoticed paddock grazed by a couple of antique piebald nags or that field or that patch of scrubby woodland can become prime real estate worth millions. It is worth reminding yourself repeatedly when dealing with developers that this is what they do, and it is all they do. Their words are honeyed, their promises alluring, their methods sometimes unscrupulous, their objectives wholly determined by self-interest.

At the start of the negotiating process they will tell you how delighted they are to have this opportunity of working with the village so that the village may rejoice in all the blessings that will arise from covering that paddock or those fields or that woodland with five-bedroom family houses. When the village – in our case, through the voice of our NDP working party – replies that what the village actually needs is two- and three-bedroom houses so that the sons and daughters of village residents might have a chance of living there, the developers smile their condescending smiles. May we remind you, they say patiently, that the district council already requires us to designate 40 per cent of the homes as 'affordable', to be handed over to the Housing Association. That, they imply, is their gift, their social conscience at work. But where is our profit to come from, they ask? And all this screening you want, and the open space, and the low density? You cannot be serious.

Behind the smiles, we know what they are thinking. Amateurs, why must we deal with amateurs? The district council planning officers are bad enough, but at least they understand the rules. But these people! Well-meaning do-gooders who think they are serving their precious communities when all they are actually doing is getting in the way of the professionals.

At the end of the meeting there are handshakes and expressions of goodwill. The developers' side go away promising to dwell on what they have heard and to come back a month or so later with their design. A month or two later they reappear and present the design, with the air of an art dealer showing off a rare eighteenth-century print to a collector. In its way it is an artefact of some elegance, certainly much superior to the crude Google Earth and OS map reproductions that we rely on. It shows access roads and avenues and closes curving beguilingly between groves of little round trees and clusters of tasteful toy red-brick houses and garages discreetly concealed behind shrubberies. There are no straight lines or right angles, nothing so vulgar as a terrace except, perhaps, where the 'affordables' have been deposited. The composition is bosky, semi-rustic in character: an invitation to believe that, once it is all done, you will hardly notice that it is no longer a paddock and that the horses have gone.

And we, by now hardened to this exercise in make-believe, look down at the bottom of the design, where the number of houses and their size are specified. We say: 'But this is not what we asked for.' And he, the man in the sharp suit, smiles his condescending smile and replies: 'That's market realities for you,' which turns out to be the answer to everything.

*

Our greatest difficulty, among many, was that for a long time we really did not know what we were doing. Looking back now, it strikes me as disgraceful that – in bestowing the right to draw up Neighbourhood Development Plans – no attempt was made to show how it should be done. The civil servants did not bother, the ministers did not care. What mattered to them was the gesture, the noise they could make about devolving power away from the centre to the people. What happened thereafter did not concern them.

There was no blueprint, no 'toolkit', to use the jargon. There was some financial help, which went on paying the consultants, but little in the way of useful guidance as to how a group of well-meaning, untrained volunteers – most of them, like me, at a fairly advanced stage in life's journey and therefore not as quick on the uptake as they might once have been – were supposed to undertake the considerable range of awesomely complicated and time-consuming tasks dumped on them. Advice was available from the district council, but it was mainly reactive. We would show them what we had done, they would point out the many defects, we would try again, they would identify more defects, and so on, like some elephantine game of patball.

Different metaphors occurred to me at different times to describe our progress. We were a caravan of camels battling our way across the dunes of the Empty Quarter towards a distant oasis, forever deluded by mirages glimmering in the haze. We were Captain Scott and his team floundering up and over the Beardmore Glacier on our way to the South Pole. We were Lewis and Clark dragging our canoes up the headwaters of the Missouri, heading for the Pacific. As with all these and every other voyage of exploration, we had our differences. Many were the rows, the explosions of angry words, the expressions of dismay. Many were the times we seemed to have reached rock bottom, only to go deeper; many the times we reflected that had we known what was going to be involved we would never have started.

But on we plodded, as much as anything because to have given up would have been to admit that all the time and effort had been wasted. Were you to have looked at our NDP website — I would not have advised it — you would have found our Draft Plan (137 pages), our Environmental Report (116 pages), our Sustainability Scoping Report (87 pages, and please don't ask me what that means) and our Basic Conditions Statement (a mere 20 pages). The Evidence Base was there, containing such jewels as the Business Survey, the Traffic Report, the Ecology Study, my own Equality Impact Assessment — no, I cannot begin to remember what was in it — the Landscape Assessment (53 pages) and much much more besides, as well as a vast array of maps, tables and other stuff.

After four years of toil and drudgery we staggered over the finishing line. We submitted our draft plan to the examiner, an independent professional planner, who ruled that, with a few tweaks, it was fit for purpose. It thus became a Neighbourhood Plan, and on 29 September 2016 – a red-letter day for us, if no one else – the village voted on it in a referendum. A final spasm of energy on the part of our working party – leaflet drops, posters banged into the verges of the main through routes, letters to the local paper and, on the day itself, the curious sight of yours truly on a bicycle wobbling along the streets with a megaphone urging the populace to exercise its democratic right – helped secure a hugely satisfying result. Almost half the registered elector-ate of 2900 took the trouble to vote. Of those, 94 per cent approved the plan. After the returning officer announced the figures, we sipped champagne, dazed by the outcome.

Our plan thus became part of the planning process. Under law, it carries weight in determining applications – no one yet knows how much, but that will become clearer as devel-opers press to build houses on sites that are not in it. The future remains clouded by uncertainty. But at least we can console ourselves in the knowledge that we have done all we could have done. The prize all along has been to give those who know the village best and who value it the highest a significant say in what happens to it. Our NDP will do that, if it is allowed to. For me, it has been comparatively easy to remain positive about what has been an absurdly extended and gruelling exercise, because I have done the least towards making the plan happen and therefore had the least to lose if it fell on its face. At times of general despair I said to the others that if we were able to get the houses built where we wanted – even if there were more of them, and some of them were bigger than we might wish – the toil and tribulation would have been justified. If we can see off the likes of Gladman and the other development companies – who would happily see our countryside annexed by bricks and tiles and concrete and tarmac and think only of how much money they had made – it will have been worth it.

If we can keep the village as a village, it will have been worth it.

22

SECRETS OF SURVIVAL

Sonning Common and Beyond

I like living in my village and always have done. It suits me and my wife, and our children have grown up here and feel at home. We have made good friends and there are abundant small pleasures around: the walks, the rides, the pubs, the shops, the accidental encounters and chats.

The fondness I have for it goes to a deepish level. I have grown to care about the place. I think that is because I have been able to get to know it, to comprehend it as a whole entity. I am on nodding terms with all of it, and with the lanes and paths and fields and woods that comprise its setting.

It has often been said that with the post-war agricultural revolution and the breaking of the link between the village and the working of the land, the relationship between the settlement and its surroundings was destroyed. This is simply not so. There are countless villagers like me, for whom walking and cycling – just being – in the countryside is a crucial part of life itself. Of course the relationship is different in its nature to that between the peasant or agricultural labourer and the fields he worked all his life, in that it is not a matter of life and death and survival. But the close embrace of the open countryside is as essential to the village as it ever was. That is why attacks on it arouse such passionate feelings.

My village is large and diffuse as villages go, but still small and compact enough to be knowable. It is also big enough to work as a community, to have life and meaning. Its schools, shops, pubs, facilities and amenities work as vital organs, pumping blood, enabling movement and activity. Because it is not pretty or old, the heavy hand of the conservers and preservers has been restrained, and it has been able to grow and sustain itself. The results are not elegant, but in the village looks count for less than life.

Inevitably that life is limited, even somewhat boring. This is a deficiency felt with particular acuteness by teenagers. There is no culture, no night- or café life, no buzz. The virtues – peace, quiet, security, cleanness, services, connections – are not exciting virtues. But you do not grow up living in a village, or come to live in one, expecting excitement.

In the course of researching and writing this book I have studied village life past and present as closely as my mental powers permit. I have read extensively about the past, and have spent much time exploring individual villages and talking to village people about the present. It is time to set down some of the lessons I have learned.

First and foremost, the village as a model of communal living is secure. It does not suit everyone, because village life is generally uneventful. But a substantial proportion of

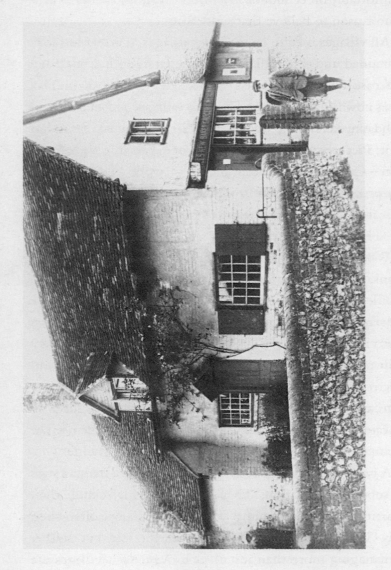

Baker's, Blounts Court Road, Sonning Common

the population – mostly white, mostly middle class, mostly comfortably off economically – find that it suits them. There is no reason to believe that will change.

All villages used to be working villages, more or less self-contained and self-sufficient. That, patently, has not been the case for a long time. Picturesque villages in holiday areas now function seasonally, busy with second-homers and holidaymakers in the season, silent and somewhat lifeless out of it. Picturesque villages in areas of especial scenic attraction – Cotswolds, Chilterns, Dales – have tended to become the preserves of affluent second-homers, retirees and those in search of a rural idyll with the funds to meet the sky-high price of a home.

Where such villages are within reach of a motorway or trunk road or mainline railway station, the demographic profile is slightly different and the age bracket lower, because the earner is able to get to where the money is earned. But that village is unlikely to be much livelier as a result, since such people tend to keep themselves to themselves behind electronic security gates protected by advanced alarm systems and surveillance cameras. They send their children to private schools, and generally have neither the time nor the inclination to enter energetically into community life.

A great many villages have gradually subsided into a state of subdued animation. They have lost their school, their sporting clubs, their young families, their shop, often their pub. The village hall and the church are left, but neither is managing more than just to tick over. Such villages are often in lovely parts of the country and are themselves lovely. They will not be abandoned as so many medieval villages were. The old houses have had much money spent on them to make them pleasant and comfortable, and having lasted for so many centuries will probably last for several more. But the heartbeat is pretty faint. The arteries are shrunken, and not much blood is circulating.

To flourish a village has to be able to sustain itself. That means at least a primary school, a shop, a well-used village hall, a pub, preferably a recreation ground cherished by an active football club and cricket club. To enable all this, it needs to be allowed to grow. New housing for young families is an absolute imperative. I am aware that in this era of inflated property prices, the notion of 'affordable' homes for local families rings somewhat hollow. But any couple with young children or the potential for young children is better than none, wherever they come from and however affluent they may be.

*

So let us pretend that I have been put in charge of nurturing village life. I have been named the Government's Village Tsar, or Commissioner for Rural Communities. I have absolute power to do as I see fit, irrespective of the howls of outrage from the lobby groups and interested parties.

First of all I would make a bonfire. I enjoy bonfires. On to this one I would throw all existing statutory conservation measures and documents affecting the whole or the greater part of villages wherever they may be. All too often the effect of such protection has been to prevent any significant new building of any kind within the existing form of the village. No village is so old, so beautiful, so historic, so special that it should be denied the means to sustain itself. Historically, the whole point of the village was that it was able to grow, organically and usually haphazardly and over extended periods of time to meet the needs of people. To cut off that growth is to turn it from living community into something else: heritage, museum, theme park, rest home.

East Hendred in Berkshire is one of the fifty or so Conservation Areas designated by the Vale of White Horse District Council. When I was there I met a friendly, elderly, long-term lady resident who told me that her father, as chairman of the parish council, had been instrumental in securing this protection for this lovely village. She was proud that this official chokehold had prevented any 'nasty new houses' being built in her village; and delighted that all the homes that the area was being forced to accept were being dumped half a mile away beside the main Wantage Road, where they would not lower the tone. That they would also be inhibited by their geographical position from making any meaningful contribution to the vitality of her village did not seem to matter to her.

There were several patches of ground within the existing form of East Hendred that could have taken a house or two, or three or four. But this is sacred ground, and no planning application would stand a chance. This is wrong, hence the need for my bonfire. Villages need to grow from within, so that those who come to live there are drawn into the community instead of being exiled on the edge of it. I used to subscribe to the general bleat against back land or back garden development. But I now believe that this can be a good way for new housing to be provided, assuming the site is suitable.

I am aware that this puts me at odds with the majority of village people, who are disposed to regard the principle of sacrificing gardens for houses with extreme disfavour and oppose them violently. Unfortunately they are often right to do so, because of the incurable urge of developers to press for the biggest and most expensive house or houses they can possibly get away with, regardless of how brutally overbearing or inappropriate they may be. But it does not have to be that way. It is not beyond the compass of a reformed planning system to ensure that such developments are modest in scale; suitable – say – for middle-income young families, or elderly couples looking for somewhere more manageable in a village context.

Our house is in the middle of Sonning Common and has a long garden. After we moved in we had several speculative approaches from companies hungrily eyeing our garden and the others along the road with a view to lucrative back land development. As it happens we would not sell our garden at any price because it gives us more pleasure than anything money could buy. The same goes for our neighbours on one side.

The situation on the other side was quite different. The building next door was at that time a solicitors' (it has now been converted back to a private house), with a truncated rear garden. Behind that and extending behind the row of commercial properties beyond the solicitors' was a tract of wilderness almost an acre in extent, the domain of foxes and muntjac deer and a favourite fighting ground for local cats. This has now been turned into a little enclave of ten semi-detached two- and three-bedroom homes. Planning permission was obtained on appeal in the face of fierce opposition from the parish council's planning committee (which I was not a member of at the time) and more muted opposition from South Oxfordshire District Council. The building work, extending over the best part of two years, was a considerable nuisance and disruption, but that is part of life if you live where we live. Now the homes are there, one of them a few feet from our boundary fence, I am glad we did not object to them.

As the national supremo in charge of the health and welfare of villages, I would therefore use my powers to compel them to find room for new homes, regardless of how picturebook charming they may be. The only exceptions would be villages with no space, if there are any; I would not be so tyrannical as to demand the razing of existing buildings. Where possible, homes should be built within the existing form of the village. But I accept that, to meet the need, space has to be found around the edges of settlements as well. Again, compulsion will undoubtedly be necessary. I do not think that Sonning Common would have got round to finding room for 140-plus homes if it had not been told to.

But it would be critical to my strategy for speculative companies of the likes of Gladman to be frozen out of this process. Their speciality is to seduce the owners of farming land on the periphery of villages and towns with visions of easy wealth, and then lobby and push and agitate for that land to be designated for building. Once that happens, the map of the village is redrawn to show the land in question swelling the overall form like a goitre. The inevitable next step is to argue that the adjacent fields could and should be built on as well, to round out the profile of the settlement. There is a classic illustration of this insidious model of expansion in and around the small market town of Buntingford in Hertfordshire, which is in the process of being encircled by new housing estates because of the inability of the local council to produce a sound, watertight plan for controlling development.

*

My way of addressing the challenge of finding space for the houses we need would be to empower local communities to find the answers, working with their district councils – with the threat of unleashing the Gladmans of this world should they be too inert or incompetent to do so. Every village in the country should be able to find residents who are sufficiently active, mentally alert and concerned to take charge of this process. If they can't, so much the worse for them.

That is the problem of land supply solved. Next we have the small matter of what kind of house should be built, and how. As supremo of village renewal, I would certainly have something to say about that.

I start with my own house. Built around 1910, it is not a thing of beauty. The basic building material is red brick. The upper part of the frontage is faced with pebble-dash, and the corners of the building and the surrounds of the windows and front door are formed from a pale and rather unpleasant yellow brick. The original roof was probably slate, but was replaced before our time by dark-brown concrete tiles whose irredeemable nastiness is at least partially concealed at the back by solar panels. We have added a single-storey extension at one side and extended at the back, but nothing else has been changed significantly.

As a specimen of design there is nothing to be said about our house except that it is not offensive. It is like millions of others of its time, serviceable, decent, run-of-the-mill, unobtrusive. Its saving grace is its distinctiveness. On either side are detached red-brick houses of about the same vintage, both more handsome than ours, wholly different from each other and ours in the detail of design. Looking down the street, most of the houses dating from the first half of the twentieth century fall into this bracket: unbeautiful but individual. There is the odd bungalow, and in places the older houses have been replaced by newer ones, utterly uninteresting in terms of design, but necessarily unlike those on either side.

This is where the charm of villages like ours lies, not in quaintness or prettiness, but in modest diversity. Sonning Common grew plot by plot, each filled with someone's idea of a decent home. Here and there are clusters or little rows of identical or very similar semi-detached houses, obviously the work of the local builder. My first home in the village was one such, half of a 1930s pebble-dashed pair whose design is replicated with variations on odd plots down the lane and around the corner.

Where the plotland model has been adhered to, this diversity has been maintained up to the present day. The houses built from the 1960s onwards are generally unexceptional at best and dispiriting at worst. But at least they stand alone, or in small concentrations, and their impact on the overall look of the village is minimal.

The key to achieving diversity is to accommodate differing concepts of what a home should be. The enemy of that interesting – if sometimes distressing – diversity is the uniformity of the modern housing estate: that deadening, dehumanising sameness that the volume housebuilders have so successfully engineered from one end of the land to the other. As the man in charge of saving the village, I would make it my business to smash the wretched monotony of estate design; and if that means striking a blow at the hegemony of Taylor Wimpey, Bovis, Barratt, Persimmon and the rest, I am ready.

The defence invariably offered by these big beasts of construction to the charge that their houses are generic, mundane, identikit and deeply mediocre is that they are giving the market what it wants. It is an insult to the buying public and the intelligence of us all. The fact is that for those on a middle-bracket income looking for a new home, the estate and the estate house is pretty much all that is on offer. They choose it because there is no choice.

This is how the system works. Planning permission is obtained for – say, for the sake of argument – eighty houses on a seven-and-a-half-acre site on the edge of the village. The development company does nothing. It sits tight while house prices go on rising, until the costs of obtaining the land and getting planning permission are partially or wholly covered. Often it will seek to increase the value of its investment by going back to the local authority to apply to increase the number or size of the houses. Local authorities – intimidated by the cost of appeals – will often roll over rather than haggle over a permission already given in principle.

At length the company that is actually going to build and sell the homes produces from its database a design for the estate – let us call it Gresham Meadows, because that is exactly the kind of name they go for. Like all its other designs, it shows a network of sinuous ribbons of tarmac and paving along and off which are distributed a selection from its portfolio of house types, each with its rectangular patch of garden. The remainder of the space is taken up by garages and parking spaces, and the trees, shrubberies and other open and green spaces stipulated in the conditions of the permission.

Over time Gresham Meadows slowly arises from a wasteland of mud and destruction until it is ready to go on the market. The brochure will describe these houses as select, contemporary, modern, traditional, exclusive and – invariably – stunning. It will claim the estate as rural, part of a thriving community, having a genuine village feel.

It is none of these things. It is an unwanted addition, in spirit and in appearance utterly divorced from the village on to whose side it has been bolted. The houses are, in essence, the same as are found everywhere else. They are warm, comfortable, perfectly pleasant to live in. But they are not part of anything, do not belong – in the true sense of belonging – anywhere.

It is time to stoke up my bonfire, still glowing a little with the embers of innumerable conservation orders. On to it – and guaranteed to produce a warming blaze – would go local authority guidelines on recommended densities for new housing developments. This is commonly twenty-five dwellings per hectare in rural areas, which frequently represents an appalling waste of space. I suspect that the obsession with low-density housing derives from the Garden City model and its guiding principles of openness and spaciousness and general leafiness. That may have been fine then, but land is simply too precious and valuable in this congested island of ours to be squandered in this way.

Under my plan – I might even call it a Masterplan – there would be a presumption in favour of building in numerical terms at higher density. At the same time I would wage war on the fixation with the detached and the semi-detached. There would be terraces, mewses and crescents of joined-together houses. They work fine in towns and cities; why not in the new estates? The majority would be of two and three bedrooms – people must get used to the notion of living in smaller houses. Detached homes would be the exception, and five- and six-bedroom excrescences would be banned.

The requirements of the motor car must be sensitively handled. It is standard for half the overall space in a new estate to be covered by tarmac in the form of roads and parking areas. This is intolerably wasteful. New solutions to parking need to be sought – for instance, in shared open-sided oak-framed barns, rather than the usual integral or detached garage. And why should it not be possible to keep some of the cars out of sight, by putting them underground, as is increasingly the case in towns and cities? The builders will howl about the cost, but they will be getting more houses on their land. Their protests will be ignored.

With cars and hideously unsightly parking areas out of the way, there will still be plenty of open space on my new high-density estate. There could be allotments or an orchard or even a football pitch created above the hidden car park. There could be a pond for fishing, a communal garden such as they have in smart city squares, a giant communal trampoline – the possibilities for bringing people together are intoxicating.

After I have amused myself watching the guidelines on densities being reduced to ash and writing new ones more suited to our time, I will turn my attention to another glaring failure of the current system. Because obtaining planning permission for large developments is so laborious, time-consuming and expensive, it follows that only big companies with big resources can do it. Smaller-scale local builders are generally excluded. Worse, so too are individuals who long to buy a single plot and build the house of their dreams. This inbuilt bias towards the volume housebuilders needs to be dismantled. Apart from the malign effect on choice, it has made them far too powerful – so powerful that local authorities who would like to challenge them tremble before them instead.

What is needed is what I believe happens in Germany, and possibly elsewhere in Europe. One company is responsible for obtaining permission for a site and preparing it and providing power and water. But it does not build the houses. It sells the land in plots so that everyone – big builders, smaller local builders, single self-builders – gets a slice of the cake.

I will also have to do something about design. Let us all agree that the general run of modern housing estates – built from the 1960s onwards – are boring and bland. Individually there may well be nothing offensive about the dwellings, which are comfortable, well appointed and perfectly pleasant to live in. But *en masse* and replicated across the country, they have a deadening effect on the localities where they are situated. Does anyone seriously dispute that?

The problem is that these houses are all born from the same restricted concept of what a house should be. The variations – some cladding here, dormer windows there, a patch of pebble-dash there, rendering here, plain red brick there, a little pattern of different-coloured brick inset here, white-PVC windows there, brown PVC windows here, a spot of mock Victorian here and mock Georgian there – are trivial tweakings of the same dull and repetitive theme. We need houses of wood, houses of glass and steel, houses of straw bales, houses of cob – as well as houses of brick and stone. We need thatched roofs, concrete roofs, slate roofs, tile roofs, regularly pitched roofs, irregularly pitched roofs, flat roofs. We need tall houses and shorter houses and houses dug into the ground and covered in a wildflower meadow.

Historically the challenge of building places to live has stimulated sharp and creative responses, resulting in dwellings of startling beauty and beguiling charm. But in our time we have lost that knack. We need to readmit into the housebuilding process a wide and eclectic range of tastes and visions. Designing and building the homes of the future is far too important to be left to the nameless employees of building conglomerates twiddling with the controls of their 3-D printers.

In the past a crucial wellspring of diversity and character came from the necessary use of local building materials. Where there was stone – pale Cotswold stone, honey-coloured Hamstone, light-coloured Yorkstone and darker Lakeland stone, rarer iron-rich Bargate stone and Old Red Sandstone – they cut it in the quarries and built with that. Where there was no available stone they built in cob, unless there was clay, in which case some bright spark would open a local brickworks. Each brickworks provided a signature for the district, just as local builders gave the houses they built their own imprint with decorative flourishes and stylistic quirks.

Most of the local quarries and almost all the local brickworks have gone. In strict conservation areas – the Cotswolds, for example – new building has to be done in what the conservators deem to be the appropriate stone, imposing another kind of monotony. Generally, though, the brick rules. In the first age of estate building the palette of colours encompassed everything from sickly-yellow to a dozen variants on shit-brown. But increasingly the orthodoxy in rural areas has come to favour a small range of red brick, machine cut in unvarying sizes, smooth textured, laid in dead straight lines, dull as ditchwater.

In the exercise of my power, I would offer incentives for the reopening of abandoned quarries and the re-establishment of brickworks using local clay. In an area such as the Chilterns there would be schemes to train a new generation of flint-knappers and revive the beautiful brick-and-flint tradition. I would look with extreme disfavour on house designs which combined excrement-brown brick with excrement-brown window frames and excrement-brown concrete roof tiles. But I would welcome the pioneer in glass and steel. I would embrace the craftsmen and craftswomen in wood. I would glory in dwellings of turf and straw. And to those who cried out that people wouldn't want such homes and wouldn't buy them, I would say: you haven't asked them yet.

I should perhaps admit here that I am not a designer. Nor am I an architect. I know very little about either discipline (although more than I did). I acknowledge that, visually, I am something of a philistine. But it would be crucial to my strategy for sustaining our villages to achieve better and more interesting design. I would need to recruit into the process designers and architects who are properly trained, have good taste and are bold in their thinking. But how to find them? And how to use them?

I am open to ideas. One of my own is to require each and every planning authority in rural England to employ an architect/designer to oversee all new-build applications, to promote new and different approaches to building homes, and to find and encourage a new breed of builders, developers, suppliers and craftsmen and women who are united in a passion to provide places for people to live that compare in charm and distinctiveness with those of the past. Where will my passionate overseers come from? I have no idea, but surely someone from the Royal Institute of British Architects would have?

*

I am a dreamer but I am not stupid. Will any of this come to pass? Of course it won't. I am not so dim as to imagine that whichever minister is given charge of local government will see my manifesto and send for me to offer me the job of keeping our villages alive and kicking.

No, we will bumble along wasting space, time, money and opportunity as we always have done. There are no votes to be gained from reforming our hopelessly sclerotic planning system. The notion of a minister summoning the bosses of Barratt, Taylor Wimpey, Persimmon, Berkeley, Bellway, Galliford Try, Redrow, Bovis and Crest Nicholson to tell them that their houses are boring and their influence on the housing market is malign is fanciful. More villages will be squeezed and suffocated by housing estates pushed through the planning system by the power of the volume builders. Local authority planning officers will continue to be half-buried in speculative applications from developers entirely free of any concern as to whether the village in question lives or dies. The whole incredibly laborious, time-consuming, incomprehensible monster that is our way of meeting the need of ordinary people for somewhere decent to live will just lumber on, regardless of the fact that anyone who has anything to do with it knows that it is unfit for purpose.

The only hope I can see lies, paradoxically, in the developing crisis in local government finances resulting from the vice-like squeeze brought about by cuts in central government support and the inexorable rise in demand for social services. This crisis is real. Ten years ago my own county council, Oxfordshire, was still happily splashing out on fatuous fripperies such as arty signs bearing the words 'Quiet Lane' which they put up beside quiet lanes all over the place to tell people who might not have noticed that these were quiet lanes. Now Oxfordshire County Council is staring into a chasm. Half of its budget currently goes on social care, a legally binding obligation which cannot be cut and will only rise in cost as the population ages. At the same time OCC's grant from Whitehall has been slashed. Into the chasm are sliding the services it can cut: schools, libraries, roads and the rest.

There is now a real chance that one of the two layers of local government in Oxfordshire – either the county council or the district councils (plus Oxford City Council) – will be abolished in an effort to make better use of the resources. Under the existing arrangements, the county council is responsible for social care and the district councils for planning. Whichever comes out on top will have to take charge of both, plus all the other services that we expect (but increasingly do not get) in return for our council tax.

Parish councils, such as my own in Sonning Common, have been able to make up some of the shortfall in the provision of services. For instance, when the county council threatened to pull the plug on our library, we stepped in with an offer of financial support and a group of volunteers was recruited to keep it open.

Across the shires there is a reserve army of grandads and grannies and retirees ready to be mobilised. We live longer, we stay fitter, we have time and energy to spare. As well as running libraries, villages could organise the cutting of grass, the repair of roads, the feeding of elderly residents, the maintenance of schools, the lopping of branches off dangerous trees, the clearing of blocked drainage holes, the provision of grit for freezing weather. And more. In fact most of the everyday tasks at present done expensively, incompetently or not at all by the local authority could be done by the village. Why should parish councils not be given the power to raise the money they need from their residents to do the things those residents want done, and face being booted out at the next election if they fail to deliver?

I am not suggesting that parish councils could deal with the challenge of providing housing. That kind of planning requires – even if it does not get – strategic thinking on a wider scale. But villages can make a vital contribution. In fact they already do – witness our own Sonning Common Neighbourhood Development Plan, and the several other

NDPs-in-the-making in our area. Somewhat late in the day, the officers of our own South Oxfordshire District Council have realised that a good deal of the tedious and burdensome background work on planning applications previously done (or not done) by them can be shovelled off on to the volunteers. Having previously been distinctly sniffy about NDPs – they didn't care for the idea of their domain being invaded by well-meaning amateurs – they are now relying upon them to head off the frontal assaults of the land predators and find the desperately needed sites for the houses.

So that is the hope: that the limp and uninspiring label of Localism can, over time, be made to mean something. The Big Society, in David Cameron's infinitely condescending slogan, has always been there, even before he was toasting crumpets at Eton. It has grown in size and importance, not because of inane government 'initiatives', but because of us; because we are here in greater numbers than before, more active for longer than before, ready and able to do what people have always done, which is to serve our communities. The prime minister who has the gumption to enlist that reserve will have achieved something truly remarkable.

POSTSCRIPT

There are some nice lines in a poem called 'The Norman Church' by A. A. Milne, the creator of Winnie the Pooh:

> *Between the woods in folded hands*
> *My accidental village stands,*
> *Untidily, and with an air*
> *Of wondering who left it there . . .*

I very much like the phrase 'accidental village'. It crystallises what is precious and special about the village – its unexpectedness, its capacity to surprise and suddenly delight. Every village is different, not just from other villages, but within itself: different houses, different gardens, different colours and textures, different heights, different angles, different people. To stroll around the village – any village – with ears and eyes on the alert is to open yourself to a rich and subtle composition of sights and sounds and impressions. It is a lesson in the most absorbing subject of them all, which is how we have lived and how we live now.

At the outset of the 1939–45 War a prolific and now forgotten writer on countryside matters, C. Henry Warren, produced a book called *England is a Village*. Warren was one of the lesser lights in a group known as Kinship in Husbandry, the back-to-the-earth precursor of the Soil Association that included H. J. Massingham, Rolf Gardiner, Edmund Blunden and Arthur Bryant. Warren's little book is a standard chronicle of village life, forgettable stuff redeemed somewhat by Denys Watkins-Pitchford's superb scraper-board illustrations. It was obviously intended as a memorial to a way of life that at that time seemed imperilled as never before.

In the foreword Warren wrote: 'England's might is in her fields and villages, and though the whole weight of mechanised armies roll over them to crush them, in the end they will triumph.'

And triumph they have, after a fashion. They are still here, and it is up to us who love and cherish them to make sure they survive and thrive. 'The best of England is a village,' Warren reflected. There is truth in that.

BIBLIOGRAPHY

Askwith, Richard, *The Lost Village*, Ebury Press, 2008.

Bailey, Brian, *The English Village Green*, Robert Hale, 1985.

Barron, Hester, *The 1926 Miners' Lockout: Meanings of Community in the Durham Coalfield*, Oxford University Press, 2010.

Baseley, Godfrey, *A Village Portrait*, Sidgwick & Jackson, 1972.

Bennett, Ernest, *Problems of Village Life*, Williams & Norgate, 1914.

Beresford, Guy, *Goltho: The Development of an Early Medieval Manor c.850–1150*, Historic Buildings and Monuments Commission for England, 1987.

Bloxham, Christine, *The World of Flora Thompson Revisited*, Tempus, 2007.

Blythe, Ronald, *Akenfield: Portrait of an English Village*, Allen Lane, 1969.

Bonham-Carter, Victor, *The English Village*, Penguin, 1952.

Boyes, Georgina, *The Imagined Village: Culture, Ideology and the English Folk Revival*, Manchester University Press, 1993.

Brace, Catherine, 'A Pleasure Ground for the Noisy Herds? Incompatible Encounters with the Cotswolds and England, 1900–1950', from *Rural History II*, April 2000.

Brown, Ivor, *The Heart of England*, Batsford, 1935.

Bibliography

Burchardt, Jeremy, *Paradise Lost: Rural Idyll and Social Change Since 1800*, I. B. Tauris, 2002.

Darley, Gillian, *Villages of Vision*, Architectural Press, 1975.

Ditchfield, Rev. P. H., *Old Village Life*, Methuen, 1920.

Dyer, Christopher, *Everyday Life in Medieval England*, Hambledon, 1994.

—— (Ed.), *The Self-Contained Village? The Social History of Rural Communities 1250–1900*, University of Hertfordshire Press, 2007.

English, Barbara, 'Lark Rise and Juniper Hill: A Victorian Community in Literature and in History', from *Victorian Studies* 29, Autumn 1985.

Ernle, Lord, *The Land and its People: Chapters in Rural Life and History*, Hutchinson, 1925.

Gibbs, J. A., *A Cotswold Village; or Country Life and Pursuits in Gloucestershire*, John Murray, 1899.

Goodenough, Simon, *The Country Parson*, David & Charles, 1983.

Gough, Richard, *Antiquities and Memoirs of the Parish of Myddle*, Penguin, 1981.

Grieves, Keith, 'Common Meeting Places and the Brightening of Rural Life: Local Debates on Village Halls in Sussex after the First World War', *Rural History*, vol. 10, issue 2, October 1999.

Grove, Valerie, *Laurie Lee: The Well-loved Stranger*, Viking, 1999.

Hall, Roger, *Bar Hill: A Social History of a New Village*, self-published, 2002.

Harrison, Fraser, *Strange Land: The Countryside – Myth and Reality*, Sidgwick & Jackson, 1982.

Hart, A. Tindal, *The Curate's Lot: The Story of the Unbeneficed English Clergy*, John Baker, 1970.

Hartley, Marie, and Ingilby, Joan, *Yorkshire Village*, J. M. Dent, 1953.

Hey, David, *An English Rural Community: Myddle under the Tudors and Stuarts*, Leicester University Press, 1974.

Hill, Constance, *Mary Russell Mitford and her Surroundings*, John Lane, 1920.

Hindle, Steve, *The State and Social Change in Early Modern England c.1550–1640*, Cambridge University Press, 2002.

Hinton, James, *The Mass Observers: A History, 1937–1949*, Oxford University Press, 2013.

Hobsbawm, Eric, and Rudé, George, *Captain Swing*, Lawrence and Wishart, 1970.

Hordon, Kathryn, and Wright, Alan, *Coal, Community and Conflict: A History of Chopwell*, Hickory Tree Press, 1995.

Hoskins, W. G., *The Making of the English Landscape*, Hodder & Stoughton, 1954.

Howat, Gerald, *Village Cricket*, David & Charles, 1980.

Jefferies, Richard, *Hodge and his Masters*, Smith, Elder & Co., 1880.

Keith, W. J., *The Rural Tradition: William Cobbett, Gilbert White and other Non-fiction Prose Writers of the English Countryside*, Harvester Press, 1975.

—— *Regions of the Imagination: The Development of British Rural Fiction*, University of Toronto Press, 1988.

Kitchen, Fred, *Brother to the Ox: The Autobiography of a Farm Labourer*, J. M. Dent, 1940.

Lane, Margaret, *Flora Thompson*, John Murray, 1976.

Laslett, Peter, *The World We Have Lost*, Methuen, 1971.

Lee, Laurie, *Cider with Rosie*, Hogarth Press, 1959.

Lord, Graham, *James Herriot: The Life of a Country Vet*, Headline, 1998.

Mabey, Richard, *Dreams of the Good Life: The Life of Flora Thompson and the Creation of Lark Rise to Candleford*, Allen Lane, 2014.

Manley, E. R., *A Descriptive Account of East Hendred*, self-published, 1969.

Marshall, J. D., *Old Lakeland: Some Cumbrian Social History*, David & Charles, 1971.

Martin, E. W., *The Secret People: English Village Life after 1750*, Phoenix, 1954.

—— *The Book of the Village*, George Allen & Unwin, 1963.

—— (Ed.) *Country Life in England*, Macdonald, 1966.

Massingham, H. J., *The English Countryman: A Study of the English Tradition*, Batsford, 1942.

Matless, David, 'Doing the English Village', from *Reconstituting Rurality*, ed. Terry Marsden and Jonathan Murdoch, UCL Press, 1994.

Mitford, Mary Russell, *Our Village* (ed. Anne Thackeray Ritchie) available online from www.archive.org

Morton, H. V., *In Search of England*, Methuen, 1927.

Muir, Richard, *The English Village*, Thames & Hudson, 1980.

—— *The Villages of England*, Thames & Hudson, 1992.

Newby, Howard, *Green and Pleasant Land? Social Change in Rural England*, Penguin, 1980.

Page, Robin, *The Decline of an English Village*, Davis-Poynter, 1974.

Parker, Rowland, *The Common Stream*, Eland, 2015.

Patton, Julia, *The English Village: A Literary Study, 1750–1850*, Macmillan, 1919.

Peake, Harold, *The English Village: The Origin and Decay of its Community*, Benn, 1922.

'Miss Read', *Chronicles of Fairacre*, Penguin, 1982.

—— *Early Days*, Michael Joseph, 1995.

Roberts, Brian, *The Making of the English Village: A Study in Historical Geography*, Longman, 1987.

Scott, J. Robertson, *England's Green and Pleasant Land*, Jonathan Cape, 1925.

Scott, S. H., *A Westmorland Village: The Story of the Old Homesteads and 'Statesman' Families in Troutbeck by Windermere*, Archibald Constable, 1904.

Sharp, Thomas, *The Anatomy of the Village*, Penguin, 1946.

Short, Brian (Ed.), *The English Rural Community: Image and Analysis*, Cambridge University Press, 1992.

Sturt, George, *Change in the Village*, available from www. archive.org

Taylor, Christopher, *Village and Farmstead: A History of Rural Settlement in England*, George Philip, 1983.

Thompson, Flora, *Lark Rise to Candleford* (with introduction by Richard Mabey), Penguin, 2008.

Turner, W. J., *Exmoor Village: A General Account Based on Factual Information from Mass Observation*, Harrap, 1947.

Waddilove, Lewis, *One Man's Vision: The Story of the Joseph Rowntree Village Trust*, Allen and Unwin, 1954.

Warren, C. Henry, *England is a Village*, Eyre & Spottiswoode, 1940.

Whitlock, Ralph, *A Family and a Village*, J. Baker, 1969.

—— *The Lost Village: Rural Life between the Wars*, Robert Hale, 1989.

—— *A Victorian Village*, Robert Hale, 1990.

Wild, Trevor, *Village England: A Social History of the Countryside*, I. B. Tauris, 2004.

Williams, Raymond, *The Country and the City*, Oxford University Press, 1973.

Wymer, Norman, *Village Life*, Harrap, 1951.

ACKNOWLEDGEMENTS

I would like to thank the following for generously taking the trouble to make their photographs available without charge: Eric Rowlands, Patrick Hellicar, Philip Lane, Jason Hawkes, Alan Franklin, Brian Liddell, Gerry Wise, Gordon Baxter, Martin Greenwood, Michael MacLeod, the Dales Countryside Museum.

I owe particular debts of gratitude to Iain MacGregor and Jo Whitford at Simon & Schuster for taking so close and supportive an interest in my work; to my priceless agent, Caroline Dawnay; to my copy editor, Sally Partington, whose attention to detail and great knowledge of history and literature has saved me from many egregious errors; and to my wife Helen, for making it possible for me to pursue my version of a writer's life.

PICTURE CREDITS

Twyford: p.10, top image © The Twyford & Ruscombe
    Local History Society; p.10, bottom image © The
    Francis Frith Collection.
Goltho: p.18, image © The Churches Conservation Trust.
East Hendred: p.34, image © The Francis Frith Collection.
Lower Bourne: p.52, image © The Francis Frith Collection.
Foxton: p.69, images courtesy of Gordon Baxter.
Bibury: p.85, image © The Francis Frith Collection.
Robin Hood's Bay: p.104, image © Jason Hawkes.
Chelsfield: p.121, images courtesy of Philip Lane.
Eversley: p.139, image © The Francis Frith Collection.
North Moreton: p.159, image © The Francis Frith
    Collection.
Askrigg: p.181, image courtesy of The Dales Countryside
    Museum.
Slad: p.214, image © The Francis Frith Collection.
Chopwell: p.229, image © Historic England.
Luccombe: p.244, image courtesy of Eric Rowlands.
New Earswick: p.268, image y58_new_5757_b © Explore
    York Libraries and Archives / City of York Council,
    2016.

Picture Credits

Bar Hill: p.274, image © Jason Hawkes.

Pitton: p.284, image © Museum of English Rural Life, University of Reading.

Troutbeck: p.297, top image courtesy of Brian Liddell; bottom image © The Francis Frith Collection.

Three Mile Cross: p.311, image © Museum of English Rural Life, University of Reading.

Sonning Common: p.327, image © Museum of English Rural Life, University of Reading; p.350, image courtesy of Michael Macleod.

INDEX

Index

Index

Index

Index

Index